Metaverse and Blockchain

Blockchain and Metaverse technologies are revolutionising the digital landscape by offering transformative potential across industries. Because of its decentralised and transparent nature, Blockchain ensures secure and tamper-proof transactions and fosters trust in such areas as finance, supply chain, and healthcare. It enables the creation of digital assets, smart contracts, and decentralised applications to pave the way for a more equitable and efficient digital economy. The Metaverse is redefining how people interact, work, and socialise by creating immersive virtual environments. It combines Augmented Reality (AR), Virtual Reality (VR), and Blockchain to enable ownership of digital assets, such as NFTs, and facilitate seamless virtual commerce. Together, these technologies are driving innovation, enhancing user experiences, and creating new opportunities for collaboration and economic growth in a rapidly evolving digital world.

Going beyond theoretical concepts, *Metaverse and Blockchain: Real-World Applications* covers the intersection of the Metaverse and Blockchain. The book offers a pragmatic exploration of how these technologies are revolutionising industries and creating tangible impact in business. Diving into the space where the Metaverse and Blockchain converge, the book explains real-world applications through case studies. It explores how Blockchain technology is reshaping the architecture of virtual worlds, providing a secure and transparent foundation for unprecedented digital experiences. Highlights of the book include the following:

- Augmenting virtual worlds with mobile edge computing
- Technological advancement of Blockchain through Metaverse in the financial sector
- Internet of Things-integrated Blockchain-based supply chain management
- Integrating machine learning and Blockchain technologies into the Metaverse

A guide to understanding and leveraging the potential of these transformative technologies, the book explains how to apply Metaverse and Blockchain in the real world so organisations and individuals can realise benefits from these innovative technologies.

Advances in Computational Collective Intelligence

Series Editor: Dr. Subhendu Kumar Pani

Leveraging Artificial Intelligence in Cloud, Edge, Fog and Mobile Computing
Edited by Shrikaant Kulkarni, P. William, Vijaya Prakash, and Jaiprakash Narain Dwivedi

Using AI to Develop Sustainability Strategies for a Changing Global Economy
Edited by A.V. Senthil Kumar, Ankita Chaturvedi, Atul Bansal, and Rohaya Latip

Artificial Intelligence, Geographic Information Systems, and Multi-Criteria Decision-Making for Improving Sustainable Development
Edited by Sujoy Kumar Jana, Kamalakanta Muduli, Indrajit Pal, and Purushottam Meena

Advanced AI and Data Science Applications
Edited by Dr. D. Sivabalaselvamani, Dr. G Revathy, and Dr. Ranjit Singh Sarban Singh

Intelligent Business Analytics
Edited by Nitendra Kumar, Lakhwinder Kaur Dhillon, Mridul Dharwal, Elena Korchagina, and Vishal Jain

Augmented Reality and Sustainability: Goals and Challenges
Edited by Sonal Trivedi, Vishal Jain, Balamurugan Balusamy, Subhendu Pani, and Danish Ather

Patient-Centric 6G: A New Era in Smart Healthcare
Edited by Rajeev Kumar, Ankush Joshi, Preeti Bajaj, and Danila Parygin

Generative AI Tools: From Algorithms to Applications
Edited by Priyanka Sharma, Senthil Kumar AV, Monika Jyotiyana, and Adnan Alrabea

IoT Cybersecurity: Trends, Challenges, and Solutions
Edited by Laxmi Shaw, D. Ajitha, Chinmay Chakraborty, and S.M. Prabin

Smarter Healthcare through Generative Intelligence
Edited by Vibha Jain, Aditya Gupta, Amritpal Singh, Prabal Verma, and Tawseef Ayoub Shaik

Metaverse and Blockchain: Real-World Applications
Dileep Kumar Murala and Sandeep Kumar Panda

https://www.routledge.com/Advances-in-Computational-Collective-Intelligence/book-series/ACCICRC

Metaverse and Blockchain

Real-World Applications

Dileep Kumar Murala and
Sandeep Kumar Panda

CRC Press
Taylor & Francis Group
Boca Raton London New York

CRC Press is an imprint of the
Taylor & Francis Group, an **informa** business
AN AUERBACH BOOK

Designed cover image: Shutterstock

First edition published 2027
by CRC Press
2385 NW Executive Center Drive, Suite 320, Boca Raton FL 33431

and by CRC Press
4 Park Square, Milton Park, Abingdon, Oxon, OX14 4RN

CRC Press is an imprint of Taylor & Francis Group, LLC

ISBN: 978-1-032-84953-9 (hbk)
ISBN: 978-1-032-85969-9 (pbk)
ISBN: 978-1-003-52070-2 (ebk)

DOI: 10.1201/9781003520702

Typeset in Garamond
by SPi Technologies India Pvt Ltd (Straive)

Contents

Preface

Introduction

Embark on an enlightening journey into the intersection of the Metaverse and Blockchain with our compelling guide, *Metaverse and Blockchain: Real-World Applications*. This insightful book takes you beyond theoretical concepts, offering a pragmatic exploration of how these cutting-edge technologies are revolutionising industries and creating tangible impact in our everyday lives. Dive into the fascinating realm where the Metaverse and Blockchain converge, unlocking a treasure trove of real-world applications. Through a series of illuminating case studies, we unveil how Blockchain technology is reshaping the architecture of virtual worlds, providing a secure and transparent foundation for unprecedented digital experiences. Learn about the real-world uses of Non-Fungible Tokens (NFTs) and see how they're changing sectors like the entertainment, gaming, and art industries. Discover the role of Blockchain in ensuring digital scarcity, provenance, and authenticity, ushering in a new era of trust and ownership in the Metaverse. From supply chain management to decentralised identity solutions, *Metaverse and Blockchain: Real-World Applications* sheds light on how these technologies are solving real-world challenges. Uncover the impact of Decentralised Finance (DeFi) in the Metaverse, where Blockchain-driven financial ecosystems are providing inclusive and accessible financial services to users across the globe.

Navigate the intricate landscape of Decentralised Applications (DApps) and smart contracts, witnessing their deployment in sectors ranging from healthcare to education. Gain valuable insights into the practical considerations, challenges, and triumphs of implementing Blockchain solutions in various industries. Whether you are a tech enthusiast, a business leader, or a curious explorer, *Metaverse and Blockchain: Real-World Applications* serves as your indispensable guide to understanding and leveraging the immense potential of these transformative technologies. This book helps individuals and organisations use the Metaverse and Blockchain in the real world by guiding them through implementation. Come experience the merging of the virtual and the tangible in "Metaverse and Blockchain" as practical applications shape our interconnected digital environment. Get ready to embark on a life-changing adventure! Make your way to the real-life Metaverse.

Therefore, this book provides a 360-degree impact on Metaverse related to avatar, content creation, virtual economy, social acceptability, security and privacy, and trust and accountability.

Objective of the Book

This book aims to provide in-depth knowledge of how the technology behind Metaverse and other virtual reality is changing the world. The primary objective of this book is to uncover the revolutionary innovation of the 21st century, Metaverse, and exhibit its wide range of applications in different domains. "Enter the future with *Metaverse and Blockchain: Real-World Applications*, a game-changing guide that reveals the revolutionary relationship between Blockchain and the Metaverse." This book is a pragmatic guide to how new technologies are changing industry. Distributed ledger technologies explore real-world applications that are shaping the future of digital interaction, from NFTs transforming art to Blockchain-securing supply chains and digital health diagnosis. This book covers cross-chain interaction schemes, multi-signature UAC locks, and Metaverse Blockchain Digital Twins. This book helps techies, business leaders, and curious minds traverse the Metaverse and Blockchain convergence, unlocking practical, significant breakthroughs.

This book provides the working principles of Metaverse and recent advancement in its applications.

Organisation of the Book

It includes the fundamentals of Metaverse, features, working principles, and its applications in different sectors. To meet the objectives, this book contains 11 chapters as follows:

Chapter 1

The chapter presents a detailed examination of Blockchain's functions and applications within the Metaverse ecosystem, with an emphasis on how it enhances critical aspects of Metaverse interactions and transactions.

Chapter 2

This chapter explores the Mobile Edge Computing (MEC)-based Metaverse and its applications. It emphasises how 6G can be integrated with the Mobile Edge Computing (MEC) paradigm and how Blockchain technology might improve MEC.

Chapter 3

This chapter provides a thorough examination of the Metaverse in education, highlighting emerging technologies, opportunities, problems, and trends.

Chapter 4

The chapter aims to comprehend the impact of Blockchain technology on financial services within the Metaverse by incorporating recent advancements and emerging trends. It illustrates how these technology advancements are generating novel corporate models and transforming global banking.

Chapter 5

This chapter investigates the potential applications of Blockchain technology throughout the supply chain of healthcare, with a specific emphasis on the healthcare industry.

Chapter 6

This chapter will talk about the problems that the previously mentioned industries are having because they still use old-fashioned supply chains. It will also talk about how the integrated Internet of Things and Blockchain-based systems in those industries can help solve those problems.

Chapter 7

This chapter analyses the role of Blockchain technology within the Metaverse, its challenges, and the incorporation of Artificial Intelligence (AI) in the advancement of intelligent Blockchain functionalities and their implications for the ecosystem.

Chapter 8

This chapter integrates Artificial Intelligence (AI), the Internet of Things (IoT), and Blockchain technologies into a unified ecosystem that is called smart farming.

Chapter 9

This chapter focuses on Network Slicing (NS) and Multi-Access Edge Computing (MEC) as 5G technologies that can enable Metaverse implementation.

Chapter 10

This chapter examines Metaverse-oriented Digital Anti-Ageing Healthcare (DAAH). It also demonstrates how Metaverse applications in chronic illness treatment, physical activity, and mental health supervision can enhance healthcare quality and extend patient life expectancy.

Chapter 11

This chapter delves into the advantages, obstacles, and future possibilities of combining Digital Twins, Blockchain, and the Metaverse. It aims to shed light on how this convergence can bridge and innovate the physical and digital realms, paving the way for a new era of interconnected, intelligent, and immersive digital experiences.

Topics presented in each chapter of this book are unique to this book and are based on our unpublished work. In writing this book, we attempted to bring into the discussion all the new trends and experiments that have been made with Blockchain and Metaverse. We believe this book is ready to serve as a reference for larger audiences such as system architects, practitioners, developers, and researchers.

Acknowledgements

The preparation of this edited book was like a journey that we had undertaken for several months. We wish to express our heartfelt gratitude to Director Prof. (Dr) K. L. Narayana, Faculty of Science and Technology (IcfaiTech), ICFAI Foundation for Higher Education, Hyderabad, Telangana, INDIA, Center of Excellence Blockchain Technology, ICFAI Society, library sources, our families, friends, colleagues, and well-wishers for their constant support throughout this journey. We express our gratitude to all the chapter contributors, who allowed us to quote their remarks and work in this book. We would like to acknowledge the hard work of authors and their cooperation during the revisions of their chapters. We would also like to acknowledge the valuable comments of the reviewers, which have enabled us to select these chapters out of the so many chapters we received and to improve the quality of the chapters. We wish to acknowledge and appreciate the Taylor & Francis team for their continuous support throughout the entire process of publication. Our gratitude is extended to the readers, who gave us their trust, and we hope this work guides and inspires them.

About the Authors

Dr Dileep Kumar Murala is an assistant professor in the Department of Computer Science and Engineering, Faculty of Science and Technology (IcfaiTech), The ICFAI Foundation for Higher Education (Deemed to be University), Hyderabad, Telangana, India. He completed his PhD at the School of Computer Engineering, KIIT (Deemed to be University), in 2020. He received a Master of Technology degree from the Department of Computer Science and Engineering, Andhra University Engineering College (AUE), Visakhapatnam, in 2011, and his Bachelor of Technology degree from the Department of Computer Science and Engineering, Gudlavalleru Engineering College (GEC), JNT University, Kakinada, in 2009. He has published 50 papers in international journals, conferences, and book chapters of repute. He holds two Indian patents to his credit. He has published the book titled *Security and Privacy Challenges in Cloud Computing Environment.* His research interests include Blockchain technology, Metaverse, AI, and cloud computing.

Dr Sandeep Kumar Panda is a professor and associate dean in the Department of Artificial Intelligence & Data Science, Faculty of Science and Technology (IcfaiTech), The ICFAI Foundation for Higher Education (Deemed to be University), Hyderabad, Telangana, India. His research interests include Blockchain technology, the Internet of Things, AI, and cloud computing. Dr Panda was recognised in the top 2% of scientists list published by Stanford University and Elsevier in 2024 and 2025. He has received five Best Paper awards from international conferences held in the UK, Singapore, Dubai, and India. He also received the Best Teacher Award and a cash prize of ₹1 lakh from ICFAI University Hyderabad during the 13th Convocation in 2023. He has published 108 articles in international journals, conferences, and book chapters of repute.

Chapter 1

Exploring the Blockchain Metaverse: Concepts, Technologies, Applications, and Challenges

1.1 Introduction

"Second Life" denotes offerings within the Metaverse. All physical components are animated and incorporated into virtual entities within the Metaverse by new technologies. This community space enables avatars to construct residences and engage with the virtual environment and other avatars. In contrast to the universe, a verse is a technologically constructed virtual realm akin to a game or simulation. A 1992 novel introduced the term "Metaverse" to denote a virtual refuge [76]. The Metaverse has been rejuvenated by advancements in virtual reality, computer vision, processing, networking, and communications. The most recent VR/AR wearables facilitate social interaction within the Metaverse. The Metaverse is a distinctive platform that integrates diverse applications with contemporary technology. The Metaverse can employ Digital Twin (DT) technology to create and modify virtual worlds utilising sensor or IoT data. DT facilitates the comprehension and enhancement of physical entities [77]. The universality of the Metaverse may have mitigated COVID-19. User avatars exhibit indoor preferences via various functionalities. Business telecommuting, virtual education, and industrial operations utilise the Metaverse. These configurations enhance teaching, communication, and the execution of challenging tasks with reduced effort and time. A Metaverse scenario features three

DOI: 10.1201/9781003520702-1

individuals residing in a house, each utilising distinct virtual worlds to achieve various objectives [1].

Virtual schools within the Metaverse have the potential to transform education for both educators and students. Students can investigate locations and do scientific experiments with lecturers and colleagues in virtual classrooms. An engaging method inspires pupils to acquire knowledge and develop [2]. Interactive graphics augment use case demonstrations. Medical schools can conserve time and offer significant experiential learning via virtual operations [7]. A digital replica of the Metaverse factory can be generated with factory sensors and actuators. Virtual processes utilising replicated factory machinery materialise instantaneously. Remote employees are also able to contribute lyrics [3]. Although they attract businesses, the majority of applications remain conceptual and are still under development. Numerous challenges must be surmounted prior to the realisation of the Metaverse. The generation and rendering in real time may be influenced by issues related to computer and networking infrastructure across various Metaverse scenarios. Users are mostly concerned about security, privacy, and trust about Metaverse integration [4]. Establish varied Metaverse ecosystems that embody user interests and behaviours. A user of an avatar must swiftly navigate virtual environments and engage with others and objects. These objectives necessitate appropriate architecture, resources, and technology inside the infrastructure. Various settings necessitate meticulous and secure synchronisation. Consequently, meticulously organised research facilitates the creation and integration of many situations within a comprehensive framework for Metaverse development. Notwithstanding the evaluations of Metaverse advancements, scholars require a definitive framework for content creation, rendering, engagement, and management. This framework delineates the primary characteristics, requirements, and obstacles of the Metaverse across several businesses. The organised Metaverse environment delineates each developmental phase and its facilitating areas. Certain Metaverse surveys are domain-specific, while others are multidisciplinary. Domain-specific studies concentrate on technologies that facilitate the Metaverse, such as AI, Blockchain, and 5G and 6G wireless. Subsequent research investigates the Metaverse market and corporate developments across several geographies and applications [5]. Transdisciplinary Metaverse research emphasises conceptual descriptions over the obstacles of technological integration and implementation [6]. No surveys have established criteria for the realisation, development, or pipeline ecosystem of the Metaverse. The Metaverse pipeline ecosystem and its difficulties must be explored due to their impact on academic and industry research. All of these factors can impede the formation of the Metaverse.

1.2 Background

1.2.1 Web 3.0

The Metaverse constitutes a wholly immersive Internet experience. Augmented Reality (AR) and Virtual Reality (VR) enable individuals to engage with diverse environments through avatars and contemporary web technologies [7]. The advancement of Web 3.0 technology is attributable to significant historical milestones. That is the Metaverse. Recent technology encompasses Web 3.0 (Web3). The Web serves as the foundation for all internet services. Web 3.0 lacks a cohesive definition due to its ongoing evolution and interpretation. Web 3.0 will facilitate decentralised software [8]. Web 3.0 will employ machine learning and artificial intelligence to develop more intelligent and adaptable software. What is the purpose of Web 3.0? HTML delineates the structure and layout of Web 1.0 and 2.0 sites. The affiliations and locations of HTML's data sources may vary from previous web versions; yet Web 3.0 will continue to depend on it [1].

1.2.2 Recent Technological Advancements Facilitate the Metaverse

This essay succinctly examines Metaverse technology. The online Metaverse comprises three-dimensional entities and landscapes. Envision remote work, digital museums, and online concerts from the comfort of home [9]. The industry employs Blockchain, augmented reality, virtual reality, 3D Reconstruction (3DR), artificial intelligence, and the Internet of Things to augment the 3D Metaverse.

- **Blockchain**: Blockchain facilitates decentralised digital ownership, collectibility, value transfer, transparency, and connectivity. Cryptocurrency facilitates multifaceted wealth transfers within commerce and society. Decentralized token can be purchased with Bitcoin. Acquire $16 \times 16\ m^2$ NFTs using in-game cryptocurrency. Blockchain safeguards digital real estate. Cryptocurrency may promote engagement in the Metaverse [11].
- **Augmented Reality (AR) and Virtual Reality (VR)**: AR and VR offer three-dimensional experiences. Augmented reality enhances reality with images and characters. Numerous cell phones and digital cameras are compatible with it, rendering it more accessible than virtual reality. Virtual reality replicates perspectives. The Metaverse is developing in augmented reality and virtual reality. Virtual reality can incorporate physical simulations into the Metaverse [10, 11].
- **AI**: Recently, artificial intelligence has been employed in corporate strategy, decision-making, facial recognition, and high-velocity computing. Recent AI research has concentrated on immersive Metaverses. Artificial intelligence expedites data analysis. Artificial intelligence systems can get distinctive insights from historical data and previous iterations. In specific Metaverse scenarios, non-player characters may possess artificial intelligence. Artificial intelligence has the potential to generate avatars for the Metaverse. Artificial intelligence can generate realistic avatars from two-dimensional and three-dimensional images [12].
- **3D Reconstruction**: Due to pandemic lockdowns restricting purchasers from inspecting houses, the utilisation of 3D reconstruction in real estate has surged. Some companies employ 3D reconstruction for virtual property tours.

Similar to the Metaverse, users can remotely explore new properties and make purchases. The Metaverse requires digital legitimacy. Three-dimensional reconstruction generates realistic environments. Specialised 3D cameras deliver lifelike representations of architecture, environments, and objects [13].

- **Internet of Things (IoT)**: Sensors and devices link our environment to the Internet within the framework of the Internet of Things (IoT). These gadgets acquire a distinct identity and are capable of transmitting and receiving data upon establishing an Internet connection. Devices such as thermostats, speakers, medical apparatus, and others are interconnected through the Internet of Things. Data from the Internet of Things is transmitted to the Metaverse. This enhances digital accuracy. Weather and other factors may influence Metaverse items through IoT data streams [14].
- **Edge Computing** employs a proximate data centre to the user, similar to cloud computing. The edge offers cloud-like processing, storage, data management, and applications. For the Metaverse to be realistic, it must fully immerse and engage people. The latency between user input and response should be minimised. Edge computing enhances response times by situating computers in proximity to users. The technology facilitating the Metaverse was referenced. Integrating these components enhances clarity. Figure 1.1 illustrates the technology underpinning the Metaverse [15].

These technologies serve as the foundation for the Metaverse. The Metaverse requires them.

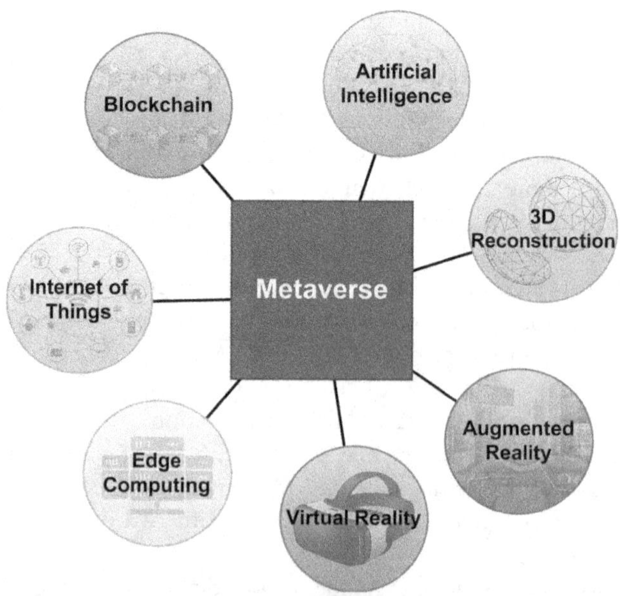

Figure 1.1 Foundational technologies of the Metaverse.

1.3 Principles of Blockchain and the Metaverse

This section presents Blockchain and the Metaverse, followed by an examination of their respective roles.

1.3.1 Fundamentals of Blockchain

Blockchain originated from Satoshi Nakamoto's 2008 white paper. The hash value of the preceding block header connects blocks inside a decentralised ledger. A block comprises a cryptographic hash, timestamp, nonce, and transactions [16]. The block timestamp is valid if it surpasses the network-adjusted time by two hours and the median of the preceding 11 blocks, thus averting Blockchain manipulation [17, 69]. The median of all node timestamps is the network-adjusted time. The Blockchain operates efficiently when each node adheres to a consensus method for the generation and verification of blocks. The consensus protocol governs the operations and legitimacy of the Blockchain. Bitcoin miners are required to utilise substantial computing power to resolve a stochastic mathematical problem employing the Proof of Work (PoW) methodology [18]. The difficulty, or nonce, for the subsequent block is adjusted every 10 minutes to avert the centralisation of processing power. Proof of Work exhibits poor transaction rates and considerable energy consumption; yet its processing power serves as a deterrent to attackers. Proof-of-Stake (PoS) enables miners to compete based on Bitcoin ownership instead of computing power, alleviating problems associated with Proof-of-Work (PoW) [19]. The enhanced InterPlanetary File System (IPFS) verifies service provider storage capacity issues through PoSpace consensus [20, 70]. Each block's transaction data is structured as a Merkle tree to enhance verification efficiency. Verification of a Merkle tree branch does not necessitate transaction data. Bitcoin is the inaugural Blockchain to decentralise transaction records. Researchers identified Blockchain technology as advantageous for asset management, family trusts, and ledgers. This resulted in the emergence of Ethereum, the second Blockchain. Smart contracts represent Ethereum's most significant invention [21, 71]. Regulations for programmatic smart contracts are present on the Blockchain. Smart contracts autonomously execute fund transfers or dispatch account notifications post-transactions. Access to smart contracts accelerates application development. Smart contracts render voting challenging to manipulate or comprehend. The insurance sector consolidates hospitals to oversee and document patient information on the Blockchain, utilising smart contracts to expedite claims processing. Smart contract derivatives and Non-Fungible Tokens (NFTs) are increasingly acquiring global prominence. Ethereum employs ERC-721 and ERC-1155 standards to differentiate NFT assets. NFTs are both indivisible and non-fungible, in contrast to Bitcoin and Ethereum. NFTs garner about $7 billion across art, gaming, sports, copyright, insurance, and various other sectors [22].

1.3.2 Fundamentals of the Metaverse

- **Definition of the Metaverse**: The Greek term "meta" signifies "more comprehensive" or "transcending." The term "verse" is derived from "universe," signifying the space-time continuum. The term "Metaverse," a fusion of two concepts, denotes a digital realm that transforms society. The Metaverse employs virtual reality, Digital Twins, and Blockchain to replicate reality [23]. Individuals can engage in employment, reside, and socialise in any location within the Metaverse. Neal Stephenson's 1992 science fiction novel *Snow Crash* established the Metaverse, whereby individuals utilise computer avatars to signify status. The Metaverse is a conceptual framework with limited protocols and implementations.
- **What Technologies Facilitate the Metaverse?** The Metaverse integrates 6G, artificial intelligence, virtual reality, and Digital Twins. Augmented and virtual reality are essential for the realisation of the Metaverse [24, 72]. Augmented Reality (AR) superimposes digital information onto the real world, whereas Virtual Reality (VR) engulfs users in an interactive digital environment. Both strategies are crucial for the Metaverse, a virtual realm where individuals can engage as if they were in reality. The second significant method is the Digital Twin, which forecasts the behaviour of physical objects utilising real-world data [25, 73]. In the Metaverse, Digital Twins can replicate reality. The Metaverse may provide experimental answers to tangible issues. Blockchain constitutes the third Metaverse technology, serving two primary functions. Blockchain has the capacity to safeguard Metaverse data. Blockchain has the potential to establish a worldwide economic framework that connects Metaverse virtual environments with physical reality. NFTs facilitate the translation from virtual to tangible assets. Virtual assets can be exchanged similarly to tangible ones. Consequently, Blockchain connects the Metaverse with physical reality [26, 74].

1.3.3 Function of Blockchain in the Metaverse

The Metaverse provokes numerous fascinating and amusing concepts. In this alternate universe, the economic ecosystem is inescapable. ERC-20 fungible tokens and ERC-721 or ERC-1155 non-fungible tokens constitute the fundamental elements of Blockchain technology. Blockchain is essential to the economics of the Metaverse. The Metaverse employs Blockchain for the following reasons [27].

- **Data Privacy and Security**: The Metaverse gathers sensitive information to enhance user experiences. This data assists companies and applications in developing targeted systems. If compromised, perpetrators may exploit the information to attack victims. The identity, access control, and consensus mechanisms of Blockchain provide users with complete data control and privacy. The Blockchain encrypts and hashes Metaverse data using asymmetric keys [28, 75].

- **Ensure Data Integrity**: The Metaverse aggregates healthcare and entertainment data. This data assists Metaverse AI models in making stakeholder assessments. Production of Metaverse items necessitates tangible user data. Blockchain enables individuals and organisations to authenticate all transactions through comprehensive audit trails. The quality of data in the Metaverse will enhance [76].
- **Enhanced and Secure Data Transmission**: AR/VR gadgets augment Metaverse connectivity and immersion. The primary advantage of Metaverse-augmented reality integration is the enhancement of both digital and physical entities. Innovative applications that address real-world issues prosper in the Metaverse due to frictionless data exchange in augmented and virtual reality. The Blockchain's sophisticated encryption safeguards data transit throughout the Metaverse [9].
- **Facilitating Data Interoperability**: Participants in the Metaverse require access to and ownership of virtual environments and application assets. The many virtual world ecosystems restrict data interchange. Cross-chain protocols provide data interchange among Blockchains operating in distinct virtual environments. Users can traverse virtual realms effortlessly with Blockchain interoperability [19].
- **Ensuring Data Integrity**: Data within the Metaverse must be precise and uniform. Impaired data integrity may undermine stakeholder confidence in the Metaverse. Due to the immutable nature of Blockchain technology, Metaverse data is copied in each block and cannot be altered or deleted without majority consent. This Blockchain technique safeguards Metaverse information. The following are examples of Blockchain applications within the Metaverse [10].
- **Blockchain in Finance Is Immutable, Accessible, Transparent, and Decentralised**. Transactions within the Metaverse are rapid, necessitating both security and efficiency. The characteristics of Blockchain render it a strong candidate for a large-scale, scalable virtual economic system. The Blockchain network's automated, programmable, transparent, and verifiable smart contracts facilitate dependable on-chain interactions without the necessity for third-party verification. Should the Metaverse financial system employ Blockchain technology, smart contracts can decentralise contractual activities in a programmable, non-custodial, verifiable, traceable, and dependable manner. This approach can markedly diminish financial, social, and gaming sector rent-seeking, corruption, and illicit activities [11].
- **NFTs**: *NFTs* are appropriate for identity representation due to their exclusivity and capacity for sale and transfer. Virtual assets in the Metaverse possess NFT ownership certificates.

1.4 Blockchain-Based Metaverse

Numerous computing specialists assert that the Metaverse will advance the internet due to its social network, which offers a cohesive, decentralised, immersive, continuous, three-dimensional virtual environment for interactions that transcend the physical realm. It garnered attention with its rebranding as Meta in October 2021 and its investment of $10 billion in the technology [12]. The Metaverse will influence IoT, big data, 6G, AI, 3D modelling, reconstruction, VR, spatial computing, and Digital Twins in the coming decades. Blockchain is the superior technology. The Metaverse facilitates NFTs, virtual reality, conferencing, digital art, and cooperation. Blockchain is essential for Metaverse applications. Blockchain safeguards and anonymises data through encryption and consensus mechanisms. The Metaverse gathers sensitive information for user experience, confidentiality, and authenticity. Secondly, Blockchain safeguards data [13]. The Metaverse aggregates critical information from banking, healthcare, government, and entertainment applications, necessitating authentication. Blockchain enables individuals and organisations to authenticate and authorise transactions via stringent review processes. Consequently, the quality of Metaverse data enhances [11]. Third, the immutability of Blockchain safeguards data. All blocks are cryptographically hashed, and participants must consent to modifications. Fourth, Blockchain ensures data interoperability across Metaverse virtual domains, where stakeholders require data, various applications, asset acquisition, and management. Virtual world apps and data are incompatible due to their disparate environments; nevertheless, Blockchain addresses this issue [9, 10]. Decentralisation, transparency, tamper-resistance, and the absence of transaction fees in Blockchain technology guarantee security, cost efficiency, performance, scalability, and efficacy for millions of financial transactions within the Metaverse. Blockchain smart contract technology independently verifies, identifies, and executes contracts, facilitating Metaverse integration in financial, social, and gaming domains while mitigating harmful and malicious activities. Metaverse technology employs NFTs and federated learning applications for digitisation, privacy, decentralisation, availability, scalability, and uniqueness. All these attributes are present in Blockchain [11, 13]. Federated Learning (FL) safeguards privacy by distributing training tasks among several clients and segregating local devices from the central server during the integration of the Metaverse into AI applications. FL possesses numerous vulnerabilities, including as single-point failure and malicious data. The deployment of federated learning is both secure and rapid when utilising Blockchain technology. NFTs necessitate digital storage, data transmission, privacy, security, automation, reduced transaction costs, and identification of participants and ownership [14].

1.5 Functionality of Blockchain Technology in the Metaverse

In the forthcoming decades, Blockchain's anonymity, security, indisputability, data sharing, privacy, traceability, immutability, decentralisation, smart contracts, and consensus will facilitate Metaverse applications and integrated technologies. Blockchain technology has enhanced digital innovation and Metaverse financial systems.

1. **Internet of Things**: Metaverse applications derive advantages from substantial volumes of IoT data. Healthcare, education, and smart city applications necessitate dependable and secure virtual environments for data, storage, hardware, and devices. The extensive range of Metaverse devices can access data from the IoT-based Blockchain, facilitating secure and immutable transactions. Individuals and applications can access IoT data without centralised oversight. The spread of the Internet of Things, Blockchain, and the Metaverse is challenging [76].
2. **Artificial Intelligence**: Data is processed and integrated into the Metaverse, becoming AI manageable and applicable. Blockchain ensures data integrity, privacy, traceability, and decentralisation. Consequently, the integration of Blockchain and AI within the Metaverse will facilitate precise digital analysis and data-informed decision-making. A multitude of users produce secondary and tertiary data, identified and traceable within the Blockchain-enabled Metaverse. Applications of AI in the Metaverse are founded on this data. Conversely, Blockchain consensus necessitates rapid block integration. A vulnerability in a smart contract might hinder the addition of a new block, enabling hackers to misappropriate hundreds of millions of dollars in cryptocurrency. Consequently, AI-Agent and federated learning are essential for rectifying smart contracts, enhancing Blockchain application security, managing dynamic scalability, and facilitating customisation and governance [77].
3. **Vast Data**: Efficient large data management is essential for integrating diverse data in Metaverse applications. Data manipulation in the digital realm facilitates comprehension of the Metaverse business model. Conversely, Metaverse data management must address heterogeneous, scalable, and rapid data. Blockchain will eradicate intermediaries and enhance the quality, authenticity, classification, retrieval efficiency, cost-effectiveness, and accessibility of Metaverse data [1].
4. **Extended Reality (XR)** employs computational technology and wearable devices to integrate real and virtual environments for Human–Computer Interaction (HCI). Metaverse platforms require XR applications for success. Nonetheless, VR, AR, and MR technologies require enhancement to integrate

virtual elements more precisely and extensively. Extended reality within the Metaverse induces anxiety at both community and individual levels. XR systems can furnish proprietary data to assist organisations in developing distinctive and recommended technology. XR user data must be secure, confidential, scalable, and transparent within the Metaverse. The Blockchain-based distributed ledger of the Metaverse would validate XR application data, facilitating an auxiliary and accurate recommendation system. Blockchain enhances data security in XR application file systems.

5. **Digital Twins**: DT signifies the digitisation of the Metaverse. All Metaverse applications necessitate a digital-physical integration for cohesive functionality. Digital Twin applications like banking, healthcare, and social media must interact and stabilise within fluctuating virtual environments. Moreover, Digital Twins must resolve connectivity challenges when transmitting real-time data. Blockchain technology, particularly the distributed Hyperledger, facilitates secure data sharing, anonymity, and transparency through Digital Twins inside the Metaverse ecosystem. No consensus is required to document and permanently record Blockchain-based Digital Twin transactions [2].
6. **Cybersecurity** enterprises and applications require data to develop Metaverse platforms. Data flow management, user interest profiling, and AI algorithm outputs could jeopardise the security and privacy of the Metaverse. Blockchain facilitates data storage, sharing, portability, interoperability, security, and privacy inside the Metaverse. Blockchain authentication, access control, and consensus safeguard user data. Blockchain employs hashing and asymmetric-key cryptography to protect Metaverse data. Blockchain technology facilitates decentralised and transparent identification of industrial equipment. This solution employs identity-based encryption and domain trust for device authentication. Preserve precise domain knowledge off-chain to minimise Blockchain storage requirements. A proof-of-concept simulation demonstrates the stability and applicability of its Blockchain privacy consensus. Blockchain guarantees dependable data sources and precise digital footprints by disseminating data among Metaverse services [3].
7. **Cloud Computing**: Digital and real-time cloud storage and processing enhance Metaverse services. In Metaverse applications, peer-to-peer Blockchains enhance cloud computing. Edge computing enhances access capacity, contextual information, secure access, and locational awareness. Network slicing orchestrates and enhances Metaverse applications across all enabling technologies.
8. **Mobile Intelligence**: The Metaverse employs Blockchain, artificial intelligence, the Internet of Things, and 5G/6G wireless communications to enhance mobile computing through distributed fog computing and Mobile Edge Computing (MEC). The MEC relocates computationally demanding tasks to the network's periphery and allocates resources in proximity to endpoints to enhance mobile devices' storage capacity, reduce latency, optimise

resources, improve computational performance, increase data rates, and boost efficiency. Intelligent mobile devices utilising 6G networks can seamlessly integrate with Blockchain, artificial intelligence, Metaverse edge computing, and other data analysis and interaction technologies to facilitate autonomous decision-making in production systems. Mining-based consensus ensures the security of MEC within the Blockchain-enabled Metaverse. Blockchain enables polynomial-time resource allocation. Blockchain technologies will be examined to alleviate MEC resource limitations [4].

1.6 Use Cases and Applications of the Metaverse

1.6.1 Use Cases

1. **Sophisticated Blockchain Applications**: The extensive integration of the Metaverse in enterprises necessitates Blockchain or decentralised technologies. Blockchain technology underpins cryptocurrencies such as Bitcoin, Ether, and Dogecoin, although it possesses numerous additional applications. Documenting peer-to-peer transactions facilitates the creation of NFTs and decentralised applications. The Metaverse can assist businesses in creating more immersive and realistic NFT markets that promote user engagement, NFT exploration, and improved purchasing decisions. Novel NFT and Blockchain games enabling players to trade in-game assets have emerged in the Metaverse. Blockchain game developers design distinctive online games utilising the Metaverse [5, 29, 30].
2. **Digital Educational and Professional Environments**: The COVID-19 pandemic has compelled international corporations to embrace digital communication. Video conferencing is prevalent in telecommuting, online education, and remote employment. In the absence of real-time audio and visual communication, these systems lack appeal. The Metaverse's stunning virtual environment, three-dimensional avatars, and immersive events effectively address this problem to engage consumers. The Metaverse enables exploration of a virtual world populated by lifelike avatars, rather than only conversing with individuals on a screen [31–33].
3. **Digital Enterprises and Marketplaces**: Businesses can utilise technology to promote their products and services in innovative ways. As the Metaverse expands, enterprises are transitioning from e-commerce to immersive virtual environments to enhance their experiences. Online entrepreneurs can assess products, negotiate terms, and execute contracts with vendors. Rather than employing digital marketing, businesses may utilise tangible content to engage customers. Metaverse technology facilitates the production, ownership, and exchange of digital assets and tokenised goods, hence enabling cryptocurrencies and NFTs [6, 34].

4. **Expanding Social Media Platforms**: Creators at Meta, such as Mark Zuckerberg, acknowledge that technology may extend beyond merely connecting individuals on social media. They assert that engagement with the Metaverse necessitates delivering a three-dimensional experience that goes beyond merely observing individuals on computers or phones and hearing their discourse. Metaverse-based solutions enhance user presence on social media, hence augmenting immersion. Virtual reality and augmented reality provide a more genuine digital experience compared to social networking [35, 36].

1.6.2 Applications

The Metaverse primarily serves gaming and social interaction. Nevertheless, numerous additional rivals demonstrate the potential of the Metaverse [7, 37]. Figure 1.2 analyses the primary commercial applications of the Metaverse.

1. **Professional Environment**: Specialised groups promote the Metaverse. Virtual reality retailers may showcase new trucks, automobiles, and recreational vehicles without the need for trade exhibitions. Engineers, marketers, sales professionals, financial analysts, and creatives enhance product development. Governments endeavour to regulate the Metaverse [19, 38]. Barbados seeks to establish a Metaverse embassy, despite the fact that the majority of

Figure 1.2 Applications of the Metaverse.

states are already present online. The Metaverse's prominence is transforming corporate operations.

a. *Ongoing endeavours will facilitate*: With the expansion of the Metaverse, certain industries will require reduced office space.
b. *Virtual offices are utilised to stay abreast with technological advancements*: Virtual and augmented reality will enhance workplace communication and collaboration, rendering physical offices obsolete. This is due to an increasing number of purchasers from various enterprises seeking tangible experience. VR-centric manufacturing encompasses system and equipment maintenance, industrial production lines, and personnel assembly [20, 39].
c. *Remote meetings*: Presently, they utilise Microsoft Teams or Zoom; however, as technology advances and virtual environments gain prominence, they will adopt a virtual room featuring avatars for each participant. Genuine 3D models of individuals can supplant avatars to accurately represent their expressions and actions.

2. **Apparel**: The innovative fashion industry consistently produces trends suitable for the Metaverse. The Gucci category "Metaverse Design" in Roblox is excellent. Users may now purchase exclusive fashion items from the esteemed vendor on the gaming platform. A computerised Gucci purse was sold for $4,000, indicating that virtual fashion is becoming lucrative. The allure of NFTs may result in exclusive virtual collections from premier fashion designers selling for millions [21, 40].
3. **Procurement**: Entrepreneurs and business proprietors anticipate that virtual reality will enhance the engagement of online buying. Access to online vendor assistance and the capacity to assess and appraise items will persist notwithstanding physical constraints. Certain academics assert that Metaverse technology facilitates both virtual and authentic transactions. Shopping malls will soon become obsolete. Virtual grocery will supplant online purchases [29, 41]. Zara introduced a new collection for individuals and avatars in collaboration with South Korean designer Ader Error. Virtual and physical apparel are marketed globally. Nike is leveraging the fascination with virtual products by launching "Nikeland," a Roblox store where users can adorn their avatars in Nike apparel.
4. **Recreation and Social Interaction**: The Metaverse has the potential to transform social networking and online entertainment. This is due to the fact that Metaverse consumers would prefer a more immersive virtual experience compared to existing social networks. Social networks will evolve into Metaverses where users will engage in dialogue and explore images using avatars or realistic self-representations. The rebranding of Facebook to "Meta" signifies the advancement of social media. Owing to its extensive accessibility, virtual reality technology is anticipated to advance, prompting consumers to transition from the web to the Metaverse [21, 42]. Numerous Metaverse games employ the "play to earn" premise, enabling players to exchange virtual assets for

actual currency. Participants may invite social media acquaintances to engage in gameplay, connect with other Metaverse users, and enhance their gaming experience. Players have the ability to construct, purchase, sell, invest, and compensate others. The Metaverse enables buyers to examine competing products using gaming, virtual reality, live streaming, cryptocurrency, and social media [22, 43]. Professional musicians execute performances in games. Lil Nas X, Royal Blood, 333, IDLES, and Ariana Grande will perform in Minecraft, Fortnite, and Roblox. Future Metaverse games could influence further genres. Virtual reality technology provides an immersive three-dimensional experience for participants at premier online casinos in the United States. Users can navigate a virtual casino floor and insert virtual chips into machines, rather than selecting a slot game from an extensive collection. The Metaverse will enable sports teams to reward fans post-game. Metaverse digital arenas provide real-time observation of teams and athletes. Multi-view camera technology enables supporters to support the football team, track players, and see the game from many perspectives. The Metaverse enables friends to convene digitally, even when separated by thousands of miles [23, 44].

5. **Travel and Tourism**: Virtual tourism represents an innovative application within the Metaverse. Technology facilitates virtual travel, obviating the necessity for international journeys. Experts assert that an immersive digital environment combining virtual and augmented reality can enhance tourism. Tourists unable to attend may purchase an interactive digital experience [30, 45]. Preliminary 360-degree virtual tours are accessible. Visitors may bypass the video tour and proceed to explore the area. Engage with family and friends to enhance the authenticity and enjoyment of your visit. Virtual reality tourism has progressed from its origin. Thomas Cook's "Try Before You Fly" initiative uses Visualise to enable prospective passengers to virtually explore destinations prior to making a reservation. The user may select the recommended destination subsequent to utilising this service. A 5-minute VR experience unexpectedly augmented excursions to New York [24, 46].
6. **Healthcare Services**: Augmented reality can enhance the competencies of medical students and reduce expenses. Clinical personnel utilise Microsoft HoloLens to expedite surgical procedures. Augmented reality headsets exhibit real-time patient metrics such as pulse, body temperature, heart rate, and respiration rate. CT, MRI, and 3D scan images are accessible [31, 47]. Augmented reality assists physicians in locating veins. This assists those with dark skin or diminutive blood vessels in locating veins. Augmented reality will assist physicians in diagnosing and treating numerous diseases, even with the use of X-rays and CT scans. Virtual reality enhances surgical training by more than 230% [25, 48].
7. **Armed Forces**: Military augmented and virtual reality technologies have progressed. Night Vision Goggles (NVGs) are categorised as Tactical Augmented Reality (TAR) but have numerous supplementary applications. It depicted military forces, allies, and adversaries on a map. Soldiers do not require GPS

position checks on the battlefield, as the helmet can incorporate the gadget. The AR Synthetic Training Environment (STE) replicates combat scenarios to provide soldiers with authentic and immersive training in challenging battlefield settings. STE assists commanders in training adaptable, prepared units [26, 49].

8. **Real Estate**: The primary advantage is the immersive property viewing experience for prospective purchasers. This technology enables real estate clients to do virtual home tours prior to in-person visits. Background music, narrative, and audiovisual elements are permitted in VR tours. Authentic and stimulating features enhance client enthusiasm and confidence prior to commitment. Virtual tours and guided walkthroughs engage clients in the property and its surroundings. This minimises trip duration and instils confidence in purchasers and tenants about traffic conditions and ambiance. Real estate brokers conserve time and financial resources by circumventing protracted showings and buyer-seller consultations [32, 50]. Virtual walkthroughs can cater to various client preferences, in contrast to tours. Visual clients have advantages from lighting, room design, Zoom, and further factors. Data-driven clients may utilise pop-up windows for statistics, spatial metrics, and additional information [10, 51].
9. **Production, Instruction, and Safety**: Individuals acquire knowledge more rapidly and effectively in immersive learning settings. Comprehensive virtual reality training conserves time and financial resources for industrial firms during employee training and onboarding. Employees comprehend safety protocols and replicate hazardous scenarios. These technologies facilitate the development of commercial products. All product attributes can be assessed using virtual reality. Virtual and augmented reality have lowered accidents across multiple applications [33, 52]. Virtual reality can assist manufacturers in designing manufacturing line layouts. They can promptly suggest optimal equipment positioning while preserving distance. Safety and the installation of appropriate equipment have been enhanced. Virtual and augmented reality enhance BMW's automotive design process, making it more efficient and cost-effective. Siemens and VRdirect developed an industrial tour. A dynamic training platform replicates industrial environments for personnel. Ford personnel utilised virtual reality and augmented reality to remotely access their vehicles during the coronavirus outbreak. Organisations, particularly those with intricate systems and substantial equipment, prioritise employee safety. Employees are required to get updates on industrial security and occupational safety. Virtual reality enhances safety training for hazardous machinery and equipment. Employees can safely undertake virtual examinations prior to assessments [16, 53].
10. **Instruction**: Conventional pedagogical methods cannot compete with the visual emphasis of the Metaverse. Students across all age groups favour videos over literature. Virtual reality may provide students with immersive, fantastical experiences that inspire them to engage in their studies. Contemporary educators encounter difficulties in fostering interesting learning environments. As virtual reality technology becomes increasingly accessible at educational

institutions, the majority of students will exchange and deliberate on their experiences, thereby mitigating the gravity of this issue. Virtual reality may assist in identifying material issues and enhancing editing, which is on the rise. It removes the linguistic obstacle that impedes the education of numerous students [17, 54].

11. **Intimate Relationships**: The COVID-19 pandemic demonstrated the transformative impact of technology. The digital realm will transform our ties inside the Metaverse, particularly those of a romantic and sexual kind. Adult closeness can be achieved through virtual business meetings, concerts, and social gatherings. Long-distance couples can engage in intimacy via the Metaverse. The advancement in HMI development is remarkable. Meta Reality Labs unveiled a prototype of a haptic glove, including ridged pads designed to sense surface textures. Advancements in display and optical technologies occur. The clear lenses of combiner optics can superimpose virtual pictures onto reality, enhancing the practicality of augmented reality glasses. Transparent surface relief waveguides on high-refractive-index glass provide three-dimensional sensing, vehicle heads-up displays, and virtual reality screens [19, 20, 55]. The integration of these technologies with the swiftly advancing domain of haptics and sensory experiences may enhance virtual intimate ties.

1.7 Technological Challenges

1.7.1 Hardware Devices

Hardware encompasses the tangible devices required to utilise, engage with, or generate the Metaverse. This encompasses VR/AR headsets, portable controllers, haptic gloves, and bodysuits, together with corporate equipment such as cameras, projectors, optical devices, tracking instruments, and scanning systems utilised for the operation or creation of virtual environments [21, 56]. Despite advancements in consumer electronics technology such as computational power, sensors, haptics, displays, cameras, and battery longevity, analysts assert that hardware constraints are hindering the Metaverse's potential. The 3D Metaverse is significantly dependent on virtual or augmented reality; nonetheless, widespread adoption remains challenging. Consequently, companies are diligently striving for enhancement. Meta has recently enhanced its Oculus VR headsets by removing the requirement for a gaming console or personal computer [22, 57]. Even sophisticated models require more rapid GPUs for head tracking. Eye-tracking technology could alleviate system strain by utilising more powerful GPUs for VR/AR headsets. The immersion in the Metaverse is constrained by cumbersome VR/AR headsets. The market demands lightweight and durable hardware. Display technology has progressed in tandem with the computational power required to develop a gadget that effortlessly transitions between digital and physical realities.

1.7.2 Network Velocity

Many individuals conflate bandwidth with "speed"; however, it is, in fact, the maximum volume of data a connection can accommodate. The maximum data transport speed is quantified in Mbps and Gbps. The Metaverse necessitates higher specifications than the majority of Internet applications and games, and these requirements will escalate as virtual operations get increasingly intricate. Certain platforms get profit from the recycling and limitation of digital assets. Roblox typically provides altered downloads. The virtual platform will necessitate several modifications and enhancements. Numerous online gamers encounter bandwidth limitations and network congestion in location-based games. The Metaverse will amplify these requirements. Global bandwidth and internet connectivity are enhancing. Machine learning algorithms can forecast results while anticipating human input due to enhanced computational power [28].

- **Latency**: The round-trip time for data transmission is a significant network concern. A delay of 100, 200, or 300 seconds between the transmission of a WhatsApp message and its read receipt is negligible in contemporary applications. The 500-millisecond interval between YouTube's skip button and the subsequent video is negligible. Netflix and Hulu prioritise seamless viewing over immediate access. Streaming providers postpone video broadcasts to enable your device to pre-buffer content. You will not perceive network congestion or disruptions. Latency adversely affects Metaverse environments, which require seamlessness and instantaneous interaction [23, 58].
- **Reliability**: Reliable connectivity signifies trustworthiness. We require dependable services to accommodate virtual trade, education, and recreation. This encompasses network availability, download and upload velocities, and latency. Netflix provides premium streaming in 1080p or 4K resolution. Note that many services employ reliability measures such as buffering, which are inappropriate for gaming or Metaverse applications [24, 59].

1.7.2.1 Design, Implementation, and Assistance

We emphasise the technological hurdles faced by stakeholders in the development and deployment of Metaverse technology for a more comprehensive analysis. The authors' domain expertise underscores critical issues.

- **Interoperability**: Technical concerns encompass interoperability among platforms, applications, and virtual environments. To prevent disruptions, alterations, and complications, parties must implement standardised data sharing protocols. Compatibility challenges and communication protocols must be addressed for avatars from disparate Metaverse platforms to engage with virtual things [25, 60].

- **Scalability and Performance**: Constructing a Metaverse capable of accommodating numerous users while delivering an exceptional experience is challenging. Enhancing infrastructure, minimising latency, optimising network capacity, and managing substantial data volumes in real time pose challenges for stakeholders. Logistics can complicate seamless interactions and responses in a heavily populated virtual setting.
- **Real-Time Communication and Networking** are essential for user collaboration in the Metaverse. Establishing communication protocols and synchronising remote systems poses challenges for stakeholders. Metaverse telephonic communications, video conferencing, and virtual events necessitate resilient networking protocols [26, 61].
- **Enhancing User Experience and Content Creation** necessitates the provision of intuitive tools and interfaces that empower and engage users. Stakeholders must develop technologies that enable users to effortlessly construct and personalise virtual things, settings, and experiences. Achieving a seamless user experience in the development and interaction of virtual materials is challenging [62, 63].
- **Developing User-Friendly Drag-and-Drop Interfaces** or interactive scripting for user-generated material is challenging. Challenges in artificial intelligence emerge throughout the development of intelligent entities within the Metaverse. Stakeholders must create AI systems that comprehend user interactions, exhibit realistic behaviour, and adjust to evolving circumstances. AI-driven virtual assistants and natural language processing entities necessitate sophisticated artificial intelligence and data management [27, 64].
- **Data Management and Analytics**: The Metaverse produces extensive user data regarding preferences, interactions, and behaviours. Stakeholders encounter difficulties in managing, analysing, and comprehending data to derive insights, customise experiences, and enhance platforms while ensuring privacy, scalability, and governance [35, 65]. Efficient data storage and analytical systems necessitate data management and analytical expertise to comprehend user behaviour and generate tailored recommendations. These constitute significant technological challenges for Metaverse players. To establish a cohesive and immersive experience, these challenges necessitate collaboration, research, innovation, and enhancements in technology and infrastructure [19, 66].

1.8 Recommendations for Future Directions

Scalability options for Blockchain-based Metaverse platforms require additional investigation. New consensus mechanisms and layer-2 solutions are required to accommodate increased transactions and assets. Standardised protocols provide asset mobility and communication inside virtual environments, enhancing Metaverse interoperability. Research on edge computing and resource-sharing is essential to enhance Metaverse apps and minimise user latency. Immersive virtual environments exert pressure on centralised cloud infrastructures. Edge computing addresses this issue by situating processing capabilities in proximity to Metaverse users and applications. Edge computing in the Metaverse diminishes latency and data transmission durations by situating processing resources in proximity to users, hence enhancing responsiveness and fluidity [10, 67].

Future advancements in AI, VR, and AR will augment user experiences and virtual environments. These technologies will employ AI algorithms to enhance the immersion and adaptability of VR and AR. Machine learning and AI-driven predictive algorithms can enhance VR/AR content. Future research may diminish processing demands and create AI models for high-fidelity virtual and augmented reality experiences. These technologies are employed in education, entertainment, healthcare, and training simulations. A cohesive Metaverse necessitates the collaboration of Blockchain, VR, and AI experts [34, 68]. This approach employs diverse expertise to develop compatible standards, protocols, and frameworks. This technique enhances AI algorithms, fortifies Blockchain security, and advances virtual reality. Users of the Metaverse require ethical and regulatory frameworks to ensure privacy and safety. Research on the significant energy and environmental costs of Blockchain network sustainability in Metaverse applications is essential. The objective is to diminish the carbon footprint of Blockchain technology. Energy efficiency in Blockchain networks is enhanced by algorithms, protocols, and hardware optimisations. Integrating Blockchain into the Metaverse sustainably and at scale necessitates an examination of consensus mechanisms, data storage techniques, and computational algorithms. These initiatives safeguard Metaverse networks and mitigate the environmental impact of Blockchain technology [2].

Practical examples are employed to evaluate how Blockchain-based Metaverse systems might exceed digital settings and transform diverse sectors. The research investigates Blockchain technology within the domains of entertainment, healthcare, and education in the Metaverse. This encompasses secure, decentralised data management, authentication, and transaction protocols. The objective is to develop interoperable systems that leverage the immutability and transparency of Blockchain technology to enhance security, privacy, and trust in practical applications. Blockchain safeguards healthcare information and authenticates educational credentials. It authenticates digital ownership of entertainment assets. The essay illustrates how Blockchain-based Metaverse platforms may transform enterprises and promote innovation, transparency, and trust [18].

1.9 Conclusion

Metaverses enable individuals to establish their own realms and enterprises, thereby unlocking novel opportunities. This paper analyses applications and formulates research criteria for future investigations into the Metaverse. The study comprehensively addressed Blockchain's role in the creation of Metaverse applications and services. This essay elucidated the function of Blockchain in the evolution of the

Metaverse. Blockchain will transform the development and governance of the Metaverse. Transparency in virtual assets and transaction flows necessitates safe, decentralised infrastructure. It tackles numerous governance challenges within the Metaverse. This study evaluated Blockchain technology and Metaverse applications, identifying issues and proposing enhancements. The expanding Blockchain-driven Metaverse necessitates research and innovation for scalability, interoperability, and edge resource distribution. This evaluation encompasses the Metaverse's developmental ecosystem, encompassing technologies, facilitating domains, and social enablers for educational and commercial applications. Our survey presents the initial projected trajectories for the difficulty of each component within the Metaverse ecosystem.

Chapter 2

The Future of the Metaverse: Augmenting Virtual Worlds with Mobile Edge Computing

2.1 Introduction

The Metaverse has emerged as a formidable alternative to the Internet. The Metaverse enables users to employ their avatars to interact with three-dimensional virtual environments for business, education, or leisure, rather than browsing web sites on laptops or smartphones [1]. Virtual visualisation technologies such as VR, AR, MR, and XR enable users to interact with realistic inputs in immersive virtual environments. Numerous multibillion-dollar corporations are keen on investing in the Metaverse [2]. Meta, formerly known as Facebook, will allocate \$10 billion into Metaverse technologies. Microsoft invested 70 billion dollars to acquire Activision Blizzard to develop its own Metaverse. The Metaverse is anticipated to fundamentally transform the Internet and influence all aspects of our lives. Potential uses include online education, remote work, and real estate. Metaverse applications must satisfy particular criteria, including minimal latency, substantial resource demands, application compatibility, and security and privacy concerns, to effectively utilise a vast virtual environment [3]. Contemporary Metaverse applications emulate avatar physics and generate images with cloud-based technologies. Elevated cloud access latency results in diminished visibility and many challenges, rendering the centralised solution inappropriate. Numerous Second Life virtual worlds are centralised. Every virtual realm has zones managed by various specialist servers. The central server of the region manages physics rendering, 3D animation, and collision

DOI: 10.1201/9781003520702-2

detection for the simulation of the virtual environment. The processing power and networking capabilities of a server restrict the number of users that can access each zone. The limitation contradicts the concept of a global virtual environment, which ought to encompass as many avatars as there are individuals on Earth [4]. Fog computing and mobile edge computing address cloud-based system challenges by relocating computationally heavy jobs nearer to consumers and distributed edge devices. Adopting this strategy can enhance system performance and diminish latency. This research presents a Fog-Edge hybrid computing architecture for Metaverse applications. An edge-enabled distributed computing paradigm employs edge devices to do intricate computations, such as 3D physics simulations and virtual universe collision detection [42, 43]. Each physical entity's terminal device manages computational expenses such as physics simulation and collision detection [5]. Users of edge devices in the Metaverse perform computing tasks associated with avatar mobility. These tasks ascertain the mass, momentum, and physical forces of the area's objects. We encapsulated our input as follows:

- Analyse the trends in Metaverse development in relation to the evolution of Blockchain technology and evaluate the likelihood of multiple fragmented Metaverses emerging instead of a singular entity.
- Researchers delineate a hybrid Fog-Edge architecture for Metaverse applications. The architecture operates the Metaverse utilising the computational capability of physical devices' endpoints [6].
- Model the proposed architecture in a distributed social Metaverse application context to evaluate the advantages of decentralisation compared to centralisation.

2.1.1 Mobile Edge Computing

2.1.1.1 Introduction to Multi-Access Edge Computing

MEC computing models are examined to optimise computational efficiency and communication. As a result, computations are carried out close to the user at the edge of the network [7, 44]. Figure 2.1 describes how edge servers optimise computational resources by situating themselves at the peripheries of networks.

Decentralised mobile communication networks are facilitated by MEC servers, which are distinct from fog and cloud computing [8, 45]. Substantial enhancements in network security and privacy are achievable, as well as a reduction in congestion during peak transmission periods. Research in mobile edge computing is expanding, especially on job offloading and system architecture design. The study [9, 46, 47] presents an enhanced auction technique for job outsourcing. This technique has two phases: outsourcing and scheduling. The methodology considers the superior computation and storage capacities of peripheral servers in contrast to the constrained

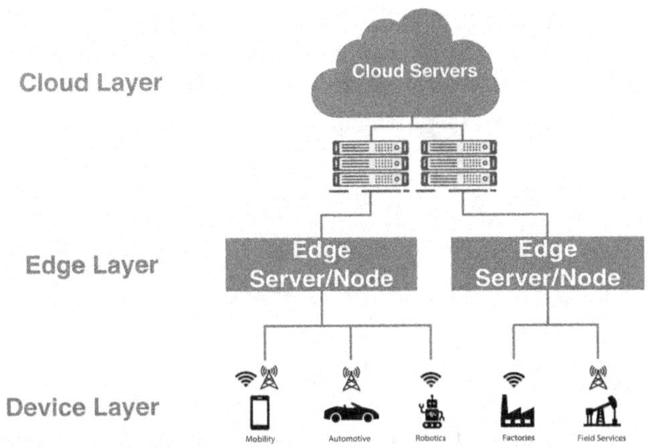

Figure 2.1 Edge servers optimise computational resources by situating themselves at the peripheries of networks.

resources of smart devices. This methodology evaluates the energy and time expenditures of local or peripheral task execution to inform offloading decisions during the decision phase. This ascertains whether the network's edge will execute the compute task. Task scheduling seeks to minimise computational latency and transmission energy consumption when delegating tasks to the edge server to get the global optimum. The journal paper [10] examines user mobility, categorises cellular networks with greater precision, and presents state transfer probabilities. This study formulates virtual machine migration as a Markov decision process to reduce energy consumption and delay, use policy iteration to identify the optimal solution. Mobile Edge Computing (MEC) is essential for service execution, particularly in task delegation and resource distribution. In order to supply computational resources and services, Vehicular Edge Computing (VEC) networks use cars as edge servers at the edge of the Internet of Things framework. Workload-specific resource distribution is made possible by the collaboration between Vehicle Edge Servers (VESs) and Fixed Edge Servers (FESs), which enables network computing offloading and computational alternatives. Articles [11, 48] demonstrate that enhancing web-based service system design with Mobile Edge Computing (MEC) technology enables edge servers to reduce core network resource consumption. MEC effectively manages real-world Web AR installations.

2.1.2 Metaverse and Mobile Edge Computing

Local XR devices or cloud servers may do all computational activities. The enhancement of battery life, reduction of device weight, and minimisation of delay are at odds with this technique. The integration of mobile edge computing with the Metaverse represents a significant advancement in MEC technology [12, 49, 50]. This method diminishes dependence on cloud servers while enhancing real-time performance and security. The rendering division is started by this convergence. Through transmission to edge clouds and IoT devices, graphic rendering improves on-device operations. In latency-sensitive systems, photonic processing improves head and motion tracking, which increases Metaverse visuals. Additionally, Metaverse systems can operate as high-performance Distributed Stream Processing Systems (DSPSs) with minimal latency thanks to the architecture of stream processing technology [16, 51].

Subsequent details of additional investigations are provided.

2.1.2.1 MEC-Oriented Architecture

The conventional cloud-based Metaverse architecture necessitates transmitting substantial data, such as avatar movements and environmental variables, to a central server, resulting in inefficiencies in virtual operations and services. Innovative Metaverse architectures utilising Mobile Edge Computing (MEC) have enhanced performance and effectively addressed limitations [13, 52, 53].

- **Metaverse Utilising Mobile Edge Computing**: This architecture employs several dynamic edge nodes to execute user commands. This design reduces user movement delays. At consumer side sensitive data is transmitted to the edge server. Optimising and dispersing edge servers provides clients with diminished latency and an enhanced Metaverse experience. Federated Learning (FL) technology is crucial for safeguarding against data breaches during the transmission of user data. The FL layer utilises parameters from analogous local models rather than private data for supplementary training [14, 54, 55]. Figure 2.2 describes the architecture of the Metaverse utilising mobile edge computing.
- **The Fog-Edge-Cloud Metaverse**: Article [15] suggests a hierarchical distributed hybrid computing architecture with multiple server tiers to mitigate Metaverse dispersion and processing constraints. Cloud layer servers replicate virtual worlds. Dedicated edge layer servers manage computational duties associated with virtual structures and the animation of virtual environments. Fuzzy servers in the fog layer do computations for virtual home environments and user mobility.

2.1.2.2 User Side Improvement

To achieve an immersive and real-time virtual world experience, it is essential to precisely forecast and assess users' behaviours, habitual preferences, and movement trajectories. Mobile Edge Computing (MEC) delivers efficient, uninterrupted services to consumer devices [16, 56]. The geographical placement of MEC servers facilitates real-time service provision. Figure 2.3 describes the BoundlessXR amalgamates XR, 5G, and edge-cloud technologies.

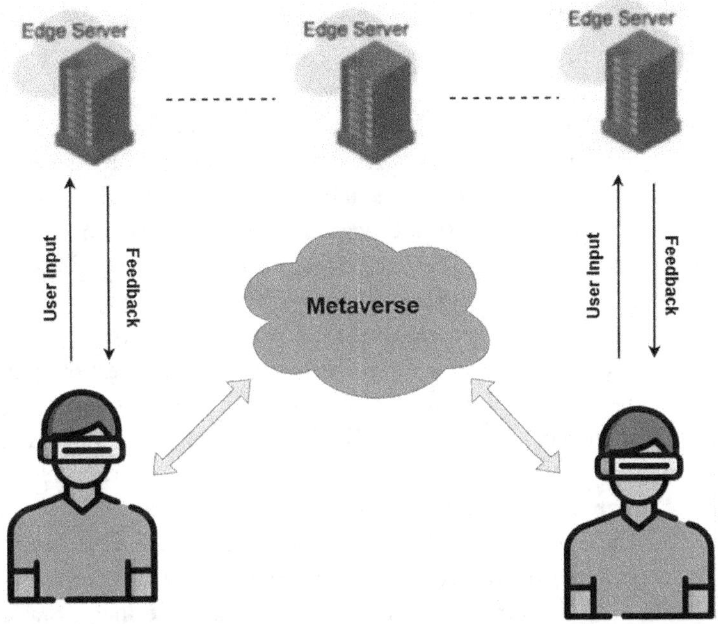

Figure 2.2 Architecture of the Metaverse utilising mobile edge computing.

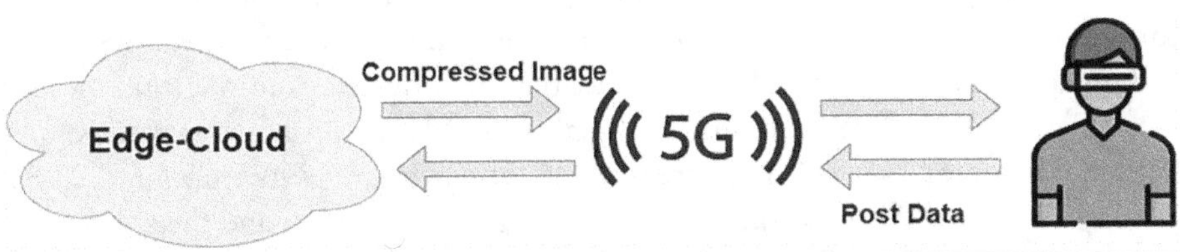

Figure 2.3 BoundlessXR amalgamates XR, 5G, and edge-cloud technologies.

Edge servers can conduct complex tasks and provide feedback to mobile devices since they have more computational power than local devices like VR headsets, HMDs, and AR glasses. By reducing latency, this improvement will ease user discomfort and dizziness.

- **System Side**: Mobile Edge Computing (MEC)-based Metaverse systems provide improved resource allocation and notably lower latency. Most Metaverse applications can be optimised for the computational capabilities of MEC servers. The diminutive size and portability of most gadgets constrain their battery life and computational capacity, a challenge that the Metaverse, utilising Mobile Edge Computing, seeks to resolve. All Metaverse components perform better when dynamic resource allocation [17, 57] and edge intelligence-based technologies [19, 58] are used.

2.1.2.3 Application Contexts

Metaverse applications necessitate on-device computation. The on-device processing unit manages all XR processing tasks. On-device processing employs edge cloud technologies to enhance power economy, performance, and minimise latency in rendering and tracking. Qualcomm's Boundless XR solution employs split rendering to distribute computing tasks across edge servers and end devices for 5G-enabled extended reality. Virtual reality devices transmit 6-degrees-of-freedom head position data to the edge cloud via 5G technology. The edge cloud transmits the compressed image to devices following input processing and image generation [18, 59]. Devices used for virtual reality also process information inside. Using 5G and MEC technology, the latency between motion, rendering, and photon transmission is less than 20 milliseconds, satisfying the requirements for Metaverse services. Any openVR/XR application running on a distant server can provide XR data using NVIDIA's CloudXR, which dynamically modifies network conditions to improve image quality and lower latency.

Academic research in edge computing is expanding concurrently with corporate advancements. The study [19, 60] introduced an innovative FACT technique to effectively address network latency, compute latency, and system accuracy, the three essential elements of an edge-based mobile AR system. The incorporation of this new paradigm into MAR applications enhanced video frame processing in the Metaverse and addressed optimisation challenges encountered by numerous mobile users. DARE, an innovative optimisation protocol [20, 61], enhanced edge server computing and augmented reality configurations. The examination of various coherence periods in MEC-based MAR indicates that the Lyapunov optimisation method [21, 62] can enhance the reliability and Quality of Metaverse Augmentations (QoA). Within an energy-aware MEC-based MAR framework, the authors of [22, 63] investigated the LEAF algorithm regarding energy consumption and the interplay of MAR system factors.

2.2 Implementation of Metaverse Computing Technology

This section examines Mobile Edge Computing technologies that facilitate the Metaverse. This essay thoroughly assesses the advancements of 5G and 6G wireless connectivity, Blockchain technology, Digital Twins, and artificial intelligence to facilitate Mobile Edge Computing (MEC) in the Metaverse [23, 64]. The Metaverse depends on Blockchain technology and cellular networks. Digital Twin and artificial intelligence technologies constitute the virtualisation engine. Mobile devices, such as augmented reality and virtual reality headsets, serve as the user interface.

2.2.1 Wireless 5G and 6G Technologies

In contrast to the 5G wireless communication network, the 6G network must tackle latency, reliability, and application contexts [24, 65]. Subsequent detailed comparisons are presented:

- **5G**: According to ITU 5G specifications, three primary use cases have been identified: Enhanced Mobile Broadband (eMBB), Ultra-Reliable Low-Latency Communication (URLLC), and Massive Machine-Type Communication (mMTC). The fifth generation (5G) network technology succeeds the fourth generation (4G) and aims to enhance data transmission speeds, decrease latency, accommodate a greater number of users, devices, and services, and optimise network efficiency. Owing to the proliferation of communication devices, the exponential increase in communication data, and the dynamic characteristics of communication networks, 5G may fail to satisfy some stringent standards [25, 66].
- **6G**: In contrast to 5G, 6G emphasises Mobile Broadband Reliable Low-Latency Communication (MBRLLC) [26]. 6G mobile communication technology, with "connected intelligence," promises improved network coverage and connectivity. 6G enhances various parameters, including a maximum transmission rate of 1 Tbit/s, which will advance current and forthcoming communication applications [37]. Moreover, holographic communication and high-fidelity human–computer interaction contexts are propelling the advancement of 6G technology. The primary objective of 6G is to provide consumers with a multifaceted and intelligent communication network through semantic communication [27, 67].

2.2.2 Blockchain Technology

Blockchain is a decentralisation technology that safeguards Metaverse user data, enhances transaction transparency, and mitigates the danger of a single point of failure. Sharding and cross-chain technology can segment the Metaverse into multiple shards to enhance its scalability and interoperability [28, 68]. Blockchain facilitates the distribution of edge resources by regulating access and identifying virtual services. Blockchain, a pivotal edge computing technology, has the potential to enhance Metaverse compute offloading, resource distribution, and edge intelligence.

2.2.3 Digital Twin

The Digital Twin is crucial for the virtualisation of tangible items, locations, and individuals. A Digital Twin amalgamates simulation methodologies across several disciplines, physical metrics, dimensions, and probabilities by utilising data from physical models, sensor inputs, and operational records. This mapping is subsequently completed in a virtual environment to precisely represent the life cycle of the actual equipment [38, 69].

2.2.4 Artificial Intelligence

Artificial intelligence technologies are employed to replicate various Metaverse scenarios. The Metaverse platform employs data inference to provide multilingual environments and tailored application services. Artificial intelligence technology is essential for the performance of Metaverse systems. Deep Neural Networks (DNNs) in visual transformer architectures can enhance accuracy and efficiency by managing variable and uncertain temporal constraints. Deep learning algorithms can categorise edge servers as either trustworthy or malevolent, hence enhancing system security and convergence [29, 70].

2.3 Investigating Research Challenges in MEC-Enabled Metaverse

Despite advancements in the aforementioned technologies, the implementation of a large-scale Metaverse system facilitated by Mobile Edge Computing (MEC) in the real world continues to pose challenges. This section will address topics related to Medium Element Computing in the Metaverse study [39].

2.3.1 Optimal Resource Allocation

It enhances computing performance and enables the adaption of Metaverse service applications. There are two categories of resource allocation challenges: communication and computing. Frequency Division Multiple Access (FDMA) bandwidth, Time Division Multiple Access (TDMA) time, and Non-Orthogonal Multiple Access (NOMA) power allocation are critical subjects in communication resource allocation [30]. FDMA, TDMA, and NOMA refer to frequency-division, time-division, and non-orthogonal multiple access, respectively. NOMA power allocation is the chosen option for 5G, rendering it noteworthy. Offloading strategies significantly influence the distribution of computational resources. Virtual reality devices and edge servers possess distinct processing capabilities; hence, local execution and offloading to edge servers are favoured [40, 71]. Both techniques must equilibrate latency and resources. The distinctive allocation of edge computing resources via device-edge association is garnering increased scholarly attention.

2.3.2 Mobility

Immersive experiences necessitate high fidelity and seamless transitions as users alter their field of view and posture. Resource allocation influences the efficiency and reliability of services, but conventional optimisation techniques necessitate increased computational resources. Deep reinforcement learning can enhance mobility and service. The prediction technology utilises historical head movements to ascertain the user's 360-degree position and precisely render the subsequent screen view [41, 72]. The ability to forecast user positions through the analysis of their physical movements might enhance resource allocation.

2.3.3 Security Protocols

Given that the Metaverse is predicated on Blockchain-based economic systems, the issues of security and privacy necessitate attention [31]. The subsequent security elements are enumerated. Individuals engaged in trading commodities, stocks, and other digital currencies must safeguard their virtual assets and transaction credentials from potential threats. Securing data transmission and server input is essential for safeguarding Metaverse users against hackers. Consequently, enhanced authentication and post-quantum cryptography serve as the primary defences against adversaries. Perpetrators in the Metaverse may conspire to pilfer or sexually assault digital avatars. Data extracted from physical devices may grant attackers entry to users' actual environments and possessions.

2.3.4 Privacy

Service providers gather diverse human biological data from consumers to tailor their service delivery, hence heightening the risk of privacy violations. Pupil spacing and size of users can be quantified through eye tracking data. Colour sensitivity and colour blindness can be assessed by evaluating user reaction times to various hues. Examining users' reaction times to various languages might indicate their nationality and native tongue. Real-Time Time (RTT) across graphical resolutions aids in evaluating the performance and cost-effectiveness of consumer-worn devices. Companies require statistics on user attention duration to enhance product marketing strategies. Nonetheless, revealing it could jeopardise users' privacy and enable perpetrators to exploit their identities in the Metaverse [32, 73]. Consequently, it is essential to analyse various methodologies and risk assessment frameworks to mitigate hazards and safeguard customers from the numerous threats they face. Federated learning and homomorphic encryption enhance system resilience and user privacy.

2.4 MEC-Enabled Metaverse Utilisation

This section delineates promising applications of the Metaverse.

2.4.1 Smart Manufacturing

The Metaverse has transitioned numerous industrial manufacturing processes to online platforms, along with altering individuals' daily activities. Virtual Reality (VR) and Augmented Reality (AR) enable individuals to do industrial tasks that are unfeasible in the physical realm, thereby establishing the "industrial Metaverse." Microsoft Hololens 2 enables proficient doctors to mimic complex procedures and assess patient risks. Automotive parts manufacturers may produce and deploy exact Metaverse components utilising Microsoft Hololens 2. This reduces the expenses associated with defective part production and enhances vehicle performance [33, 74].

2.4.2 Intelligent Urban Environments

Future cities will be digital. Future smart cities may utilise the Metaverse platform to amalgamate IoT, Blockchain, AI, VR, and AR technologies, facilitating social activities such as healthcare, economy, education, and entertainment within a virtual environment. Prior to the implementation of the virtual city, its operations must be strategically administered, and the rights and interests of its people must be meticulously evaluated. Augmented reality devices enable individuals to select furnishings and integrate décor and colours. The Metaverse will enable individuals to conduct commercial and academic meetings in a virtual environment while engaging in face-to-face communication [34, 75].

2.4.3 Play-to-Earn Games

Blockchain technology and play-to-earn games are revolutionising the gaming business. The Metaverse, because to its decentralised architecture, provides users with tangible rewards for their gameplay duration. The transition in the gaming business is referred to as "Play to Earn" (P2E). In Peer-to-Peer (P2P) games, participants can log in to complete the game or engage in combat with other players for digital assets. The predominant digital assets are cryptocurrencies and Non-Fungible Tokens (NFTs). Decentralised marketplaces enable participants to exchange NFTs within games and transfer them to alternative digital platforms. The contemporary, unrestricted, internet-based economy has heightened expectations for increased digital engagement [35].

2.5 Future Research Challenges

This section analyses MEC-based Metaverse challenges from the subsequent perspectives.

2.5.1 Analysis of Computer Resource Allocation

Current articles emphasise computational allocation. Tang and colleagues [55] devised an optimisation technique for computation offloading and resource allocation. This solution eradicated load-induced interuser interference. In order to improve MEC server collaboration, paper [36] examined cached content by assessing four decision parameters: whether a specific task needs to be cached, the optimal transmission power for offloading, and the distribution of MEC resources for task execution. However, the dynamics of Metaverse systems are not taken into account in these investigations. Instead of being static, the computational resources of each node are dynamic. Consequently, idle computing resources will be squandered when Mobile Edge Computing (MEC) addresses computationally intensive activities following the pre-determination of nodes. The fundamental problem of dynamic computing resource allocation necessitates additional investigation.

2.5.2 Mobility Management

Applications for the Metaverse depend on user circumstances and past actions. Mobility is therefore essential when creating continuous, real-time apps. However, user mobility and efficient mobility management ensure uninterrupted service, improving service quality and user experience. Present options comprise caching and Software-Defined Networking controllers. Effective caching necessitates accurate assessment of the material's popularity and collaborative caching among cells to enhance web caching efficiency. This supports Software Defined Network (SDN)-based Mobile Edge Computing (MEC) in 5G vehicular networks in the article [6].

Four proprietary software modules enhance QoS policy formulation within the SDN controller. The suggested SDN controller may federate and coordinate Mobile Edge Computing (MEC) resource allocation, ensuring mobile consumers receive uninterrupted service and superior coverage. The integration of AI in mobility management represents a promising area of research. The integration of these technologies enables the Metaverse system to independently learn from user behaviours, predict movements, and proactively interact with the SDN controller, hence enhancing its reliability.

2.5.3 Assessment of User Experience

Sensor-integrated digital avatars execute various functions within photorealistic sub-Metaverses. The primary objective of the Metaverse is to merge with the physical realm and include malevolent entities into virtual reality. Robberies in the Metaverse and vehicular collisions affect individuals in the physical world. Unregulated avatars function as a form of psychological sexual assault, victimising users. Therefore, a code of ethics to regulate avatar conduct is essential for establishing a secure virtual society. User addiction adversely affects emotional well-being in the Metaverse [2].

2.5.4 Information

Data leakage and data reliability are two significant concerns in the Metaverse. Data leakage: the MEC-based Metaverse is distinct from Bitcoin's decentralised framework. The edge cloud acquires avatar identification numbers, passwords, digital assets, and currencies from endpoint devices. These technologies are susceptible to significant assaults by prospective adversaries. The main risks of advertising fraud are identified in article [10] as blind-spot tracking, gaze and controller cursor jacking, and inappropriate content sharing with aided display.

The quality of data significantly influences the Quality Of Service (QoS) in Metaverse applications. Superior data quality enhances user Quality of Experience (QoE), but worse data quality diminishes it. The dependability of data is compromised by deceptive sources and transmission inconsistencies associated with data origins and generation methods. In Metaverse development, prioritisation of data leakage prevention and the assurance of data quality and dependability are essential.

2.5.5 Postponement

The Metaverse's main goal is to instantly generate the virtual spatial environment and provide processed data to the XR device via the downlink. Virtual reality systems must maintain latency under 20 milliseconds to prevent spatial disorientation and nausea among Metaverse users. Researchers consistently investigate computational workload partitioning [4]. Furthermore, work distribution and time lag must be equilibrated. Lightweight, wearable XR systems require less processing power and are comfortable to wear.

2.5.6 Privacy

Metaverse security emphasises the protection of user identity and data confidentiality. Users' virtual assets, facial and retinal information, and transaction records are all at risk due to the Metaverse's susceptible data processing and transfer. After obtaining and analysing a user's behavioural information and interactions with other avatars, hackers will construct a fake avatar that may take part in Metaverse social events and commit crimes.

The privacy of bystanders in the Metaverse is likewise at risk. Consequently, data and identity security are the sole pathways for advancement.

2.6 Convergence of Emerging Technologies

This section analyses the convergence of emerging technologies.

2.6.1 Mobile Edge Computing in 6G Wireless Communications

Enhanced traffic applications encompass AI-driven intelligent decision-making, cellular network connectivity, shop-floor contact for information exchange, and the gathering and processing of traffic, vehicle, and environmental data. These applications can improve traffic flow and reduce accidents by performing numerous traffic-related functions and assessing traffic conditions. 6G networks can link intelligent devices to utilise peripheral computing, artificial intelligence, Blockchain, and other technologies for data monitoring and interaction. Delegating decision-making facilitates self-organisation within production and diminishes human involvement. Most 6G performance metrics will enhance by a factor of 10–100 compared to 5G. The highest transmission speed of 6G will reach 1 Tbit/s, in contrast to the 10 Gbit/s of 5G. The anticipated outage probability for 6G is projected to be below one in a million. Consequently, positioning-related applications are anticipated to proliferate in 6G, enhancing positioning accuracy by several centimetres indoors and 1 metre outdoors. This is an order of magnitude more precise than 5G. 6G will facilitate ultra-high-density connections, accommodating over 100 devices per cubic metre. 6G will utilise the terahertz spectrum for transmission, hence enhancing network capacity. Given the stringent requirements of 6G applications, researchers must investigate the prospective integration of Mobile Edge Computing (MEC) technology into 6G environments to deliver highly dependable and low-latency services to customers.

2.6.2 Enhance Mobile Edge Computing with AI

Article [27] presents a machine learning predictive method for mobility management. Utilising machine learning to predict uncertainty and reference signal received power can resolve mobile device service interruptions. This research forecasts unit Restricted Static Pseudo-Partitioning (RSPP) means and standard deviations utilising neural networks. Analysis of results identifies MEC servers. Facilitating the advanced transfer of cached content to MEC servers minimises disruption. The integration of mobility management with artificial intelligence is a prospective research subject. Artificial intelligence may analyse user behaviours and anticipate user actions, relaying information regarding the user's status to the SDN controller, hence enhancing service reliability.

2.6.3 Augmenting Mobile Edge Computing with Blockchain Technology

The constrained computational and energy resources of MEC servers diminish system efficiency. Blockchain technology enhances the security, resource efficiency, and energy efficiency of mobile edge computing. A novel consensus process utilising Blockchain mining to enhance system security is detailed in a recent academic report [28]. Paper [29] additionally introduces an innovative polynomial-time resource allocation mechanism. Consequently, the research concentrates on advancing Blockchain-based technologies to address impending resource limitations in mobile edge computing.

2.6.4 Technological Convergence

Mobile edge computing for the Metaverse was facilitated by artificial intelligence and Blockchain technology over 6G wireless connectivity. This study encompasses AI, Blockchain, mobile edge computing, the Metaverse, and 6G wireless communications. The preceding sections have elucidated mobile edge computing, the potential enhancements through artificial intelligence and Blockchain technology, and its prospective applications in the Metaverse and 6G wireless communications. We advocate for the integration of AI and Blockchain to enhance Metaverse mobile edge computing utilising 6G wireless connectivity. Advancements in 6G wireless networks and Mobile Edge Computing (MEC) incorporate artificial intelligence and Blockchain technology. 6G and Mobile Edge Computing enhance the Metaverse's immersion and realism. A recent research article indicates that AI can manage the Metaverse utilising 6G networks. Blockchain and mobile edge computing have the potential to enhance the system referenced in [30]. Further investigation is required. A recent survey [3] addresses 6G-enabled edge AI for the Metaverse; it omits Blockchain. Furthermore, Ref. [31] examines the application of 6G technology in the Metaverse, reference [32] explores wireless systems, and reference [33] elucidates the edge-enabled Metaverse. We examine the potential of Blockchain and AI to enhance Mobile Edge Computing within a 6G-enabled Metaverse.

2.7 Conclusion

This study conducts a comprehensive examination of the Metaverse enabled by mobile edge computing. MEC employs a Metaverse edge server in proximity to a data source for instantaneous data processing. This approach may diminish latency, enhance wireless transmission bandwidth efficiency, and secure the involvement of Metaverse participants. This article addresses the enabling technologies of MEC, research challenges, and applications inside the Metaverse. We also demonstrate how MEC, AI, and Blockchain could advance the Metaverse and 6G communications. The article emphasises future research challenges and opportunities associated with the implementation of a large-scale Mobile Edge Computing-enabled Metaverse system, utilising constrained network resources and diverse traffic patterns. This vote aims to clarify the future of the MEC and Metaverse and stimulate further exemplary research moving forward.

Chapter 3

Education in the Metaverse: Vision, Opportunities, Real-World Applications, and Challenges

3.1 Introduction

The Metaverse concept was first introduced in 1992 and garnered popularity with the release of the film *Ready Player One* [1]. The Metaverse is a virtual universe that is inextricably linked to real life. It seeks to create a digitised realm composed of digital material. The way the real and virtual worlds interact shows how virtuality can affect reality through day-to-day activities and business dealings. "A three-dimensional virtual realm where daily activities are conducted by avatars representing real individuals" is how research studies [11, 36, 37] describe the Metaverse. Stated differently, the Metaverse presents a more convenient environment for him or her to realise who they are than the real world does. Moreover, the research [2, 38, 39, 40] offers a deeper, different explanation of the "Metaverse." It is characterised as "a realm where virtual and physical realities engage and develop concurrently, facilitating social, economic, and cultural activities that create value" [3]. In summary, as previously articulated, the actual world and virtual reality constitute interactions inside the Metaverse rather than existing as two separate realms. More broadly, the Metaverse might be defined as a world in which everyday life and economic pursuits are synced. Several companies are using the Metaverse for employee training, student education, and amusement. The Metaverse is integrating into

DOI: 10.1201/9781003520702-3

daily life. Realising Metaverse potential requires understanding it. Oral transmission has been employed in natural settings for centuries in human education. In the absence of a dependable medium for information transmission, predecessors were compelled to convey their narratives orally, as exemplified by Homer's Epics and the Classic of Poetry. These survival stories are characterised by simplicity, significance, inspiration, and memorability. Nonetheless, information distortion inevitably occurs during dissemination, necessitating that the listeners fully engage their imagination to comprehend the narrative [4, 41, 42]. This circumstance significantly constrains individuals' pursuit of knowledge. The subsequent invention of paper enabled individuals to document nearly anything with ease. Paper is more trustworthy and practical than spoken communication since it can store information longer.

Furthermore, the author may employ an extensive vocabulary to elucidate the picture, thereby reducing information entropy to some extent. In recent decades, the globe has entered the Internet era, with rapid progress. Individuals are increasingly dissatisfied with acquiring knowledge solely from written materials. Novel technologies, such as 4G, streaming media, and Bluetooth, enhance individuals' perceptual experiences. We can see high-resolution images or seamless videos on a computer or mobile device. Internet technologies facilitate effortless access to global events. Only a network wire separates us from the world. New education paradigms include distributed classrooms and immersive learning in the Metaverse [5, 43, 44].

The term "meta" signifies first, starting, important, and culmination. It signifies a new beginning; nevertheless, from the standpoint of wholeness, its implications encompass not only the virtual and historical realms but also the tangible and forthcoming realms. The Internet of Things (IoT), Virtual Reality (VR), Augmented Reality (AR), Mixed Reality (MR), Digital Twin (DT), 3D virtual environments, Blockchain, and AI are among its emerging technologies. Overall, it combines human, virtual, and physical realities across temporal and spatial dimensions. The Metaverse education emerges from traditional educational practices, such as knowledge dissemination and learning, while simultaneously transforming other aspects, including the dynamics between educators and learners, as well as constraints related to time and physical location.

Research gap: So far, numerous scholars have performed literature reviews [10, 45–50] pertaining to the Metaverse in a generic context. Many basic Metaverse technologies have been investigated and discussed. These include big data, the IoT, VR, AR, MR, DT, 3D virtual environments, Blockchain, 6G mobile communication technology, security and privacy issues, and more. Even though the word "Metaverse" is used a lot, most people still don't know what it means. Should the Metaverse be used in schooling, or should it not be? What new ideas or roles come up when the Metaverse and education are combined? Is it going to lead to more fights and make things worse? These questions have gone on for a long time without being solved.

3.2 The Metaverse in Education: Definition, Framework, and Characteristics

3.2.1 Definition of the Metaverse in the Context of Education

One of the most significant uses of the Metaverse, according to the writers of article [3], is education, which has a lot of promise for the near future. Since we suggest that the Metaverse can be a new learning environment [1, 31, 51], its use in education can be regarded of as a learning environment augmented by Metaverse technologies that mix real and virtual learning settings. It lets students use wearable technology to access time- and location-independent learning environments and engage with digital identities, intelligent NPCs, and avatars in real time. Children can feel as present as in a real learning environment. From this perspective, integrating the Metaverse into the classroom offers students many unique educational opportunities.

3.2.2 Education's Metaverse Structure

The author presents a Metaverse framework with hardware, compute, networking, virtual platforms, interchange tools and standards, payment systems, content, services, and assets, as well as a brief explanation of its thinking [4, 30, 52]. Nevertheless, there are no additional elucidations regarding the detailed implementation of the Metaverse. In articles [5, 53, 54], the Metaverse was divided into hardware, software, and content and three approaches: user interaction, implementation, and application. Article [6] projects another small Metaverse contribution to schooling. They discussed the duties of intelligent tutors, tutees, and peers in imparting instruction and possible Metaverse AI uses. Still, the Metaverse is created by combining several advanced technologies rather than by single technologies like artificial intelligence [37, 38, 55, 56]. Based on the limited studies addressing the Metaverse's educational applications, we suggest a paradigm for its implementation in education, informed by the perspectives gathered from the research publications. This section will explain the fundamental elements of the Metaverse in education, as illustrated in Figure 3.1.

Initially, the Metaverse comes from technological advancements in article [2], demonstrating that its adoption in education is strongly reliant on current technologies. As a result, multiple technologies can serve as the foundation of the Metaverse in education, providing significant support for aspects in both the physical and virtual realities. This text delves into each aspect of the Metaverse's technological architecture in schooling.

1. **Rapid Communication and Networking**: According to researchers [29, 57, 58], the Metaverse requires fast communication and networking, including wireless connectivity and high-speed networks (6G or 5G). In the Metaverse, high-speed networks provide stable data transfer, scene rendering, real-time

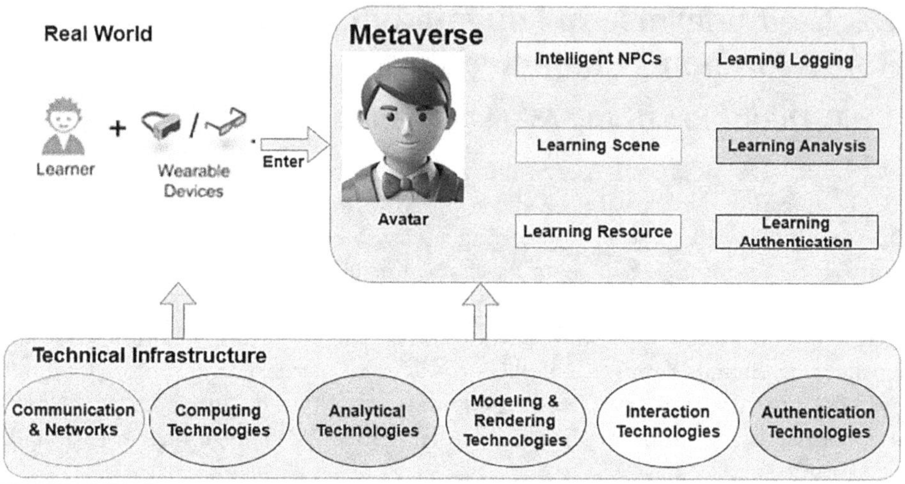

Figure 3.1 The structure of the Metaverse in educational contexts.

feedback, and user interaction. In contrast, high-speed networks enable students to seamlessly transition from physical to Metaverse schooling.

2. **Computational Technologies**: Edge, cloud, and distributed computing enable processing, calculation, storage, transmission, and exchange of data and information in the Metaverse, created by several actors. In article [13], these technologies can help learners save, use, and exchange learning data (e.g., learner information, learning records, learning resources) more correctly, efficiently, and concurrently.
3. **Analytical Methodologies**: AI, big data, and text mining are valuable in education due to increasing analytical technology [27, 59]. By offering intelligent NPC tutors, tutees, and peers, Metaverse AI can improve arbitration, simulation, and decision-making education [28]. Metaverse analytical tools track, gather, and assess learners' behaviours, emotions, preferences, and performances. The Metaverse can let teachers assess students and personalise tools and services using this data.
4. **Technologies for Modelling and Rendering**: The Metaverse combines virtual and real-world aspects into a 3D digital environment with various simulated or replicated settings, avatars, non-player characters, and more. SketchUp, Unity, and Blender are virtual object modelling and simulation software [26, 60]. The global trend in VR and AR research has enabled lifelike 3D material [20, 61]. Supporters of the Metaverse argue that it is more like XR. Digital Twins, holography, and Mixed Reality (MR) can represent and portray the Metaverse, according to other authors [11, 62]. Dynamic, high-fidelity instructional environments require modelling and rendering technology. They also enable Metaverse visualisation of educational settings and items that cannot be seen in the physical world.

5. **Technologies for Interaction**: Embodied, multimodal interaction distinguishes the Metaverse from the Internet. Metaverse user manipulation, navigation, collaboration, and sensory feedback require VR, XR, sensors, real-time tracking, IoT, and Brain–Computer Interface (BCI) [21, 63, 64]. Interactive technologies allow students to participate in exploratory learning, cooperation, and socialisation, exciting their senses and providing rapid feedback. The Metaverse can provide authentic and immersive learning experiences.
6. **Authentication Technologies**: Researchers [12] suggest that Blockchain is the best authentication solution for the Metaverse due to its transparent, open, decentralised, and reliable services, while safeguarding user privacy to support the ecosystem. Blockchain can permanently record learners' Metaverse data and works, eliminating fraud and plagiarism. The Metaverse in education's technological infrastructure and components depend on current technology and will evolve.
7. **Intelligent Wearable Devices**: These include headsets, HMDs, and smart glasses, which can be non-see-through, optical-see-through, or video-see-through [22, 65]. Smart wearables are crucial gear for digital-physical integration [12, 66]. The smart wearable device lets learners navigate the Metaverse without restriction.
8. **Avatar**: Teachers and students' avatars represent them in the Metaverse. Using real-time tracking, identification, and simulation technology has made avatars more realistic. Learners and educators can customise their avatars' dress, gender, and complexion to match their own. Article [1] noted that scanning users' faces can accurately and vividly show avatar learners' facial emotions and behaviours. Sensors, controllers, and real-time tracking let users swap avatars [2]. Avatars give learners a sense of presence and embodiment in the Metaverse while allowing them to express themselves in an innovative, pleasant, and totally immersive way.
9. **Non-Player Character (NPC)**: In Metaverse learning, AI-driven roles such as intelligent NPC teachers, learners, and peers are used [2]. Article [3] says intelligent agents enhance educational arbitration, simulation, and decision-making. Any time, educators can request support or simulate lessons with intelligent NPC learners, while learners can receive tuition, dispute, or practise skills with Metaverse NPCs. Intelligent agents satisfy unique requirements and engage students and teachers.
10. **Educational Environment**: The Metaverse produces realistic learning environments using technologies like as Digital Twins, VR, AR, and XR [4, 67, 68]. The universe, marine ecosystems, woods, and historical places are hard to witness, but they can be recreated as realistic 3D classroom layouts or constructed as partially or fully virtual settings based on educational material [2, 69, 70]. Learning environments promote texture, colour, and decoration [5]. Seoul National University (SNU) Bundang Hospital held a virtual meeting using XR [6].
11. **Metaverse Education**: Modelling and rendering technologies can depict unseen or abstract concepts, items, or events in the physical domain [7].

Multimodal learning resources can provide real-time feedback and immersive sensory experiences by engaging learners' bodies using VR, AR, XR, or sensors [8]. Astronomy students interacted with the lunar system using AR [2]. Decentralised technology should let learners edit, create, and share educational content in the Metaverse [10, 71]. Roblox lets players collaborate on virtual projects [9]. Users can make and sell augmented reality fashion products on ZEPPTO for digital currencies [11].

12. **Learning Logging**: The Metaverse roadmap [12, 72] recommends lifelogging, saving, and sharing daily experiences and information about goods and people. This strategy lets learners communicate their real-time status information via storage, databases, or tracking technologies while storing their history data (e.g., footprints, assignments, and virtual creations) in the Metaverse. It allows learners and educators evaluate the learning process and assist critical activities (e.g., assessing conduct or interaction patterns) based on personal experiences [13, 73].
13. **Analysis of Learning**: For massive data processing in the Metaverse, computation, databases, and AI are essential [14, 74]. Learning analysis uses substantial data to evaluate and report learners' performance and achievements per unit or generally. Moreover, it facilitates the evaluation of learners' performance and furnishes educators with credible evidence to deliver tailored services for students. Classting AI is an online educational community program that analyses learners' performance and generates visual, personalised analytical reports [15, 75].
14. **Acquisition of Authentication Knowledge**: The Metaverse is a more accessible, communal, and decentralised digital environment compared to conventional virtual environments [16]. In the Metaverse, the management and security of learners' information must adhere to stringent standards akin to contemporary cloud applications, ensuring the protection of user privacy using mechanisms such as authentication and authorisation to delineate accessible content. Furthermore, users' virtual works or digital inventions may be shared with others, with the expectation that they will be traceable and secured. Technologies like Blockchain and Non-Fungible Tokens (NFTs) facilitate the authentication and traceability of learners' inventions, thereby contributing to a secure, enduring, and sustainable Metaverse [17].

3.2.3 Metaverse Characteristics in Education

The Metaverse education framework predicts Metaverse learning will differ from classrooms and screen-based video conferencing. Metaverse-based learning may improve in-person and screen-based remote learning. Thus, each trait and its relevance are explained:

1. **Schedule and Location for Student Participation in Class**: The class calendar and school timetable determine when teachers and students meet in a classroom or via video-conferencing [18]. Thus, time and place limit

classroom and screen-based remote learning. In the Metaverse, fast networks and computing unbind people by time and place. The Metaverse can provide practically constant education. According to [19], smart wearable gadgets allow learners and educators to interact in educational situations at all times. A teacher invited to an out-of-town conference, unable to return during class hours, may request that students utilise wearable devices to participate in classes within the Metaverse, regardless of their physical distance. Eliminating the trip will result in less time wastage and increased opportunity for meaningful activities. Fast networks provide seamless transitions between the physical and Metaverse and formal and informal learning [20]. Teachers can rethink synchronous and asynchronous learning with the Metaverse. Avatars let students connect with intelligent NPC educators in the Metaverse. Consequently, a flexible approach to involvement can provide convenience and autonomy to educators and students. Moreover, it can offer significant potential for the sustained execution of education in the post-pandemic period.

2. **Learner Identity**: Regardless of whether in a physical classroom or on a video-conferencing network, students participate in classes using their own identities. In the Metaverse, individuals can embody themselves in an entirely distinct manner. They participate in classes using customised, lifelike, and dynamic avatars. Metaverse avatars are digital representations of player characters. By manipulating and maintaining their avatars in a unique, entertaining, and fully immersive Metaverse, learners can feel present [21].
3. **The Individuals with Whom Learners Engage**: Students engage with actual instructors and classmates in both physical classrooms and video-conferencing platforms. Apathy, emotional detachment, and social isolation occur from video-conferencing platforms' lack of face-to-face interaction with peers and educators [22]. Metaverse students can interact with avatar and intelligent NPC professors and peers. Using avatars or intelligent NPCs to communicate with teachers and classmates provides more emotional support and faster responses than viewing a grid of faces or monotonous presentations on video conferencing services. Smart NPC teachers and peers can aid pupils individually in class or afterwards. Social constructivism states that knowledge is created through social interactions [23]; hence, the Metaverse can improve students' cognitive and social skills.
4. **Educational Environment**: Traditionally, there are authentic learning environments in physical classrooms and virtual learning environments on video-conferencing platforms. During the COVID-19 pandemic, the establishment of educational environments, including conventional settings (e.g., traditional classrooms) and specialised venues (e.g., laboratories), has encountered significant obstacles [24]. In contrast, the Metaverse may recreate varied learning scenarios from real learning environments or create them from scratch. A history lecture on ancient Rome shows how the Metaverse allows technology to reconstruct and represent old Roman sites, something that is difficult to do physically. It allows learners to engage with the educational process through

visualised and immersive environments, simulating real-world experiences. Researchers have demonstrated that participants' sensation of presence and immersion can be substantially heightened while engaging in learning tasks within a simulated and vivid environment.

5. **Educational Material**: Conventional educational resources typically manifest in static formats, including printed textbooks, articles, electronic books, shared course materials, images, videos, or other things. Students are less inclined to engage with those educational tools. Metaverse-based education visualises and decentralises learning resources to encourage student involvement. A textbook discourse plus a terrestrial globe and map presentation are typical Earth lessons. AR, however, can transform education by adding a 3D rotating Earth image improved by technology. Students may see 360-degree by zooming, panning, and rotating the virtual Earth. Modelling and depicting abstract knowledge in the Metaverse help learners understand. Participants can collaborate with classmates and teachers to create or improve instructional resources, potentially improving traditional materials.
6. **Educational Endeavour**: Traditional classroom learning relies predominantly on teacher-led lectures, facilitating student engagement in various activities and peer collaboration; however, the initiation of these activities has proven challenging during the pandemic [25]. Video-conferencing platforms impose certain limitations, rendering screen-based remote learning predominantly lecture-oriented, with minimal opportunities for complex learning activities like collaboration; consequently, learning on these platforms often becomes passive [26]. Initially, the learning activities within the Metaverse appear to be situated in vibrant and colourful environments, significantly improving cognitive representation through interaction with virtual objects in three-dimensional views [2]. Free access and quick engagement in the Metaverse enable real-time collaboration among learners through virtual formats like meetups, conferences, idea sharing, group discussions, presentation panels, and debates, providing emotional support from peers rather than a grid of screens [27]. They can also schedule virtual companion sessions outside of class. Additionally, a digital environment with game-like components like avatars, NPCs, or digital items might enable inquiry-based or problem-solving activities [28]. The Metaverse also allows learners to create virtual works in a decentralised and customisable creative environment [29]. Following the learning from errors concept, it lets students change their actions during the learning process [30].
7. **Educational Engagement**: Students connect largely through video and audio on video-conferencing systems, but in traditional classes, they interact mostly in person [31]. Sensors, BCI, VR, AR, and XR enable embodied and multi-sensory participation in the Metaverse, stimulating and motivating

vision, audition, and kinaesthesia [9]. Article [10] claimed that multimodal and embodied learning boosts student interest and performance.

8. **Educational Goal**: The new Bloom's taxonomy includes six hierarchical learning objectives: remembering, comprehending, applying, analysing, evaluating, and producing [8]. Traditional classroom and screen-based remote learning are limited to low-order cognitive progress (remembering, understanding, and applying) by time, distance, and resources Therefore, traditional lecture-based classrooms impede students' ability to analyse, evaluate, and produce [7]. The Metaverse's distinctive qualities allow learners to participate in varied learning activities (e.g., collaborative work, creative exploration, or inquiry-based learning) outside of the classroom, potentially boosting their capacity to apply, analyse, evaluate, or develop information [12]. Research [6] showed that challenging tasks like problem-solving are necessary to master all learning objectives. Thus, the Metaverse may simplify cultivating higher-order thinking in students. It will, to a certain degree, produce a sequence of "ripple" impacts on the objectives of emerging learners, transitioning from higher-order to lower-order goals [32]. In the Metaverse, learners can acquire fundamental knowledge while simultaneously enhancing their skills and competences for future endeavours, facilitating holistic development throughout the learning process.
9. **Evaluation of Learning**: In traditional educational settings, instructors frequently evaluate students summatively through learning outcomes (e.g., examinations) because of the challenges associated with documenting student performance and gathering learning data. In article [5], in this scenario, scores will serve as the sole measure of learners' comprehension, leading to adverse consequences such as educational inequity. In the Metaverse, employing learning tracking and analysis enables educators to evaluate learners' performance more thoroughly through both formative and summative data [33]. It prioritises learners' development over outcomes, therefore transcending certain constraints of conventional assessment.

3.3 Potential Metaverse Education Applications

During Mark Zuckerberg's live-streamed presentation of Facebook's rebranding initiative, it was noteworthy that several prospective applications of the Metaverse, such as gaming, professional activities, and education, were prominently showcased. In the Metaverse, students and teachers can transcend time and place. The Metaverse's unique qualities will allow students to observe, investigate, and construct the cosmos in new ways. Thus, the Metaverse may offer new educational opportunities [34]. This section will discuss several Metaverse education applications based on its features and affordances, however it is not exhaustive.

3.3.1 The Metaverse Facilitates Hybrid Learning

The educational model of blended learning combines face-to-face and online training [4]. Screen-based remote instruction via Zoom, Google Meet, or Teams is common because of COVID-19 [3]. Some schools have invited students and teachers back as the pandemic has subsided, although some lockdown zones will continue to use remote or hybrid learning. Due to COVID-19 ambiguities, remote and in-person education may remain viable for post-pandemic education [2]. Scholars have identified various issues associated with learning via video-conferencing systems, such as video-conference fatigue, exhaustion, diminished motivation, inability to concentrate, desocialisation, and depersonalisation [1].

Professor Jeremy Bailenson launched Stanford University's blended learning course "Virtual People" in autumn 2021. Two hundred sixty-three VR-equipped students met in the Metaverse using Zoom and ENGAGE. The reading assignment was due before class. Metaverse learners must perform virtual and remote activities like large group field trips, small group panels, quizzes, and individual and collaborative virtual environment development. The Metaverse allows educators and students in different locations (home, lockdown zones, and abroad) to participate in educational environments utilising wearable technology. This approach holds that the Metaverse supports in-person and remote learning simultaneously or asynchronously. Avatars can be used in lectures, assignments, group debates, and collaborative projects to communicate with real and virtual teachers and classmates [35]. Instead of a grid of faces or dull slides, individuals will view themselves as in the same area, conversing and bonding. Educational initiatives may increase student engagement and passion. We can tackle modern video-conference learning problems. Given this trend, the Metaverse may offer new blended learning paradigms to boost learner engagement and experience [20].

3.3.2 The Metaverse Facilitates Virtual Experiential Learning

Virtual experimental learning is crucial in the curricula of natural sciences, encompassing both physical and life sciences [22]. Scholars [12] say that virtual experimental learning is hindered by low financing for materials and equipment and the lack of alternatives to COVID-19-related lab closures, which undermines actual experiment training. The Metaverse may model and render a lab and experimental instruments in 3D for virtual studies. Students can participate in real-time virtual experiments using interaction technology.

Given the Metaverse's educational benefits, various position papers list its potential uses for virtual experimental learning [29]:

- Facilitate experiments with risks, irreversibility, or toxicity in real-world scenarios, such as explosion hazards.
- Facilitate experiments that require a vacuum or other non-real-world settings.
- Facilitate experiments that require significant financial resources, such as expensive equipment and materials.

Virtual experimental learning using the Metaverse allows students to observe, measure, document, and manipulate experiments remotely, overcoming physical constraints like space, money, location, equipment, and hazards [36]. It promotes error-learning and skill acquisition through practice. Given these benefits, Metaverse application in virtual experimental learning seems promising.

3.3.3 The Metaverse Facilitates Language Acquisition

Language acquisition has been vital for bilingual or multilingual competency in K-12, higher education, and professional fields since the 21st century [28]. Due to various issues, including insufficient contextual practice or engagement, traditional language learning has typically been addressed passively in and out of the classroom [26]. Article [27] believes that the creation of the Metaverse holds significant promise for enhancing language acquisition. Numerous justifications exist for the integration of the Metaverse in language acquisition. Initially, language acquisition necessitates a rigorous learning environment, particularly for auditory and verbal instruction [25]. A speaking lesson may teach verbal skills by discussing flight information in an airport. Taking a class to the airport or welcoming airport staff to school is unrealistic for educators. Learners can role-play and practise dialogue with avatar partners or intelligent NPC airport staff or flight attendants in a virtual airport environment in the Metaverse. Language learners can immerse themselves in the Metaverse and build skills with instructors and classmates. Language acquisition requires ongoing practice outside of class. An English as a Foreign Language (EFL) learner on summer vacation may struggle to find acquaintances for English practice (listening, interpreting, and speaking). This learner may ask their partner to use an avatar to join the Metaverse and debate a pre-designed or recreated setting remotely. When a partner is unavailable, clever language peers can help learners practise. Language learners can practise and interact with real-world or NPC characters outside of the classroom in the Metaverse, which may help them apply their language abilities.

3.3.4 The Metaverse Facilitates Competency-Based Education

Competence-Based Education (CBE) is a dominant reform framework in Vocational Education and Training (VET), where competencies (e.g., knowledge and skills) required for vocational practise underpin curriculum development [23]. Theoretical and practical knowledge often underpin Vocational Education and Training (VET). CBE adoption is complicated by the COVID-19 epidemic [24]. A Metaverse solution for CBE is expected. It helps students transition from classroom to professional settings by providing broad and specialised information through remote observation in a virtual environment. It immerses learners in a professional training atmosphere, allowing them to practise skills with target audiences at any time and place without travelling, saving time and money. Preservice nurses may need to practise first aid or nursing, but obtaining patients is hard. They should interact with clever NPC patients in Metaverse hospital or clinic simulations.

3.3.5 The Metaverse Encourages Inclusive Learning

All children, regardless of their requirements, are guaranteed to receive instruction and support in regular classrooms thanks to inclusive education [22]. Special needs children are usually disabled, but they can also be abandoned, abused, or mentally sick [21]. Nonetheless, it is difficult for many educators to facilitate the acceptance of kids with special needs by their general education peers and to promote collaborative learning without obstacles. The unique characteristics of the Metaverse suggest that it could serve as an optimal environment for children with special needs to learn alongside their typically developing peers [20].

The initial identification difference hinders special-needs students' incorporation into conventional classrooms [12]. With the use of digital identities in the Metaverse, learners can erase discrimination and identity labels by having their photos recreated. This gives them the confidence and sense of belonging to study alongside regular students. The organs and senses of these learners can then be enhanced by Metaverse technology (such as AI, sensors, or BCI), allowing for regular communication and interaction with a wider student community as well as giving sensory stimulation and cognitive advancement throughout the educational process. Because special needs students learn differently from other students, the Metaverse can use big data, learning analytics, and computing technologies to deliver specialised services and individualised education based on emotional and physical data. The Metaverse supports inclusive education, which encourages student diversity and gives all students equal access to mainstream education.

3.4 How Is Schooling Affected by the Metaverse?

Over the ages, the educational system has evolved to incorporate new ideas. We present a brief comparison of three educational approaches. Beyond scholars and educators, we must acknowledge and prepare for an educational paradigm shift. Online education is accustomed to Generation Z. The digital and physical worlds have always existed side by side. Smartphones, the Internet, and computers have been a part of our lives since we were born. Digital native Generation Z is challenging in terms of efficiency and desire in schooling. Metaverse is a broad framework for future digital qualities. Metaverse benefits include engagement, authenticity, and portability. Thus, the new educational system must be reevaluated to ensure accessibility and sustainability.

- **Interactive Immersion**: Metaverse education offers an immersive interactive experience beyond Web 2.0 limits. Research indicates that learners derive greater enjoyment from instructional settings and thus achieve enhanced learning outcomes in realistic experiential environments that incorporate observation and practice.

- **Visualisation**: The Metaverse allows learners to study chemicals and living cells from a microscopic perspective using digital technology. It can also reproduce optimal physics circumstances, making abstract theories like Einstein's relativity palpable [6].
- **Minimal Learning Expenses and Hazards**: Typically, certain subjects, such as chemistry and physics, require the execution of experiments. Digitisation, a key part of Metaverse education, can reproduce all these trials. It may reduce resource use. Operational risk is low for trainees who conduct flammable and explosive substances or air crash exercises.
- **Unconstrained Temporal and Spatial Dimensions**: Metaverse education can overcome time restrictions. Reenacting historical events eliminates the need for students to visualise or see through books or media. Instead, it removes geographical barriers. Students from temperate locations want to study equatorial environments. If students have digital simulations of the tropics, they can use the Metaverse to accomplish this.
- **Reducing Academic Misconduct**: The Metaverse detects academic dishonesty using Blockchain technology [7]. For instance, Blockchain requires timestamp-based chronological ledgers for information generation, release, and transmission. This functionality allows copyright protection and easy tracking and oversight of academic journal production, distribution, and dissemination [3]. Smart contracts only work when parties keep their promises. When an author submits a manuscript to this system, new blocks are created, and transaction data is dispersed and stored in the level block. This example assures that the author's submission behaviour is unique and reduces academic dishonesty.
- **Personalisation**: Utilising Digital Twin generators or simulators, similar to the Metahkust7 pupils, learners can create customised avatars that align with their preferences, so enhancing their confidence and engagement in the educational experience. If users consent to the use of their personal information, the educational system can provide legal instructional content and curriculum.
- **Enhancing Communication**: The existing online classroom suffers from inadequate contact and communication due to physical distance [8]. Students are unable to evade distractions, and educators cannot timely assess the effectiveness of their instruction based on students' responses, such as facial expressions and body movements. The Metaverse enables educators to establish virtual spaces for conducting internal meetings. Simultaneously, learners can establish study rooms for collaborative work, studying, and social interaction. Everyone can see each other, trade data, and play games with their avatars. These factors build the bonds between students and teachers, as well as the camaraderie among classmates.

Thus, our Metaverse education vision is bold. As said, the Metaverse's peak must be decentralised, yet Web 2.0's network ecology doesn't match its requirements. Web 3.09 can serve as a fundamental component of the Metaverse, enabling machines to process information similarly to humans. In this context, we anticipate that the innovative educational paradigm will yield several benefits:

- **Economical**: The Internet of Everything makes information retrieval and learning easier, lowering educational costs.
- **AI Search**: The AI search system exclusively presents results deemed urgent by users. The search system will autonomously categorise all distinct communications and alert users to pertinent topics and resources.
- **Instructional Transformation**: Utilising tools for big data analysis and instructional behaviours, educators can offer pupils intricate, tailored assignments that foster greater independence.
- **Learning**: Students require minimal time to gather and arrange essential learning points. Moreover, people can study or review at any time and at any location.
- **Personal Learning Network**: The personal learning network will automatically gather information relevant to the user's educational goals and offer monthly reports.
- **System for Managing Personal Education**: This system will generate individualised study schedules for each user, allowing for modifications at any time and from any location, contingent upon the user's current circumstances.

We believe that the Metaverse's transformative changes in education will progress the Metaverse. Many students will profit from Metaverse-based education, thus contributing to the promotion of the Metaverse. Conversely, youngsters educated through the Metaverse will become increasingly acquainted with its various facets. This indicates a higher likelihood of their development of the Metaverse.

3.5 Industry Case Study of Metaverse Education

Metaverse development in schooling is expected. The Metaverse has great promise, and several groups are developing educational programs in it.

3.5.1 Metaverse Education inside Technology Corporations

Recent developments in Metaverse schooling have garnered the interest of numerous technological firms. Roblox, as a prominent entity in the Metaverse sector, possesses distinct benefits in Metaverse schooling. Conversely, its multiplayer gaming system offers learners opportunities for social connection. Conversely, it enables users to develop without restrictions, significantly enhancing the content of educational scenarios. Roblox pledged nearly $10 million to nonprofits and three educational games in November 2021. Nonetheless, the Metaverse can also advantage other industries beyond gaming. Strivr is a firm committed to delivering virtual reality training solutions to enterprises. Their products provide immersive learning through virtual reality, engaging employees in practical learning experiences. Results show increased employee learning retention. Managers may measure the effectiveness of staff training and competence by gathering specific learning and assessment data, claims Strivr. Users can construct and digitally display 3D creations with the JigSpace software. It effortlessly integrates digital information with the user's surroundings by using augmented reality. Innovative 3D educational modelling lets students explore interests [1].

3.5.2 Metaverse Education in Higher Education

The Metaverse's educational benefits are becoming more apparent as it gains popularity. Some colleges have tried Metaverse education to test these hypotheses. All participants want immersive experiences to improve academic memory and efficacy. With the novel *Neuromancer* as inspiration, Stanford University Professor Jeremy Bailenson created "Virtual Human." The "Virtual Human" course lets all students transcend space. VR headsets can establish a "classroom" anywhere. Instruction is purely virtual. This "classroom" can be in a museum, lab, underwater, or "hazardous" crater. Immersive encounters let students see phenomena they only imagined. Aviation accidents and safety investigations are Embry-Riddle's main focus [2]. The headmaster wants to create a virtual collision lab and a Metaverse University. Students can view flight accidents, listen to pilot-air traffic control communications, analyse emergency response techniques, examine accident sites, and gather data in the simulated aircraft control room. Digitally accessing the accident scene, they can investigate. They can take pictures, provide the professor survey data, and make quick changes. Furthermore, the School of Medicine at Case Western Reserve University makes substantial use of Metaverse technology in its teaching. Students studying anatomy utilise Microsoft's "Hololens," a wearable mixed reality device. Medical students can examine body parts in three dimensions thanks to this groundbreaking holographic visualisation technique, which also improves perceptual skills that are hard to achieve with traditional approaches. With "Hololens," students may easily pan and zoom the hologram, which enhances their anatomy lessons. After examining pertinent tools and techniques, we feel that the following is the ideal order for Metaverse education:

- The Connect phase prioritises immersive experiences through the utilisation of Digital Twin technologies and simulation exchange, such as XR.
- The interaction phase focuses on intricate simulation through the use of Digital Twins, real-time rendering, and a 3D engine.
- The production phase creates content, such as items and surroundings, by utilising the platform's large data and stable functionality.
- Identified virtual world users and entities through the use of Web 3.0 and Blockchain technologies.
- Significant transmission capacity, computational power, and energy are required to carry out large-scale activities.

3.6 Challenges and Concerns

In this section, we shall present many challenges and issues. There is a substantial volume of pertinent stuff to address. Consequently, we identify five critical issues (privacy threats, inclusiveness, technological implementation, addiction, and governance challenges) that require immediate resolution.

3.6.1 Technical Execution

1. **Immersion Technologies**: It, including VR, AR, and MR, forms the backbone of the Metaverse. The three technologies make up Extended Reality (XR). We carefully study them as instructional tools.
   a. *Virtual Reality*: Currently, virtual reality is a comparatively advanced technology in Metaverse schooling. Prior research [6] has demonstrated that virtual reality possesses significant promise for enhancing educational outcomes by providing a more immersive environment. Nevertheless, we require further comprehensive investigation on this novel pedagogical approach. The fundamental hardware for executing virtual reality is the Head-Mounted Display (HMD), which facilitates complete immersion by simulating reality within a 3D virtual environment. HMD lacks visual and dynamic interaction realism, which is concerning. Current VR visual generation and presentation methods are limited. The brain is very change-sensitive, which is why we think this. The immersion might be ruined by the smallest detail. Consequently, in a virtual reality environment, optimising the semblance of realism is an essential yet unresolved task.
   b. *Augmented Reality*: Predominantly, AR gadgets offer more comfort for wear compared to VR equipment. Nonetheless, employing identical instructional content across various AR devices is challenging due to the absence of a standardised protocol among numerous vendors [5]. The lack of content portability is currently one of the foremost issues facing augmented reality. The study [2] also found that separating the real and virtual worlds reduces user engagement in education. Augmented reality sensing and virtual information integration require local and cloud computing capabilities and high-bandwidth, low-latency communication.
   c. *MR*: In mixed reality, users can engage in real time by merging actual and virtual items. MR is more immersive than VR or AR but requires specific technology. Smartphones need great resolution and contrast to see real objects. The gadget must present the virtual object as stable or attached to an actual thing, hence the system must carefully monitor physical object positions [4].
2. **AI**: AI improves Metaverse education by providing virtual teaching assistants, language processing for diverse learners, and learning outcomes assessment. Three principal challenges that must be solved in educational AI systems are

the generation of virtual teaching assistants tailored to individual learners, the facilitation of seamless communication across diverse languages, and the equitable assessment of learners' educational outcomes. In the Metaverse, ethical AI decision-making and AI misuse prevention (such as employing AI code to cheat on tests or steal assignment solutions from peers) are major issues.

3. **Digital Twins**: The Metaverse replicates real-world objects in real time. Many Metaverse schooling projects demand precise Digital Twin accuracy and real-time performance. Digital Twins must find and remedy faults [19]. Security and privacy are important concerns when using real-time data to create Digital Twin models. Section V-B has specifics.
4. **Blockchain**: With more students enrolling in Metaverse schooling, Blockchain's computational speed (three to seven transactions per second [13]) may not be enough to examine enormous amounts of data. Blockchain integration with Metaverse schooling depends on scalability. Scalability increases the number of Blockchain nodes, increasing fork risk. Blockchain decentralisation and security will decrease, making it difficult to balance these three attributes (e.g., the Blockchain impossible triangle) [5]. Mining costs will rise as the Blockchain grows [6]. The Metaverse always involves humans, who make mistakes, especially inexperienced learners. Although Blockchain's immutability prevents data manipulation, it is untraceable. New information takes up space and may reveal sensitive information, making it ineffective [7]. Metaverse computational demands present a major technical challenge. The integration of education into the Metaverse requires significant computational power to simulate and render instructional scenarios, facilitate educator-learner interactions, and manage human–computer interactions, which challenges network throughput and cloud computing power.

3.6.2 Privacy and Security

The Metaverse will increase online time. Metaverse firms will collect consumer privacy data to identify cognitive and behavioural trends. Unmatched data will be collected. These organisations must comply with personal data protection rules and have systems to manage data regulatory hazards. Future improvements to the Metaverse education system's user data collection, storage, and management are needed. The importance of information security is clear. Thus, Metaverse education must include Confidentiality, Integrity, and Availability (CIA) [9]. Metaverse schooling may have numerous options for these three qualities:

- **Confidentiality**: To improve educational outcomes, Metaverse education must protect sensitive personal data, such as identifying information or monitoring emotions. Information gathering is optional. Allowing people to keep their data for a better experience is logical.

- **Integrity**: The educational system must ensure the integrity of all data, including Digital Twins, by meticulously scrutinising submitted files to prevent tampering. Information changes may harm the Digital Twin [16]. Integrating the Metaverse with Blockchain technology is an interesting experiment.
- **Availability**: Users can access Metaverse's educational system at anytime and anywhere. Some Metaverse schooling systems can endure DoS and DDoS.
  1. *Inclusivity*: The Metaverse and education aim to increase participation. Therefore, an inclusive virtual environment that meets a variety of participant needs is vital. It is hard but loving. Poor people want to change their lives via education, yet affordability is a major issue. Exceptional learners, such as those with impairments or religious beliefs, are sometimes prioritised over high-quality education.
  2. *Addiction*: As the saying goes, addiction is two-sided. Immersive user engagement may lead to "cyber-syndrome," a range of physical, social, and emotional difficulties caused by excessive cyberspace use. However, XR provides a wealth of visual and aural stimulation that may increase cognitive workload [4, 6]. Metaverse schooling now uses immersive gaming. Thus, Metaverse education must create a game that improves learning while reducing learner addiction. Metaverse education should be a tool, not a cure. Certain instructional content that does not require Metaverse simulation will improve physical education and reduce addiction risk.
  3. *Governance Challenges*: Community governance should be prioritised over other Metaverse components due to learners' moral differences. To avoid ethical difficulties like slang, insulting, bullying, and shaming, community rules of conduct must be established and improved [8]. Governance costs are high because the Metaverse is larger than Web 2.0. The weak regulation of social media reveals that internet businesses prioritise revenues before ethics. Companies offering Metaverse education platforms should act as operators, not regulators. The majority of users should determine a violation. It must balance corporate and user interests.
  4. *Ethics and Morality*: The Metaverse is accessible worldwide due to freedom [12]. Due to the virtual "I" emergence, conflicting beliefs and worldviews, simulated experiments, data theft, racial issues, religious conflicts, bullying, and violence may pose ethical challenges across national, ethnic, religious, and gender boundaries [22]. How to develop a Metaverse with controls and ecosystems is also crucial. Additionally, Metaverse citizenship must be fostered through ethical and legal instruction.
  5. *Identity and Social Interaction*: Digital identities can reflect users' egos in many activities in the Metaverse [12]. As reality and virtuality blend, people may confuse their "real-me identity" with "virtual-me identity" [20]. Using avatar and NPC social interactions in the virtual environment may develop emotional and social boundaries that hinder real-world

relationship building. Additionally, NPC educators may criticise professors. Thus, society, schools, and families need a timely guide to identify reality from virtuality, intelligently approach the Metaverse, and prioritise real-world interactions.

3.7 Potential Metaverse Education Research Areas

The Metaverse in education has many possibilities as technology advances. Few education Metaverse studies exist. Articles on this topic are expected to proliferate significantly in the future years. Thus, the following are potential Metaverse in education research topics:

1. **Create Educational Metaverse Models or Frameworks**: Metaverse development [23] requires high-quality infrastructure that follows best practices. Educational methods are based on Metaverse hardware and software architectures. For school administrators, instructors, and students, the Metaverse architecture must have accessibility, safety, humanity, trust, instructional capacity, and cognitive abilities. Additionally, education design should emphasise unique and extra aspects. A specific environment may allow learner avatars to airdrop "class notes."
2. **Education Using Metaverse Rules and Concepts**: The Metaverse is a promising digital environment for teaching, but the previous section discusses privacy, security, and moral concerns. Teens are in a crucial physical and cognitive stage. Educational obstacles can greatly impact future outcomes. Therefore, Metaverse-based educational environments must have strict controls.
3. **Examining School Administrators, Educators, and Parents' Views on Metaverse Integration for Education**: Teachers and administrators will face both possibilities and obstacles with Metaverse implementation. The Metaverse could also change how students study in schools and at home. School administrators, educators, and parents' views on using the Metaverse for education should inform its design, management, and pedagogy.
4. **Metaverse-Related Educator Training**: Effective teaching and educational transformation depend on teachers. The Metaverse, an emerging educational technology, provides many possibilities for educators. Thus, preparing educators to use the Metaverse in their lessons is complex. Additionally, the Metaverse offers novel virtual teacher education approaches. Metaverse education study may focus on teacher training and development.
5. **Assessing Cognitive and Non-Cognitive Effects on Metaverse Learners**: Educational scholars may find this fascinating. Exploratory study using Metaverse and conventional technologies is needed to compare students' academic achievement across grades and ages because the Metaverse's educational

framework and methods may differ from traditional schooling. In such an innovative setting with high immersion, presence, and autonomy, the Metaverse's impacts on learners' cognitive (attention, memory) and non-cognitive (learning attitude, motivation) elements must be examined. Examining students' activity in the integrated smart environment's virtual and real worlds helps educators understand the Metaverse's social effects and improve learning methodologies.

6. **Compared Metaverse Learning and Teaching to Other Educational Platforms**: Comparisons are needed to determine the optimum teaching and learning environments using modern technology in education. Will Metaverse learners outperform classroom or screen-based remote learners? Will Metaverse learners behave similarly? Which learner performance component improves in different environments? We recommend exploring the previously mentioned themes.
7. **Innovative Metaverse-Based Methodological and Educational Frameworks**: The Metaverse, with its unique properties, is ideal for future education, where the traditional pedagogical model will become dynamic and place learners at the centre of the teaching-learning process [24]. Traditional education will change. Thus, Metaverse-appropriate methodological and pedagogical frameworks must be explored.
8. **The Current Pedagogical Ideas for Metaverse-Based Schooling**: The education Metaverse will stimulate new educational discussions. Reevaluate and modify technology-enhanced teaching. Since the Metaverse is new, scholars are anticipated to contribute new insights on pedagogical theories including embodied cognition, situated cognition, extended cognition, distributed cognition, flow theory, cognitive load theory, and the technology acceptance model.
9. **Develop a Metaverse-Based Educational Assessment System or Use It for Evaluation**: Researchers [25] claim that in both conventional and modern educational environments, educators struggle to evaluate student performance and obtain learning data, therefore learning outcomes are prioritised over performance. The Metaverse reliably records and analyses student performance using AI, computing, and storage. Learning analytics reports with formative and summative data might be assessment outcomes. Metaverse assessment can be objective and rigorous. Due to Metaverse implementation, indications must be added or adjusted, needing a clear assessment system.
10. **Innovative Metaverse Applications and Case Studies across Disciplines and Sectors**: We examined Metaverse usage in blended, competency-based, inclusive, and virtual experimental learning in the fourth segment. Learning physics, chemistry, geography, EFL, medical and nursing education, and communication in the Metaverse will differ from traditional methods. Scholars should provide Metaverse design case studies in various educational fields.

3.8 Conclusion

The Metaverse creates immersive, interactive, and collaborative learning experiences that transcend traditional classrooms, transforming education. Through virtual campuses, augmented reality-based content, and gamified learning environments, the Metaverse can enhance student engagement, promote experiential learning, and facilitate global collaboration. These opportunities align with evolving pedagogical approaches, enabling more personalised, student-centric education. However, the successful adoption of Metaverse technologies in education faces multiple challenges. Critical issues include high infrastructure costs, the need for advanced hardware and network support, and the digital divide, which may exacerbate inequalities in access. Additionally, concerns about data privacy, cybersecurity risks, and mental health impacts demand careful consideration. Educators must also undergo training to adapt to this new paradigm, requiring significant shifts in teaching practices and curriculum design. While current use cases illustrate the potential of Metaverse-based learning ranging from virtual classrooms and remote field trips to hands-on STEM education widespread implementation requires strategic collaboration among educational institutions, governments, and technology providers. Policymakers need to establish guidelines for equitable access and ensure responsible data management. Looking ahead, continuous innovation and research will play a pivotal role in refining the integration of Metaverse technologies into education. Future efforts must focus on addressing the technological, social, and ethical challenges while fostering inclusive learning environments. By doing so, the Metaverse can move from concept to reality, offering sustainable, engaging, and accessible educational solutions for learners worldwide.

Chapter 4

Technological Advancement of Blockchain through Metaverse in the Financial Sector

4.1 Introduction

The Metaverse is a swiftly advancing digital realm where immersive virtual experiences intersect with human activities, including finance. Blockchain technology propels innovation in financial transactions, asset management, and economic relationships inside this vast digital ecosystem [1]. Blockchain and the Metaverse are creating decentralised, secure, and transparent value management and exchange systems that are changing finance. Blockchain technology, characterised by its decentralised ledger, smart contracts, and tokenisation, supports numerous financial innovations within the Metaverse. Decentralised Finance (DeFi) systems provide financial transactions and services devoid of intermediaries. Virtual currencies, tokenised assets, and decentralised exchanges operate collaboratively within the Metaverse [2]. These technological advancements are revolutionising the finance sector. Blockchain technology within the Metaverse enhances the efficiency, security, and inclusivity of financial services. Virtual banks, decentralised markets, and Blockchain-based financial instruments are transforming financial transactions and consumer engagement with digital assets.

DOI: 10.1201/9781003520702-4

This analysis examines technological innovation at the convergence of the Metaverse and Blockchain within the banking sector [3]. This article analyses the financial implications of decentralised finance, tokenisation, and virtual asset management. The poll indicates that these technologies provide transparency, reduced transaction costs, and enhanced financial inclusion [4]. Integrating Blockchain and the Metaverse presents regulatory challenges, cybersecurity threats, and scalability concerns. This survey will elucidate the intricacies and resolutions to these problems. This assessment consolidates recent developments, trends, and emerging applications to elucidate how Blockchain technology in the Metaverse has transformed banking. It underscores the digital transformation of financial services and delineates avenues for research and innovation [5].

4.2 Review of Literature

4.2.1 Governance of Blockchain Finance and the Metaverse

Embedded supervision could supplant regulation in a decentralised financial system. Article [6] asserts that Blockchain technology in finance would enhance supervisory efficiency. Blockchain technology's autonomous monitoring would render embedded supervision unnecessary, establishing a regulatory framework in which a ledger requires no verification. Nonetheless, the requisite criteria remain ambiguous and must take into account [7, 40]. Auer [8] asserts that embedded supervision must: (1) necessitates a comprehensive regulatory framework and legal system; (2) be engineered to achieve economic finality when a transaction is no longer beneficial to reverse; (3) be formulated for economic consensus, acknowledging market regulation; and (4) promote cost-efficient compliance to guarantee equity for both large and small enterprises. Its advantages are apparent since it, akin to Blockchain, necessitates no oversight, which is the primary grievance of competitors [9, 41]. This integrated oversight might be readily included into gaming-inspired e-commerce strategies. Blockchain technology has enabled play-to-earn games with token economies. Decentralised Finance (DeFi) and GameFi show how gamification affects Blockchain developers. The simultaneous advancement of gaming and Blockchain technologies renders integration unavoidable. Blockchain serves as an effective decentralised finance solution for the Metaverse due to its:

- **Digital Proof of Ownership (DPoW)**: Digital wallets authenticate ownership of Blockchain assets.
- **Digital Collectibility**: Similar to the physical realm, NFTs facilitate the creation of distinctive items that can be amassed [10, 42].
- **Transferable Value**: Contemporary online multiplayer games facilitate value transfer. This strategy can be implemented via Blockchain when Metaverse monetary transactions increase.

- **Governance**: Blockchain has the potential to supplant elected authorities and guarantee regulatory adherence in a decentralised society.
- **Accessibility**: Blockchain-based digital wallets are accessible to the public, in contrast to traditional banks that restrict account establishment [11].
- **Interoperability**: Custom Blockchains like Polkadot (DOT) and Avalanche are being developed. The Metaverse requires interoperability, and Blockchain has shown promise.

A robust, resilient, and stable economy will enable the Metaverse, a parallel realm for human engagement, to thrive. Author in reference [12] asserts that the Metaverse economy will mirror real-world tendencies, notwithstanding its unique characteristics. A thriving economy exhibits competitiveness, lucrative enterprises, set regulations, a feeling of equity, sustained consumer expenditure, and rights.

4.2.2 Payment Rails

The growing digital world will influence currency exchange for goods and services through payment infrastructure. Advancements in communication technologies have established numerous new payment systems. Cash transactions have diminished. Article [13] indicates that cash transactions in the United States decreased from 40% to 20% from 2010 to 2021. The primary payment systems in the United States include CHIPS, Fedwire, ACH, credit cards, and peer-to-peer payment platforms such as PayPal and Venmo. In evaluating these transactions for software licensing, one may anticipate more adaptable and innovative advancements owing to the rise of the virtual domain. In 2021, digital-only video game sales surpassed $50 billion, and the sector's GDP has increased fivefold since 2005. The mandated integration of services such as PlayStation's wallet, Apple Pay, and in-app payment systems renders virtual economy payment mechanisms more constrained than those of the physical market. Xbox and PlayStation permit customers to download games exclusive to their respective systems. Valve launched Steam in 2003 as a companion platform for PC gaming [14]. Valve employed a "game launcher" to catalogue and centrally administer game installer files for the updating and installation of multiplayer online games when they transitioned to a "games-as-service" paradigm. The system additionally managed game rights and facilitated automated downloads upon request. Similar to console gaming platforms, Valve's business strategy ensured a consistent 30% revenue from each transaction. The 30% payment systems constrain Apple, Google, and their app stores, hence restricting virtual world platforms [43–45].

4.2.3 Emergence of Metaverse Retail

The phrase "Metaverse," albeit prevalent in financial news, has been associated with retail for nearly two decades. Bourlakis and Papagiannidis [15] categorised Metaverse retailing into three phases with the advent of smartphones: traditional, electronic, and Metaverse. Retailers must employ innovative strategies to function in three distinct yet interconnected realms. Traditional brick-and-mortar businesses, online e-commerce platforms, and Metaverse vendors have distinct promotional obstacles. The researchers examined Second Life's "Metaverse phenomenon" and found *World of Warcraft*, *EverQuest*, *Eve Online*, and *Star Wars Galaxies* essential to the "third dimension of commerce." The majority of Metaverses originated as games, particularly MMORPGs. These rapidly transformed into novel virtual and electronic environments for participants. Due to the substantial number of customers dedicating over 12 hours to these virtual environments, novel social and commercial contexts have emerged to provide expanded opportunities. As participants in these games and Metaverses engage economically and socially, there is a convergence of real-world and virtual enterprises. The new multidimensional, multispatial economic environment has become more difficult due to these advancements. It is essential to delineate the electronic, virtual, and physical characteristics of the contemporary corporate environment to understand its economic, social, and regulatory implications. Promote a tri-domain advertising initiative for success [16]. The roots of the Metaverse are frequently employed to contextualise arguments. Second Life, founded in 2003, enabled individuals to monetise their virtual endeavours. Users may monetise their platform content due to their ownership of copyright. Linden Lab's Second Life provided content producers with three options to safeguard their works, permitting or restricting copying, modification, or transfer of their creations or purchases prior to the advent of NFTs and Blockchain technology [17, 46]. The device monitored commodities and manufacturers while generating distinctive digital items. The Linden Dollar facilitated all transactions within Second Life. These can be exchanged for goods and services in the virtual realm or converted into real currency for tangible creators. Due to the absence of a firm licence for virtual entrepreneurs, quantifying their numbers or assessing their success is unfeasible. Positive Linden Dollar Flow (PMLF) assesses more than 66 million "entrepreneurs" within the network. Businesses recognised the significance of client engagement on this platform and commenced operations. These firms include ABN AMRO, Adidas, American Apparel, Dell, Harvard Law School, IBM, Microsoft, Pontiac, Reuters, Sony Ericsson, the Swedish Government, and Toyota. The majority of organisations utilise Second Life for promotional purposes, but a select few want to conduct business within the platform. The widespread adoption remains insufficient [18, 47, 48]. The main difference between Metaverse retail and traditional or e-retailing is customer brand engagement expectations. In two-dimensional marketing and advertising, paper, photographs, films, and music express the product's essence; in the Metaverse, people expect a three-dimensional simulation. The practice aligns with [20]'s forecast of "retail theatre." According to [19], certain Second Life retailers created experiences that enabled consumers to engage with things, hence facilitating purchases. Merchants can cultivate a sense of community among their clientele. Despite enhanced accessibility and the capacity to tailor marketing to particular consumers, firms must exercise caution regarding the repercussions of overwhelming prospective customers. An automated system can provide product or service information while traversing congested Metaverse platforms. Users have the capability to mute bots and automated agents, although persistent silence may be bothersome. Well-designed 3D information can boost sales and improve the retail buying experience. Virtual retail incorporates augmented reality and virtual reality to facilitate a cohesive purchasing experience. Virtual environments facilitate the observation of virtual entities and data. Products can be rendered in three dimensions or crafted for size and fit, rather than being displayed on a flat screen, billboard, or printed medium, which presents clear advantages. Product experiences can enhance purchasing decisions and bolster client confidence [21, 49].

4.2.4 Legal and Financial Challenges in the Metaverse

Digitalisation triggered new laws and regulations. The Metaverse's economic and social changes require an understanding of its disruptive effects on law. An AI precedent for the Metaverse will change conduct and require new antitrust or contract laws [22, 50]. The Metaverse and XR will change how objects interact in real and virtual spaces, affecting how people use these products. AR apps overlay digital components on the actual world, whereas VR immerses users in a simulated environment and lets them interact with avatars and virtual items. Augmented Reality (AR) and Virtual Reality (VR), like AI, may upset legal categories by distinguishing tangible and virtual entities, complicating ownership concerns. Different interpretations of virtual and social spaces increase legal risk. Avatars, which may be digitally altered to resemble any character, worsen the dilemma. Virtual and augmented environments can present unexpected relational and legal issues. As virtual entities such as NFTs integrate with tangible objects, the legalities of ownership will become increasingly ambiguous. The augmented duration of engagement in virtual environments for social and business purposes will amplify legal complexity issues [23, 51]. To safeguard the Metaverse identity embodied by avatars, considering data protection legislation and the adaptability of avatars and virtual conduct, article [24] poses two significant enquiries. How should property law evolve to integrate Blockchain-based virtual land and real estate?

4.2.5 Acquisition of Metaverse Real Estate

Various Metaverse iterations possess distinct land acquisition histories. Second Life incorporated digital land "ownership" into its premium gameplay tier [25, 52]. Premium members receive a complimentary plot of land for development and recreation. The term "owned" was eliminated from Linden Labs' marketing materials because to several legal disputes about digital property ownership. Anshe Chung, an entrepreneur and real estate magnate in Second Life, emerged from land "ownership." BusinessWeek highlighted Ailin Graef's avatar, Anshe Chung, on its cover, while CNN referred to her as the "Rockefeller of Second Life." Fortune referred to Anshe Chung as the "first virtual millionaire" for her acquisition and leasing of virtual real estate while incurring taxes on it [26]. Before expanding between worlds, Entropia Universe was known as Project Entropia. It holds several Guinness World Records for "the most expensive virtual item," a digital asset. Jon Jacobs' avatar NEVERDIE bought an asteroid space resort at a 2005 public auction for US$100,000 (1,000,000 PED). Like Second Life, Entropia Universe converts PED to US dollars at 10:1. The Crystal Palace space station sold for $330,000 in 2009 and Calypso for $6 million in 2010, setting the record. NFTs, denoting 16 × 16 metre^2 land plots, can be acquired on Decentraland utilising MANA cryptocurrency. This acquisition enables proprietors to construct virtual spaces and generate revenue through leasing or alternative methods, so establishing a multidimensional cryptocurrency economy [10]. Decentraland, The Sandbox, Somnium Space, OVR, SuperWorld, Axie Infinity, Bloktopia, and Next Earth offer virtual land. These marketplaces require a digital wallet to buy land. Users can explore groups and buy virtual property plots with the platform's cryptocurrency via the digital wallet. Samsung in Decentraland opened stores because of its worth. Virtual land becomes more valuable and expensive as it approaches Paris or New York. Attributes, dimensions, and additional elements on the property may enhance its value [27, 53]. Numerous individuals critique virtual real estate companies such as Decentraland for their initial constraints and instability. The value proposition of Decentraland lies on land acquisition; nevertheless, the process is intricate. Prospective virtual landowners are unable to purchase tokens using cash. Even Ether (ETH), Bitcoin's leading competitor, is incapable of purchasing virtual real estate. Decentraland, similar to other cryptocurrency initiatives, necessitates MANA, its ERC-20 token. The most affordable virtual land parcels on the site are priced at 4,000 MANA, equivalent to $2,489, reflecting a two-thirds depreciation in value over the past year. A non-fungible virtual land parcel remains under ownership until another user expresses a desire to purchase it. MANA can be sold to consumers purchasing land and transferred among site users [28]. Various factors can rapidly influence land prices due to Bitcoin market volatility. The earning potential of virtual shopfronts varies, experiencing a fivefold increase within a month followed by a substantial decline.

4.2.6 Non-Fungible Tokens and Ownership

Blockchain has the potential to facilitate the Metaverse and supplant current payment systems; yet ownership cannot be effortlessly transitioned from the physical realm to the virtual. Despite Blockchain facilitating decentralisation, it is imperative to examine the terms of service of Metaverse platforms prior to obtaining digital assets. Proponents of cryptocurrency assert that decentralisation and interoperability facilitate NFT ownership. Tokens are seen as non-fungible evidence of digital asset ownership within Metaverse systems [30, 54]. Decentralisation enables Blockchain users to transact virtual products without authorisation. Nonetheless, ownership of Metaverse assets is governed by contract law rather than property law, resulting in increased complexity. Article [29] explained that virtual and real ownership diverge, leading to customer confusion. Acquisitions of Metaverse objects are documented on a Blockchain, a decentralised digital ledger that guarantees immutability. The method allocates NFT ownership to the user's private digital cryptocurrency wallet. Access to the NFT is exclusively granted to the wallet owner through the private key. Nonetheless, NFTs and digital assets must be differentiated, as virtual ownership contrasts with physical ownership. Service agreements define "ownership" differently. All Metaverse platforms need users to agree to the terms of service, use, or end-user licensing agreement during registration. These contractual contracts define user rights. The majority of individuals disregard these Terms and Conditions. Merely 1.7% of consumers identified and enquired about a terms-of-service contract's "child assignment clause," which forfeits their firstborn child [5, 55, 56]. These extensive and complex contracts delineate ownership specifics, and in contrast to Blockchain, platform terms of service are centralised. The existing Metaverse is unconnected, therefore users cannot transfer avatars or other digital assets between virtual domains. One entity owns them. Platforms continue to link NFTs to exclusive digital assets. Service laws show that Metaverse platform NFTs and digital assets are rarely the same. NFTs are on the Blockchain, whereas digital assets and real estate are on private servers in inaccessible databases. Digital asset servers can sever connections and isolate owners, inhibiting usage. Users are infrequently obligated to receive notification of modifications to the terms of service of these services. Users must refresh and review the Terms of Service to identify any new text that may result in their expulsion from the site and the forfeiture of their assets.

4.3 Key Meta-Economic Sectors and Enablers

The study must define its application domain to predict Metaverse financial services. This section describes the Metaverse ecosystem's main sectors and enablers. Industry experts say the Metaverse's virtual economy will surpass the actual world's. With five billion Internet users, the Metaverse economy digital assets and marketplaces is expected to produce $8 trillion to $13 trillion in market opportunity. An estimated 25% of the worldwide population will use the Metaverse for at least one hour by 2026, making markets more accessible. This broad virtual performance requires real-world currency, fair trade and exchange of virtual commodities, ownership rights protection, and virtual acquisition financing. Financial service firms view gaming and virtual real estate as established and promising. Virtual commerce, education, tourism, healthcare, and event planning are promise yet unknown. Discourse shows that Blockchain, NFTs, DeFi, and AI are essential to the Metaverse economy. Figure 4.1 describes the key meta-economic sectors and enablers.

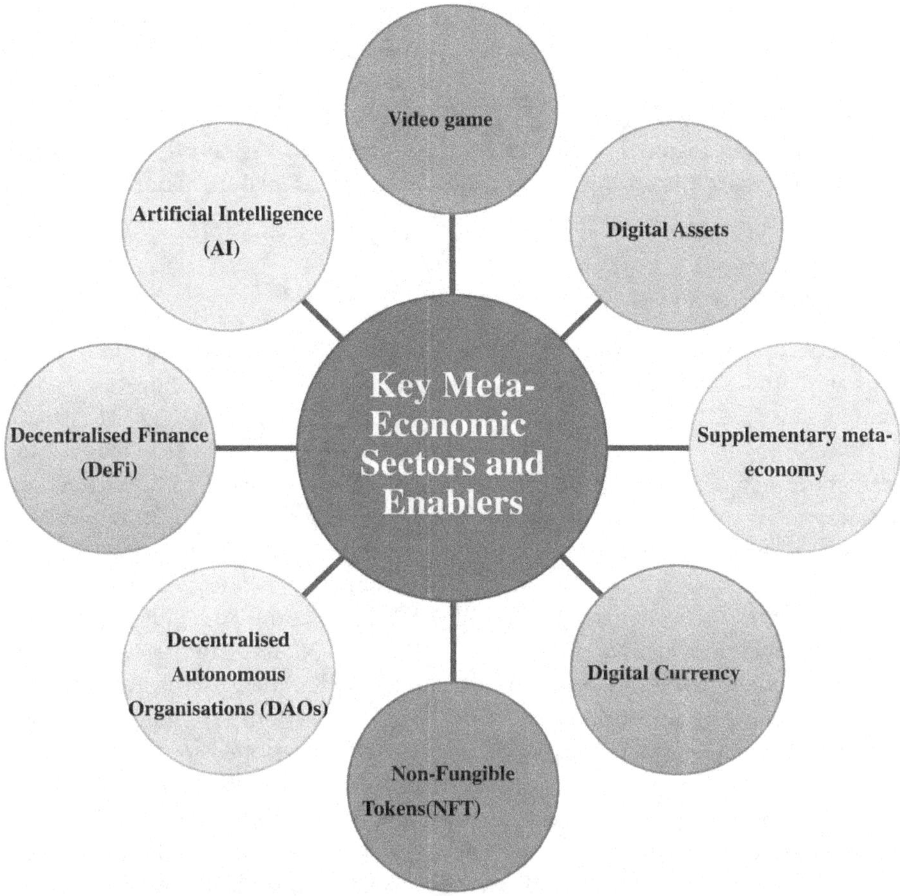

Figure 4.1 Key meta-economic sectors and enablers.

4.3.1 Video Game Sector

During the COVID-19 pandemic, internet gaming surged in popularity, with worldwide gaming length increasing by 39%. By 2030, over 3 billion individuals will engage in online gaming, constituting 38% of the global population. Microsoft anticipates exceeding 4.5 billion by 2030. In-game marketing revenue is projected to attain $18.4 billion by 2027, with yearly expenditures on virtual products totalling $54 billion, of which $40 billion is allocated to gaming skins. Consequently, this emerging meta-economy domain necessitates an in-game economic framework that provides sustainable and efficient financial services [11, 39, 57]. For Meta economy growth, many platforms must be integrated. Allowing users to "transfer" assets to other virtual venues should boost Metaverse trading [2, 38].

Monetising gaming labour and time may propel the business forward. Play-to-earn is supplanting pay-to-play, wherein players purchase games. Emerging gaming modalities necessitate financial systems that effortlessly transfer virtual earnings into tangible money [22, 37, 58]. Virtual reality and augmented reality technologies could enhance global GDP by $1.5 trillion. Apple's Vision Pro device's global introduction suggests strong demand despite user complaints about ergonomics and price.

4.3.2 Digital Assets

Metaverse business and events require virtual land. Second Life has made virtual land and products commerce viable, with major participants making up to $1.5 million annually. Real estate transactions exceeded $1.4 billion in 2022 [31, 59, 60]. The Non-Fungible Token (NFT) virtual land represents a digital parcel of real estate with coordinates. Sandbox, the leading virtual platform, had 65,000 virtual land sales for $350 million in 2021, while Decentraland recorded 21,000 transactions worth $110 million. Average sandbox land price rose from $100 in January 2021 to $15,000 in December 2021. Although activity is high, virtual real estate sales ($100 million monthly) are a small fraction of NFT transactions ($2 billion) [12, 61], demonstrating the Metaverse's real estate potential. Virtual land is valued by its proximity to landmarks, NFT collections, and seasonal trade patterns. Adidas, PwC, and McKinsey buy [23, 62]. Most virtual land acquisitions are long-term investments or speculative, with a smaller percentage being developed [24]. Virtual mortgages from TerraZero meet the growing demand for virtual real estate. Purchasers consent to regular Bitcoin transactions and a long-term obligation to acquire virtual assets. Upon completing the final payment, purchasers obtain complete ownership rights, facilitating the acquisition of virtual real estate. The Meta economy may lack resource scarcity characteristic of the real economy. Artificial territorial limitations imposed by platforms such as Decentraland may be evaluated. The evolution of virtual lands and their impact on the secondary market will be intriguing to observe. Certain scholars contend that the Metaverse economy will entail numerous transactions, potentially complicating Blockchain storage and maintenance. Virtual real estate may attract financial service providers due to its investment potential. Smart contracts and artificial intelligence can enhance the transparency and inclusivity of virtual land and space finance.

4.3.3 Supplementary Meta-Economy Sectors

The meta economy enhances virtual commerce and trading, among other sectors. The COVID-19 pandemic also led to an increase in virtual meetings. Simultaneously, virtual education and healthcare received acknowledgement. Supplementary sectors contributing to the expansion of the Meta economy encompass:

- **Retail and Commercial Engagements.** Rapidly expanding Metaverse commerce include user-to-user and business-to-user transactions [25, 63, 64]. YouGov believes that 10% of individuals engage in shopping within the Metaverse, and the value of virtual fashion is projected to reach $50 billion by 2030. Gucci, Burberry, and Adidas established Metaverse offices and marketed virtual apparel. Utilising Metaverse data for targeted advertising will expedite virtual commerce.
- **Telemedicine and Virtual Learning.** Virtual healthcare and education will improve public health and education by providing remote medical services and self-directed training for varied vocations. Tele-surgeries are available with Microsoft's HoloLens.
- **Digital Tourism.** Research indicates that virtual tourism can supplement and potentially supplant physical travel. Virtual reality can enhance vividness and engagement, resulting in increased consumer satisfaction. Virtual reality enhances traveller liberty and personalisation [26, 65]. This form of tourism is more economical and environmentally friendly than traditional travel.
- **Virtual Conferences and Meetings.** Virtual events and gatherings expanded during the COVID-19 epidemic, similar to other areas of the Meta economy. Even with the removal of physical separation limitations, hybrid labour continues to be pertinent [27, 66]. Meta (Horizon Workrooms) and Microsoft (Mesh for Microsoft Teams) spend heavily in virtual meeting and conference systems. The Metaverse hosts major sports tournaments like the Australian Open. All Metaverse economy divisions will form a virtual financial system requiring financial transactions. Cryptocurrency, NFTs, Decentralised Autonomous Organisations (DAOs), DeFi, and AI power the Metaverse. All these facilitators employ Blockchain technology, or Distributed Ledger Technology (DLT), to store, secure, and decentralise Metaverse data. Blockchain technology safeguards the standardisation, composability, traceability, and immutability of digital assets by guaranteeing transaction transparency.

4.3.4 Digital Currency

Metaverse virtual economy prioritises digital asset management. Protecting and transferring ownership of these assets is crucial to the Metaverse economy. Two types of Blockchain tokens represent assets digitally and address these issues. In the Metaverse, fungible and non-fungible tokens dictate financial dynamics. This chapter examines fungible tokens, namely cryptocurrencies. The meta-economy requires a currency for the exchange of products and services, akin to any other economy. Numerous online platforms utilise Bitcoin, a money based on Blockchain technology. For example, Sandbox employs Sand, a distinctive cryptocurrency that varies in value between $1 and $5 per unit, as assessed in transactions within Sandbox. Users were willing to spend 3.4% more for Sand compared to Ethereum (ETH). Researchers credit Sandbox's open economy, flexible exchange rate, and lack of capital restrictions for its recent increase against ETH [28, 67, 68]. A significant Metaverse platform, Decentraland, and its native currency, MANA, demonstrate virtual liquidity dynamics. First, MANA provided 2,644,403,343 units [29]. The MANA contract called for 8% inflation, while community agreement was 0%, making MANA's supply deflationary. The circulation is diminished by a 2.5% marketplace fee through the "burning" of MANA after each transaction. The European Central Bank categorises virtual currency schemes as closed, unidirectional, and bidirectional. Closed schemes restrict cryptocurrency to platform-specific applications and prohibit conversion to fiat cash. Unidirectional schemes let transactions using real currency without the option for conversion back to actual money. The final category, virtual currency transactions, may attract financial service firms. Although cryptocurrencies may serve as the currency of the Metaverse, they elicit apprehensions. In his Metaverse research on fungible tokens, article [11] used Decentraland's MANA to show that cryptocurrencies' volatility prevents them from functioning as a unit of account and medium of exchange. The author supported Metaverse stablecoin currency. Numerous experts study decentralised finance's money supply and deflation in addition to cryptocurrency volatility [12]. Establishing a new virtual currency necessitates the trust and approval of platform users. Fractional reserve lending in a virtual banking system can augment the money supply, as stated in [13]. Nonetheless, virtual banking presents regulatory challenges. The government may need to act as the "lender of last resort" in the precarious financial environment of the Metaverse. Linking virtual currency to fiat currencies or commodities represents an alternative method of currency management. Bitcoin developers must innovate to address these and other cryptocurrency challenges as the market expands. Interoperability solutions that enable seamless Bitcoin transfers within platforms or through financial service providers are needed in some gaming scenarios. Cryptocurrencies in alternative financial institutions, often linked with high-risk investments, raise concerns. Analysis of cryptocurrency fraud and its likely spread in the Meta economy [14, 69].

4.3.5 Non-Fungible Tokens

The Meta economy developed with the introduction of Non-Fungible Tokens (NFTs), a Blockchain-based representation of digital ownership that is not interchangeable on a one-to-one basis. NFTs facilitate virtual ownership and commerce by generating value for digital assets. NFTs can assign monetary value to digital art, designer clothes, and virtual real estate in a context where economic worth does not consistently dictate value. The predominant category of NFTs consists of collectibles, succeeded by ownership of digital art [15, 70]. NFTs are attractive because of their lucrativeness. In 2021, NFT sales totalled $25 billion. One hundred one NFTs from the "Bored Ape Yacht Club" were auctioned for $24.4 million. A Blockchain documents all NFT activities, encompassing minting, storage, and trading, to avert corruption and fraud. Since the advent of the internet, artists have grappled with generating value in the absence of scarcity. NFTs provide a resolution. A digital artwork can be reproduced indefinitely. A file that can be reproduced endlessly should be free; instead, NFTs are exchanged for positive values due to the artificial scarcity created by digital ownership, exemplified as artist-certified copies. NFTs, similar to cryptocurrencies, exhibit volatility. The inaugural day of NFT trading yielded an average raw return of 130%. NFTs exhibit an annualised volatility of 175% in daily returns, while oil demonstrates 30% and the S&P 500 index shows 15%. In July 2021, a CryptoPunk was valued at $100,000, increased to $500,000 in November, and subsequently decreased to $350,000 in December. NFT proponents highlight the ease of claiming ownership, enabling fast, transparent transactions. NFTs bypass clearance and settle in seconds. NFT ownership is verifiable; yet replicating the underlying assets is challenging due to the uniqueness and scarcity of virtual things. The NFT community must determine how to safeguard the properties of transferred items [16, 71].

4.3.6 Decentralised Autonomous Organisations and Decentralised Finance

DAOs and DeFi are utilise Blockchain technology to coordinate and administer various Metaverse platforms. A DAO is founded on protocols and smart contracts. Decentralised voting authority is typically predicated on user tokens. Each DAO member possesses the ability to vote transparently, rendering DAOs genuinely democratic. Blockchain-based Decentralised Finance (DeFi) offers financial services in a decentralised manner. DeFi, originally designed to eradicate financial intermediaries, now guarantees application composability and programmability to alter and adapt basic protocols. JPMorgan Chase wants to tokenise large assets like US treasury funds as collateral in DeFi pools to facilitate crowdfunding and microfinancing. Decentralised exchanges managing DeFi will enhance Metaverse liquidity by utilising fractionalised NFTs as collateral.

4.3.7 Artificial Intelligence

Generative AI can accelerate Metaverse evolution. Generative AI creates virtual cities, landscapes, and architecture quickly. It also lets people with different tech skills create, improving user experience and coding operations. Generative AI-powered chatbots and digital assistants provide tailored support and timely feedback, improving project quality. AI algorithms improve payment processing efficiency. Historical data and consumer behaviour in instant payment networks and infrastructures may help detect risk and fraud [17, 72, 73]. Generative AI will merge physical and virtual worlds in the Metaverse [18, 74]. The eventual elimination of human involvement in financial procedures like loan approval raises ethical concerns about artificial intelligence.

4.4 Effects on the Digital Economy and Governmental Policy

Numerous Metaverse applications seek to transform the perception, execution, and monetisation of economic activities, particularly services, in both real and virtual realms. Numerous enquiries persist regarding the technology and adoption of applications, notwithstanding the hyperbole of Metaverse proponents. We examine a minimum of three economic ramifications of utilising the Metaverse for economic services in the future, refraining from adopting a stance or making forecasts. The domains of application for these technologies, the individuals who construct and govern virtual environments, and their motivations provide numerous implications. Services within the Metaverse may obscure the distinctions between tradable and non-tradable segments of the economy. Tradables are commodities that can be exchanged across great distances and are regulated by the law of one price. Price arbitrage can occur in efficient, integrated markets for tangible commodities such as oil and financial instruments like stock shares. Non-tradable assets such as real estate and services can exhibit significant price fluctuations [19, 75]. Information technology has rendered non-tradables, such as education and marketable. The Metaverse can expedite this process by facilitating genuine interactions among users in various locales. It may also facilitate novel virtual goods and services, encompassing virtual experiences, entertainment, and digital art. The Metaverse's lack of borders may promote global economic convergence. This could enhance global resource allocation. As geographic boundaries diminish, educational institutions, music and language instructors, healthcare experts, financial and tax advisers, among others, may provide services to clients in foreign nations. While several contemporary applications emphasise gaming, we have examined educational and healthcare applications that may prove advantageous. Individuals can enrol in courses at prestigious universities or consult leading experts without the necessity of travelling to their respective countries. Flexibility may enhance resource utilisation, hence augmenting economic output. Consequently, labour dynamics may evolve. As the Metaverse expands, there may be a demand for virtual object designers and virtual event planners. As global connectivity expands, employment opportunities may rise [10]. Individuals from any location may submit applications for positions within the Metaverse. Globalisation diminished expenses as industries relocated production to nations with lower labour costs. The Metaverse may extend into further sectors. The examples of Roblox and Axie Infinity illustrate that users' capacity to monetise their creations might result in an increase in project-based or "gig" employment opportunities. Analogous to informal employment arrangements in emerging markets and impoverished nations, similar agreements may proliferate in mature economies. The integration will complicate the application of domestic rules and regulations in virtual situations. Which jurisdiction regulates a virtual service contract between customers from the United States and Vietnam? Retail customers planning to engage in the Metaverse may be unaware of cross-border service obligations under regulatory frameworks. Will authorities have the resources to monitor compliance across sectors? Can they enforce labour rules and other regulations? Third, Metaverse services may boost real-time and international transactions. Traditional payment cards, rising digital payment providers, cryptocurrencies, CBDCs, and integrated rapid payment systems compete to meet this demand [12]. If the Metaverse attains macroeconomic status, the payment mechanisms associated with this competition may gain increased popularity. This may also affect practical application. Consequently, central banks and financial authorities may seek to enhance their comprehension and influence on the selection of payment instruments within the Metaverse. Authorities must enhance initiatives to promote more efficient and interoperable payment systems that meet user requirements, while preventing the fragmentation of virtual environments and financial resources under prevailing business entities. To safeguard market integrity, authorities must adhere to anti-money laundering and counter-terrorism financing regulations, irrespective of payment methods. Public policy concerns regarding new Metaverse application developers and their intended applications arise alongside these three impacts. Prominent corporations and venture capitalists are the primary investors in virtual reality, augmented reality, and Metaverse applications for commercial purposes [13]. Commercial motivations frequently propel innovation; nevertheless, the network ramifications of technological advancement are a concern. Private organisations may possess significant motivations to create proprietary applications and inhibit interoperability with competing applications. They might also commercialise user data. Virtual reality presents online privacy concerns due to its immersive nature. Private enterprises may collect and analyse highly invasive data from transactions, biometric information, wearable metrics, and additional sources. Proponents of a decentralised Metaverse frequently articulate apprehensions over these vulnerabilities; yet it remains ambiguous if proposed Blockchain-based alternatives, many of which depend on token speculation, will more effectively foster competitive markets or safeguard data privacy. Many writers have called for industry-wide or public policy Metaverse governance frameworks and norms [14]. Some critics compare it to internet governance frameworks that standardise visual representation, file transmission, graphics, and data exchange. The Metaverse seeks open standards and protocols to improve platform compatibility. In Metaverse systems, messaging and file formats facilitate data sharing and commodity mobility. Analysts say Metaverse virtual property requires data privacy, consumer protection, and ownership rights restrictions from public authorities and regulators. Both scenarios contend that such activities must be implemented promptly to influence field innovation. The technology and applications utilised by private Metaverse users are still evolving, complicating the ability of public authorities to impose regulations. Should these applications proliferate and gain popularity, policy discussions will arise. Anarcho-libertarian commentators distrustful of governmental policies and regulations may influence the discourse surrounding cryptocurrency and distributed ledger technologies. When dangers inflict harm on consumers, the public and governments are likely to demand regulatory measures to avert future damage. In this context, assertive government involvement could be beneficial. Public sector enterprises adhere to societal public policy objectives, resulting in distinct motives compared to technology firms, venture capital investors, and other dominant stakeholders. Public sector bodies can enhance market results through active participation, acquiring knowledge about technology and uses, and fostering transparency, competition, and adherence to regulations. Responsible innovation can leverage current laws and regulatory standards, notwithstanding uncertainties around technology advancements [15].

4.5 Monetary Applications of Blockchain Technology

Blockchain technology is revolutionising finance through decentralised, transparent, and secure transactions. The technology, initially created for the Bitcoin market, has transformed payments, asset management, and insurance. This article examines significant Blockchain applications within the financial sector. Financial transactions and remittances constitute prominent applications of Blockchain technology. Blockchain technology facilitates near-instantaneous international payments, thereby diminishing both time and expense. Blockchain-based distributed ledger systems verify and facilitate transactions, removing the necessity for banks, payment processors, and remittance services [16]. The rapid, secure, and cost-effective Blockchain-based payment solutions provided by Ripple and Stellar are gaining increasing popularity. These technologies enable instantaneous cross-border transactions with minimal fees and transparent processing. Contemporary banking necessitates secure and dependable identity verification to mitigate fraud and adhere to regulations in the management of digital identification. Blockchain can address this issue by offering a secure, immutable decentralised identity management solution. Blockchain-based identity management solutions enable individuals to manage and securely disseminate their identification data to banks and financial institutions. Identity data is preserved on a tamper-resistant distributed ledger utilising Blockchain technology, guaranteeing optimal security. Smart contracts are self-executing agreements with buyer-seller conditions encoded in a programming language. Contract negotiations, validation, and execution are their responsibility. Insurance claims, asset management, and supply chain finance use smart contracts. Smart contracts are secure, transparent, and automated with Blockchain technology, saving time and resources. Smart contract automation obviates the necessity for solicitors to oversee and execute contracts, hence accelerating processes and reducing expenses [17].

Blockchain technology is transforming asset management. Blockchain digitises assets through tokens on a decentralised ledger. These tokens streamline trading, transferring, and settlement, hence conserving time and resources in asset management. Tokenisation enables investors to acquire and liquidate fractional interests in assets such as real estate and art without necessitating substantial capital investments. Financial institutions such as Securitise and Harbour are utilising Blockchain-based asset management platforms to provide investors with a broader array of assets and opportunities. International trade depends on trade finance to facilitate imports and exports between enterprises and financial institutions. Due to intermediaries, traditional trade finance is slow, inefficient, and expensive. Blockchain eliminates intermediaries and speeds up trade finance [18]. Blockchain-based trade finance platforms like we.trade and Marco Polo are becoming popular due to their efficiency and cost-effectiveness in global trade. Blockchain is disrupting the insurance industry. Enhancing policy transparency and security with Blockchain technology helps mitigate fraud and optimise the claims process for insurance firms. Blockchain-based insurance solutions safeguard policyholder data from loss and tampering by offering a decentralised platform for storage and management. Smart contracts automate and guarantee precise and prompt claims processing, enhancing insurance claims management.

The finance sector is heavily regulated, governed by an intricate framework of laws and regulations. Blockchain technology can assist financial institutions in adhering to these regulations, hence reducing non-compliance and associated penalties. Blockchain clearly and securely records regulatory compliance data. Blockchain can streamline compliance processes for financial organisations, resulting in time and cost savings. Startups and small enterprises frequently secure capital via crowdfunding. Conventional crowdfunding platforms may incur high costs and restrict access to capital. Blockchain technology can enhance the efficiency and reduce the costs of crowdfunding. Blockchain tokenisation enables investors to acquire and trade ownership tokens of companies or projects, hence enabling crowdfunding. Blockchain-based crowdfunding platforms such as ICOBox and Swarm are increasingly popular, providing startups and small enterprises with additional investors and funding alternatives [19].

4.6 Blockchain Applications in the Financial Sector

Finance has encountered numerous hurdles throughout history. Technology has resolved numerous issues, but certain advancements have generated new challenges. Financial service organisations face challenges in selecting from the several fintech options available. Consequently, they pursue a comprehensive resolution to all significant difficulties. Blockchain possesses significant potential to address challenges within the financial services sector.

4.6.1 Security and Transparency

Global financial services are centralised and multi-tiered. Financial data is predominantly maintained centrally and must traverse multiple intermediaries, encompassing both front and back offices. Data protection is contingent upon intermediaries and database security, hence constraining transparency. Notwithstanding great database protection, data breaches and server assaults remain probable. Lack of system openness heightens security risks, since users remain oblivious to issues until they arise or data is breached. While not all individuals desire financial record transparency, a degree of systemic transparency is advantageous and crucial for financial service providers and their clients [21].

Solution: Blockchain provides transparency and security in financial services.

- **Immutability**: Data on the Blockchain is unalterable. It guarantees data security, authenticity, and precision.
- **Privacy**: Two cryptographic keys—public and private. The public key is accessible to all users of the network. The private key is exclusively disseminated among transaction participants. All network users can view the transaction via the public key, but only individuals possessing the private key can access the stakeholders and transaction specifics. It safeguards stakeholders' sensitive financial information while ensuring system transparency.
- **Zero-Knowledge Proof Technology**: Numerous Blockchain networks employ it for privacy purposes. This facilitates the validation of financial data while maintaining confidentiality.

4.6.2 Expenditures Diminished

Centralised financial institutions allocate substantial funds towards central databases, bookkeeping, database operations, labour, security, intermediary commissions, and value transfer systems. Recurring expenses necessitate consistent financial allocation. The additional expenses render the system costlier without averting data breaches. Blockchain technology has the potential to reduce financial expenditures. According to studies, DLT could reduce financial services infrastructure expenses by US$15 billion to US$20 billion by 2030. Distributed Ledger Technology (DLT), such as Blockchain, enhances transparency, security, and cost-efficiency. Financial institutions, such as banks, can employ smart contracts to minimise intermediaries, transfer costs, and expenses associated with recordkeeping. Blockchain technology in financial services can significantly decrease costs [22].

4.6.3 Efficient Risk Mitigation

Loans present numerous risks for financial service providers, including counterparty default. Credit risk arises from information leak and the counterparty default. Oversight and assessment of loan utilisation in commercial banking are unreliable and inefficient, as they necessitate reliance on an intermediary. Consequently, the risk is significant as providers will incur substantial expenses if issues arise [23].

Solution: Blockchain financial services regard stakeholders as nodes. Consequently, intermediaries can be eradicated in Peer-to-Peer (P2P) transactions. As all network transactions are documented, the management of funds and credit risks is mitigated. Smart contracts expedite transaction settlement. Immutable data enhances reliability. Financial service organisations can mitigate risks via Blockchain technology.

4.6.4 Immediate Settlements

In the existing banking system, some transactions may need up to a week for settlement. The numerous intermediates inside the system are the primary culprit. Every transaction in our intricate financial system passes through multiple middlemen for settlement. These intermediaries may include banks' front and back offices or other entities such as currency exchange firms for cross-border transactions. Various intermediaries guarantee security and authenticity within a centralised system; yet they may prolong settlement periods and elevate expenses [31].

Solution: Blockchain facilitates peer-to-peer financial transactions. Smart contracts regulate transactions, indicating the necessity of eliminating intermediaries. Minimised "layers" will facilitate expedited payment settlements. Blockchain payment solutions facilitate instantaneous cross-border transactions. Consequently, Blockchain technology in financial enterprises facilitates instantaneous payments.

4.6.5 Enhanced Auditing

Auditing is labour-intensive and costly. The centralised structure lacks transparency. Consequently, accountants and compliance officers of financial service providers may present specific information during audits. It fosters deception, nonconformity, and protracted audits [24].

Solution: Blockchain enhances financial audits. Blockchain records are immutable, enabling auditors to validate compliance and financial organisational activities. Blockchain will guarantee that financial service providers operate with ethics and transparency. Any questionable transactional behaviour can be immediately observed. Access to information accelerates audits, hence diminishing procedural duration. Consequently, Blockchain technology in finance can enhance auditing processes. We will now examine several applications of Blockchain technology in financial services following our comprehension of its resolution of banking issues. Obtain tailored Blockchain solutions for your enterprise.

4.6.6 Applications of Blockchain in Finance

Cross-border payments, lending platforms, credit scoring, invoice administration and billing, fund investment, government expenditures, political contributions, financial record keeping, stock exchanges, and ICOs use Blockchain. Figure 4.2 explains applications of Blockchain in finance sector [25].

- **Cross-Border Transactions**: International money transfers are expensive and time-consuming due to bank fees. US–Russian funds must pass through one or more financial institutions before reaching their destination. Blockchain lets people move money autonomously. Stellar and Ripple-supported Blockchain payment solutions enable fast, affordable international transactions [26].

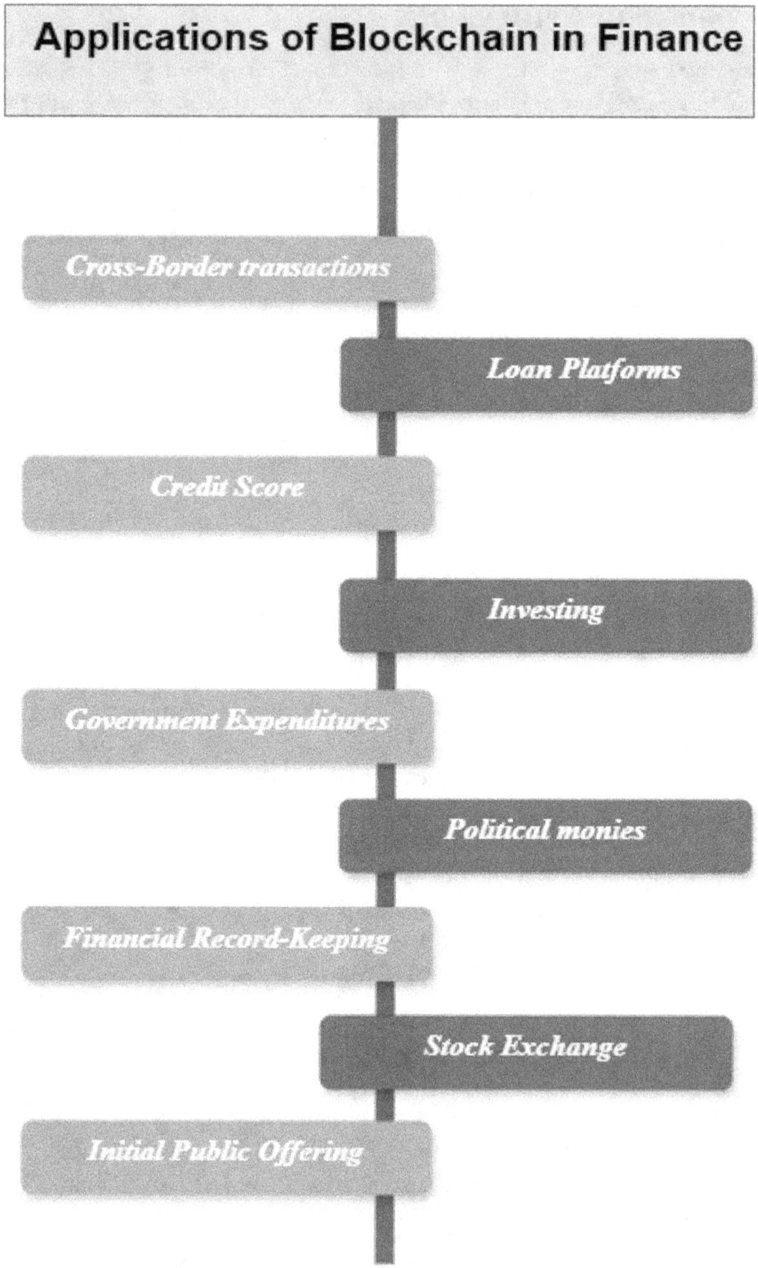

Figure 4.2 Applications of Blockchain in finance.

- **Loan Platforms**: Before Blockchain, customers needed middlemen to trust and transact. Immutable smart contracts let borrowers negotiate interest rates, repayment schedules, and transaction durations with lenders on Blockchain. Lenders and borrowers can negotiate smart contract terms [32]. Noncompliance with smart contracts results in late payment fees on the total amount owed to lenders. Blockchain-based loan applications have facilitated ING and Credit Suisse in trading high-quality liquid assets amounting to EUR 25 million. Blockchain enhances system trust and optimises the process by removing intermediaries.
- **Credit Score**: Financial institutions necessitate a credit score prior to advancing a loan application. The present credit management is constrained by the rigidity of credit ratings. A person's credit score is not applicable internationally. Consequently, a universal credit score is essential. The Equifax breach, which exposed the personal data of 143 million American consumers, underscores the necessity for systemic reform. Employing Blockchain for credit score management may enhance transparency. Blockchain enables lenders to assess creditworthiness through unalterable financial transaction records [33]. Smart contracts safeguard applicants' personal information. Electronic invoicing is being implemented by Invoice Management and Billing Solutions, but they lack the criteria for efficient invoice-backed finance. Smart contracts let banks post invoices on the Blockchain. Blockchain can store client data, payment due dates, and amounts. The smart contract updates invoice status to "paid" and notifies companies of client payment. Financial services Blockchain technology can assess client trading security [27].
- **Investing**: Fund investing is labour-intensive and costly. The existing approach employs numerous databases and manual procedures. Blockchain enables financial institutions to keep individuals' legal, personal, and public information in a decentralised ledger. It may diminish errors and fraud, enhance transparency, and augment data accessibility. Investment firms can rapidly retrieve consumer data through an immutable smart contract. Users who decline to give data will be prohibited from access [34]. Users can monitor information access and its intended use. Blockchain technology in financial services can enhance transparency in fund investments.
- **Government Expenditures**: Digital efforts are modernising legal processes and enhancing public engagement globally. Technological advancements have enhanced the openness of public money, hence augmenting faith in the system. Envision inhabitants overseeing expenditures related to road construction. Governments could mitigate corruption by employing public Blockchain technology to monitor urban development expenditures [35]. Consequently, Blockchain technology in governmental financial services would enhance efficiency.
- **Political Monies**: Blockchains can demonstrate the expenditure of public monies by a political party. Blockchain enables voters to select political parties with greater discernment [28].

- **Financial Record-Keeping**: Financial record-keeping organisations intend to utilise Blockchain technology for the immutable storage of financial history, month-over-month profitability, and dividend distribution. Smart contracts assist shareholders in acquiring pertinent info [36]. Shareholders ought to have access to sensitive information, while interested parties should be limited to public information. Consequently, Blockchain enhances financial transparency within financial services organisations.
- **Stock Exchange**: The stock market's regulators, brokers, and exchange cost money. A decentralised stock market management method improves efficiency. Blockchain-based smart contracts could eliminate third-party regulators [30].
- **Initial Public Offering**: Fees from venture capitalists, private investment firms, and banking bureaucracy make the IPO expensive. The decentralisation of equities markets is forthcoming. Blockchain enables investors and organisations to interact safely and thoroughly without intermediaries, resulting in cost savings [31].

4.7 Conclusion

The amalgamation of Blockchain technology and the Metaverse has tremendous potential for the banking sector. Utilising the decentralised, secure, and transparent characteristics of Blockchain, financial services can provide creative solutions that correspond with the expanding digital economy of the Metaverse. This convergence is poised to transform transactions, improve security, lower operational expenses, and enable novel digital assets and services. Furthermore, smart contracts and Decentralised Finance (DeFi) in virtual environments may facilitate users' participation in intricate financial transactions without intermediaries, promoting inclusivity and accessibility. The extensive implementation of Blockchain in the Metaverse necessitates addressing legislative obstacles, scalability issues, and the establishment of interoperable standards. As the Metaverse advances, Blockchain's function in safeguarding and facilitating financial transactions will be essential, leading to a more decentralised and transparent financial future.

Chapter 5

Blockchain in Pharma Supply Chains: A Comprehensive Survey on Impact and Innovation

5.1 Introduction

Supply lines are complicated, and people who work in the healthcare and medical supply chain today face a lot of problems. Healthcare services depend on getting medicines, medical equipment, and other healthcare goods to people when they need them and as quickly as possible. To make this work, transactional data like orders, inventory levels, and events like shipments being loaded or received at a certain place are now shared [1]. This old way of managing the supply chain often needs help with problems like information packets going missing or being lost, not being clear, tracking that doesn't work well, and counterfeiting. The use of Blockchain technology in digital supply chain management could help solve these problems by letting the system share risk management information that is based on the situation. According to a new study from Gartner, more than 40% of people will invest in apps and services that use Blockchain technology as a secure data platform by 2030. As more machine-to-machine digital data sharing takes place in supply chains, the need to coordinate IT strategy for efficiency, innovation, risk management, and purpose becomes the most important factor in Blockchain adoption [2].

DOI: 10.1201/9781003520702-5

The medical supply chain is made up of many interconnected steps, such as making, distributing, storing, transporting, and delivering medical supplies to patients and healthcare workers. Because there are so many players and stakeholders, the process faces many problems. When fake drugs get into the supply chain, they put patients at great risk because they might not work or contain dangerous substances. Tracking stock poorly and not being able to see how much is in stock can cause shortages or too much stock, which can raise costs and hurt patient care. A lack of transparency is also caused by unclear pricing systems and data silos, which make it harder for fair market practices to work [3].

5.1.1 Health Supply Chain Management Issues

The health supply chain management method has some of the following problems:

- In smart transportation, strong cryptography is needed to make sure that data and information are not changed by someone who isn't supposed to. As a result, a good car identification method is needed.
- It has to make sure that the information gets to the right person.
- Another problem is availability. This means that smart devices must be open 24 hours a day, seven days a week.
- These days, some supply chain systems use IoT devices to move medical equipment. One problem with IoT devices is that they don't have a lot of storage or working power, which makes them easy targets for security attacks. It is important to have security and privacy options that work.
- For a supply chain to be smart, the goods must be sent to the right person at the right time and place. This can only be done with a safe system.
- Tracking medical parts through the supply chain is hard because of centralised control, a lack of accurate information, and parties acting in ways that are at odds with each other [12].
- The structure of healthcare supply chains is complicated because they join many different organisations and places. Because of this, it is hard to find information and make sure it is correct [2].
- Fake drugs are now the biggest problem in the current system for managing the healthcare supply chain. Many people have died because of fake drugs, and the healthcare industry has lost money [4].
- To get around these issues, the health supply chain management system uses fresh technologies to boost safety, trust, tracking and tracing, awareness, and workflow [8].

5.2 Background of the Research and Definition of the Concept

If Blockchain technology can stop people from changing or forging information, then this is a good place to start using it in supply chain management. Additionally, the recent global spread of COVID-19 has opened up a new way for Blockchain technology to be used in supply chain management. The global supply chain broke down because of COVID-19, and large-scale regional blockades Consequently, the flow of commodities throughout the supply chain was impeded. The efficiency of the food and medication supply lines has a direct bearing on people's well-being and longevity. Blockchain technology monitors the flow of products along the supply chain, ensuring that the correct quantity and quality of commodities reach their intended destination on time. This is why the potential applications of Blockchain technology in Supply Chain Management (SCM) have garnered so much attention in recent years [4].

5.2.1 The Supply Chain

Peter Drucker first suggested an economic chain as the basis for the supply chain. This changed into a value chain, which Michael Porter [25] then expanded upon and finally arrived at its present form. The supply chain has always been an interesting topic for management study, and the idea and meaning of it have grown over time. There is a consensus among the majority of academics on a description of a supply chain. In its most basic form, the supply chain begins with the core business and encompasses the management of the flow of information, transportation, and cash. Subsequently, it proceeds to the process of purchasing raw materials and transforming them into intermediate and final goods. The final step is for the sales network to deliver these products to the end users. It is made up of suppliers, manufacturers, distributors, stores, and end users. The supply chain connects all of these groups. The supply chain connects people to nature and offers many goods and services, such as clothing, food, housing, and transportation [5].

5.2.2 Managing the Supply Chain

Supply chain management is the process of planning, organising, running, controlling, and improving the whole system of the supply chain so that business partners can get the best service at the lowest cost. "5 rights" must be met for supply chain management to work well: it is important to have the appropriate people, the right number, the right amount of product, the right time, and the right place. The purpose of supply chain management is to improve the efficiency of the supply chain to provide end customers with a greater amount of value. For businesses to use supply chain management, they need to work on both making smart partnerships and integrating themselves from a management point of view. In the supply chain, the bullwhip effect is a way that changes in demand are amplified. As information moves from the final customer to the original supplier, it can't be shared accurately. As a result, the real information gets distorted and amplified step by step. This causes demand information in the supply chain to change more and more, which is the biggest problem with making it work more efficiently. New tools need to be used in the supply chain so that real information is shared quickly and widely [6, 36].

5.2.3 Blockchain

It can make up for the flaws in traditional credit systems, stop people from changing or forging information, and lower the cost of credit for everyone [16, 37, 38]. Blockchain technology is a new technology that acts like a distributed ledger that can be tracked. Satoshi Nakamoto first wrote about the idea of Blockchain in the article "Bitcoin: A Peer-to-Peer Electronic Cash System" [17, 39]. Since then, experts from all over the world have become interested in it. Blockchain technology is a way to store, verify, send, and receive network data that doesn't need a third party. It does this through its spread nodes. Furthermore, only authorised users of the network can access the data stored on the immutable ledger that Blockchain technology employs. There is complete transparency and this data is shared immediately. Data transferred through Blockchain technology is more likely to remain in circulation and keep up with strong commodity demand information thanks to the introduction of a search encryption method based on Blockchain technology. Figure 5.1 describes the flow of transaction in Blockchain.

Before being included in the Blockchain, a transaction must go through numerous phases, including authorisation and confirmation. Key steps in a Blockchain transaction are listed in the following:

1. New transaction
2. Transaction transmission to a worldwide peer-to-peer network
3. Computer peers verify the transaction.
4. Blocks contain verified transactions.
5. Chaining blocks creates a long transaction history.
6. Transaction completion

5.2.4 Characteristics of Blockchain

Blockchain technology provides various characteristics; Figure 5.2 represents characteristics of Blockchain technology. Here are a few things about the Blockchain that make it such a groundbreaking technology:

- **Consensus**: Consensus means that all nodes in the network must agree that a transaction is valid.
- **Provenance**: Everyone in the network can see how an object that is recorded on the Blockchain got there.

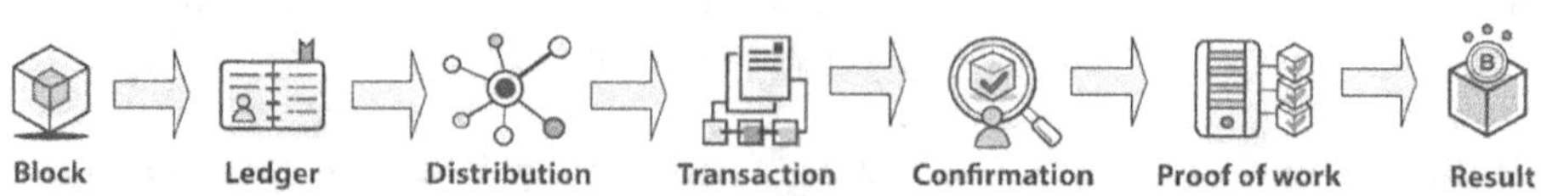

Figure 5.1 Flow of transaction in Blockchain.

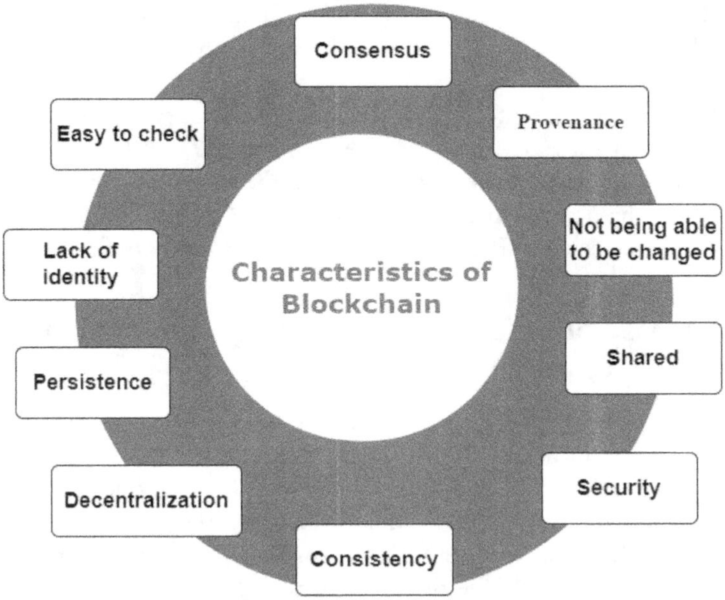

Figure 5.2 Characteristic of Blockchain technology.

- **Not Being Able to Be Changed**: No one can change any activity on the Blockchain. Anytime a transaction goes wrong, a new transaction needs to be made to fix the problems with the old one.
- **Shared**: The Blockchain network is a shared network that works between people. It doesn't fail at a single point. What if some of the nodes stop working? It won't change how the network works. The whole network can't be run by a single group.
- **Security**: Public key cryptography makes sure that the deals are safe. To secure data and create digital signatures, each person in the network has a public key and a private key [7, 40].
- **Consistency**: In the Blockchain, there will always be one value of truth. The distributed log is seen by everyone in the network in the same way.
- **Decentralisation**: In a traditional centralised transaction structure, transactions need to be cleared by a trusted body (like the National Bank), which slows down and costs a lot of money on central servers. Unlike the centralised mode that was launched earlier, the Blockchain does not need outsiders. To keep track of information in Blockchain networks, agreement calculations are used.
- **Persistence**: It's easy to check transfers, and honest miners won't say that they've done anything wrong. Once a transaction is added to the Blockchain, it is very hard to undo or delete. You can quickly find blocks that have transactions that aren't valid.

- **Lack of Identity**: A client may be able to join a Blockchain and use a randomly created address that doesn't show who they are. Blockchain tech is something we should know about [8].
- **Easy to Check**: The Bitcoin Blockchain keeps track of changes made by clients based on the Unused Transaction Performance (UTXO): Every trade affects exchanges that haven't been used before. If the current transaction is added to the Blockchain, the transactions that haven't been spent yet are changed from "unspent" to "spent." There is also the chance of easily confirming deals.

5.2.5 The Use of Blockchain Technology and Managing the Supply Chain

Supply chain management is much more efficient now that Blockchain technology is being used. All information about a product's lifetime in the supply chain can be recorded using Blockchain technology. The data will be accessible to all participants in the supply chain in a very short amount of time. The "bullwhip effect" in the supply chain is eliminated as a result of this continuous interchange of data, which also ensures that buyers provide manufacturers with correct demand data. Using Blockchain technology, it is feasible to trace problematic commodities back to their origin in the supply chain. The issue of data manipulation in the supply chain is also resolved by this technology [9, 41].

When a customer gets a bad product, the company in the supply chain that caused the problem needs to be held responsible. Data about the supply line that can be faked doesn't have enough information to hold people accountable. Distributed Ledger Technology (Blockchain) can monitor and record specific information about items as they move through the supply chain. In the chain, it functions as a public ledger that makes it easy to monitor defective items and hold those responsible accountable for their actions. Sharing information along the supply chain makes shopping better for customers, and being able to track products lets customers buy safer and healthier goods. Blockchain technology makes supply chains more competitive, which opens up a lot of possibilities for how it can be used in supply chain management [10, 42].

5.3 Related Works

To ensure that data sources, Internet of Things devices, sensors, locators, and QR codes are genuine, the authors of the paper [11] proposed a supply chain for pharmaceuticals that is based on Blockchain technology and the Internet of Things.

To make this possible, a distributed ledger was set up to store and share data. This kept the data consistent and made the goods safer. In paper [12], authors suggested using Gcoin Blockchain as the foundation for the flow of drug data. It's a mix of an open government and a decentralised autonomous organisation regulation plan that makes sure drug transactions are clear. Another thing that makes it different from the Ethereum and Hyperledger Blockchain is that it can handle millions of transactions every day. In article [13], the authors suggested a Blockchain-based approach that would use the features of smart contracts in the Ethereum Blockchain. It handles the business between the writer and the receiver. IoT devices are used to keep an eye on and record shipping conditions like temperature, humidity, pressure, location, broken seals, light exposure, and more.

In article [4], the authors talked about how important it is for any supply chain management system to be open and easy to track. They also talked about how Blockchain can be used to make the supply lines for food, drugs, electronics, and cars more traceable. The Proof of Concept was achieved by exploiting the capabilities of the Microsoft Azure Blockchain Workbench to implement solidity smart contracts. The modum.io system, which utilises the Internet of Things (IoT) and Blockchain Technology to provide quality control while medications are being sent, was developed by IoT sensors. These sensors are used to assess the temperature and humidity of pharmaceutical containers while they are being shipped. This information is kept on a public Blockchain architecture that Ethereum provides for its users. Specifically, the HyperLedger Blockchain Framework and the Ethereum Public Blockchain were discussed in article [6], which discussed two different ways that Blockchain frameworks can be utilised in the pharmaceutical company chain. Following their investigation, they realised that the HyperLedger Blockchain Framework possessed superior transparency, scalability, and an identity management system.

A public Blockchain built on Ethereum was suggested in [17] for the organic food supply chain. When a product is deployed, it sends back an address that can be used to make a Quick Response code that can be used to find the real product. To show how well known a farmer was with their products, a token method was used. To make sure the goods were good, a solidity-based smart transaction model was made. IoT devices were used to keep track of where products were. In paper [18], the authors suggested using a permissioned Blockchain based on Ethereum to stop people in the pharmaceutical business from making fake drugs. People think of drugs as digital assets, and each bit has its key. A key in the form of a QR code will be put on the item so that it can be tracked. The hash digest of the drug is made and linked on the chain, but any extra information about it is kept off the chain. It is recorded how the drug works, which the doctor will then use to figure out what amount to give a patient without invading their privacy. In their paper [19], the authors suggested using IoT edge devices and Blockchain to make the medicine supply chain more traceable. Because of the need for such a system, the ecosystem of the pharmaceutical business is broken down. Edge devices bring together data from different sources, which helps automate the process of gathering, processing, and checking data. The data that is saved on edge devices is also sent to the cloud for storage. Doctors and other recipients are also asked for their opinions on how to improve things even more.

A comprehensive and well-planned mapping of all the criteria that are significant in the design of the supply chain system based on Blockchain was carried out in the study [10]. In a manner that is consistent with logic, the purpose of a bubble plot is to arrange the subjects into different study categories. We mapped subjects such as tracking, safety, management, performance evaluation, and quality management to categories such as validation, evaluation, solution, and other categories. A significant number of the components were derived from other solutions, such as Ethereum and the Blockchain ledger. A suggestion was made in the study [21] that the supply chain could be made more secure by the implementation of Blockchain technology. Around 53 different Blockchain applications were investigated for use in the field of supply chain management. Most of the time, Blockchain applications are used to track where resources come from and automate jobs in the supply chain. However, some parts of the supply chain account are only handled occasionally. Applications of Blockchain are limited to taking advantage of the benefits of using a new, widely useful technology. These problems are linked to the way information is managed and the fact that information quality is usually bad in supply chain settings. The main topics of this study were problems with putting things together and working together in SCM.

5.3.1 Consensus Methods for Use in the Supply Chain

The Consensus Algorithm (CA) is an important part of Blockchain technology that can't be left out. A large number of academics, researchers, and businesspeople have worked on making Blockchain possible, as shown by the large number of consensus methods open source. There are pros and cons to each, and none of them work well in all cases or applications on their own. The next few lines give an overview of the most well-known chartered accountants [12, 32, 43, 44].

Proof of Work (PoW) does a lot of work, but it's done, and there's no need to do any more work to check the proof. The heavy and honest chain is now the only one left in the competition. PoW limits how often new blocks can be added, and it costs a lot to add a bad block. The GHOST consensus method is a type of PoW. The greedy heaviest-observed sub-tree approach is what it's based on. This method doesn't use the longest chain agreement rule. Instead, it follows the path of the subtree with the hardest proof of work altogether. Proof of Stake fixes PoW by not requiring as much computing power or energy because the amount of stake used to create a block is linked to that amount. As per BFT, the new block is not accepted until all the nodes have voted on who should be the trusted validators. So, entities that can be trusted work together to add records [13, 33, 45, 46].

Based on both BFT and Proof of Work, the Stellar Consensus Protocol (SCP) combines the two. Both are necessary for the agreement process, but the first one deals with identities. The Pi Consensus approach complements SCP and is tailor-made for devices with little computational capability, such as mobile phones and home PCs. While it may not be as fast as SCP, it certainly outpaces PoW. Additionally,

SCP aids in eliminating the hefty expenses associated with communication and other instruments. Two BFTs that improve SCP are CheapBF (trusted hardware) and Cross Fault Tolerance (XFT) [15, 34]. A wide variety of BFTs, each with its own set of advantages and disadvantages, are detailed in the literature: There are a plethora of additional protocols that are compatible with the public chain. Some examples include Linear Byzantine Fault Tolerance (LinBFT), which is a linear communication protocol for the public chain [17]; Democratic BFT, which solves the consensus deterministically with multiple proposers [18, 47, 48]; Aleph, which views the BFT protocol as a composition of abstraction instances [19, 49]; BFTRaft, which combines the original Raft algorithm and the Practical Byzantine Fault Tolerance (PBFT) algorithm [10, 50]; and countless others. To increase throughput and decrease latency, the BitCoin-NG consensus algorithm [14, 35, 51] employs a leader voting technique to incorporate micro-blocks.

The authors of [22] built their distributed program using smart contracts and Swarm, a distributed file system. Since PBFT's Delegated PoS method is more scalable and would function well in the pharmaceutical supply chain, they intended to switch it out for Ethereum's Proof-of-Work consensus process. They planned to put their Blockchain's consensus algorithm through its paces using a set of "simulation nodes" that included the FDA, manufacturer, wholesaler, store, and customer portal.

In paper [23], the authors came up with a new way to trade food using Blockchain technology called Food Trading System with COnsortium blockchaiN (FTSCON). Getting rid of the lack of information in the food trade is meant to create a stable and trustworthy trading atmosphere. Practical Byzantine Fault Tolerance was used to create the new consensus algorithm so that it works better. The idea behind it is to use the system's automatic transaction tool to check the transaction information. Drugledger is the name of a scenario-based Blockchain system that suggested for tracking drugs and regulating them [24]. In their redesigned service architecture, they separated the service provider into three distinct parts to safeguard the confidentiality and veracity of traceability data. The communication function sets up a P2P network utilising gossip. For the consensus module to function, the coin Algorand is utilised. The number of successful transactions a user has completed in the past is the basis for their rating in Drugledger. Members' status in Algorand is determined by the amount of money they own [16, 52, 53].

5.4 The Importance of Blockchain Technology for Healthcare Supply Chains

Blockchain technology looks like it could be a good way to solve all the problems that the current healthcare supply chain is having. Blockchain in healthcare can change the way we manage supply chains by solving important problems and making different parts of the system better. Please read on to learn more about the part Blockchain plays in the medical supply chain:

To get things started, Blockchain technology provides a cutting-edge method that makes it simpler to trace the origin of healthcare supplies and to record their history. The implementation of Blockchain technology in the healthcare supply chain enables the recording and monitoring of every transaction and movement of healthcare products, beginning with the makers and ending with the end users. Blockchain is a decentralised and open ledger [17, 54, 55]. This process creates a trustworthy record that proves the product's identity, quality, and reliability. As a result, using Blockchain in the healthcare supply chain is an important way to deal with problems like fake or low-quality medical goods, all to keep patients safe.

Second, because Blockchain technology is spread and can't be changed, it can improve the integrity of the supply chain. Because Blockchain is decentralised, data can't be changed or messed with without the right permissions from the right users. By using Blockchain's immutable ledger to record transactions, healthcare organisations can set up a strong system for keeping track of and managing goods, which lowers the risks of fraud or data manipulation [18, 56, 57].

In addition, using Blockchain technology in the healthcare supply chain helps the business be more efficient and cut costs. Using Blockchain for the healthcare supply chain automates and streamlines important tasks like transportation, inventory management, and purchasing, getting rid of the need for time-consuming paperwork and lowering the costs of running the business. Blockchain improves operational performance by making the best use of resources, which saves a lot of money in the long run [19, 58].

These cost cuts and increased efficiency lead to better care for patients because healthcare organisations can better use their resources and put the money they save on patient-centred programs and services.

5.5 Blockchain-Based Software Features for the Medical Supply Chain

Blockchain-based medical supply chain management software has several features that can make the healthcare industry safer and more efficient as a whole. Figure 5.3 describes features of Blockchain technology in medical supply chain. Among these traits are the following:

- **Immutability**: It is very important that the Blockchain-based medical supply chain management system can't be changed. Once data is saved on the Blockchain, it can't be changed. This feature makes sure that the data is safe, correct, and reliable, which lowers the chance of data breaches or manipulation [18, 59, 60].
- **History of Transactions**: In a Blockchain-based medical supply chain, everyone can see every exchange that has ever happened with any drug or medical device. This makes things more open. Because everything is clear, there is no

Figure 5.3 Features of Blockchain technology in medical supply chain.

fraud, waste, or corruption in the supply line. It also makes everyone in the supply chain more responsible and lets patients check that the goods they receive are real [61–63].

- **Smart Contracts**: Smart contracts are contracts that run themselves. They are built on the Blockchain. They are also based on predetermined criteria and can automatically carry out certain jobs, like sending payments or packages. In the medical supply chain, smart contracts can be used to automate several tasks, such as making sure that things are real and that legal requirements are met [19, 64, 65].
- **Tracking**: One of the best things about using Blockchain in medical supply chain tools is that it makes following things very simple. As the product moves through the supply chain, the Blockchain keeps track of where it is and what its state is. This tracking makes sure that everyone is honest and responsible, so everyone can see the full history of all the transactions for any drug or medical gadget [2, 66].
- **Compliance with Regulations**: The Blockchain-based medical supply chain follows the rules, such as the FDA's track-and-trace guidelines, so it is safe for everyone. These regulations, such as the Health Insurance Portability and Accountability Act (HIPAA) and the General Data Protection Regulation (GDPR), assist the healthcare industry in adhering to the law and safeguarding individuals from receiving pharmaceuticals and medical supplies that are counterfeit or of poor quality [21, 67].
- **Verification of the Patient**: When used in the medical supply chain, Blockchain can also be used to find patient information. Once the item is delivered, they will be able to see all of its transaction history on the Blockchain.

This openness makes patients safer and boosts trust in the healthcare system by letting patients check that the product is real and follows all the rules [68].

- **Making Records**: The process starts with the company that makes the medicine or medical equipment entering information about the product on the Blockchain, such as what it is made of when it expires, and what batch number it has. Then, the other sites on the network check this record and save it. This makes sure that the data is safe and correct [22, 69, 70].

5.6 A Software Development Life Cycle for Medical Supply Chains Using Blockchain Technology

It is important to hire a well-known Blockchain and healthcare software development company with years of experience in the field, like Appinventiv, to make sure that the Blockchain-based healthcare supply chain management software fits the needs of the healthcare industry, follows the rules, and works well with other systems. Here's a quick look at the normal steps we take for development:

- **Getting Requirements**: The first step is to get detailed requirements from all parties, such as healthcare providers, manufacturers, distributors, and regulatory authorities. We will have a better idea of the project's scope and features once we know more about their specific needs and challenges [23, 71].
- **Planning and Building**: The needs are used to make the design and architecture of the software. It's important to pick the right Blockchain platform (like Ethereum, Hyperledger, or Polygon), decide on the consensus method, make the data model, and organise the smart contracts and user interfaces [72].
- **Smart Contracts Are Being Made**: Smart contracts are the most important parts of Blockchain software. They spell out the rules, logic, and automation that guide transactions in the supply chain. In the process of making Blockchain-based software for the medical supply chain, experienced Blockchain engineers build and use smart contracts to manage tasks like checking products, keeping track of inventory, and settling payments [73].
- **Use of APIs and Integration**: Software built on Blockchain needs to be able to talk to other systems, like inventory management software, ERP systems, and EHR systems. Developers create Application Programming Interfaces (APIs) so that the Blockchain software and many other systems can easily share data and work together [24].
- **Assurance of Quality and Testing**: To make sure the software works is safe and can be relied on, it goes through strict testing and quality assurance. This includes testing the whole supply chain process from start to finish, testing smart contracts on a unit level, and testing how different parts of the system work together. To find and fix possible risks, security audits and vulnerability tests are done [74].

- **Setting Up the Network and Deploying the Program**: The program is put on the chosen Blockchain platform, and the network infrastructure is set up. This includes setting up nodes, configuring network settings, and making sure that only authorised participants can join and use the Blockchain network [25].
- **Ongoing Maintenance and Upgrades**: After the software has been released, it needs to be properly maintained and updated. This is the last step in the process of making medical supply chain management software. Regular upkeep and updates are needed to keep the software safe, up-to-date, and in line with changing government rules. Comments from users and changing industry standards are used to lead ongoing improvements and monitoring [75].

5.7 Healthcare Companies Using Blockchain for Supply Chain Management

Companies that are early adopters of Blockchain technology are showing how useful it can be. By using the right Blockchain in medical supply chain solutions, these companies have made themselves more accountable and open, and they have set up a supply chain that works very well and accurately across many industries.

The following are the few companies that have used Blockchain in their medical supply chain solutions:

1. **DHL**: The well-known shipping company DHL has released a new prototype that uses Blockchain technology to make supply chains for pharmaceuticals better. This software helps them keep track of and verify their drug goods, which lowers the chance that fake drugs will get into the supply chain [1].
2. **Blockmeds**: A French company called Blockpharma is using Blockchain in its medical supply chain to fight fake drugs. Their creative answer makes it easy for people to scan unique QR codes on drug packages. This makes sure that the products are real and haven't been tampered with.
3. **Walmart**: Walmart is running a pilot project using Blockchain technology to keep an eye on and track food items as they move through its supply chain. There may be effects on medical supplies as well from this effort. By using the power of Blockchain, the project can make the supply chain more open, accountable, and efficient as a whole. Making the distributed ledger work means that food safety steps will be stronger and quality control systems will work better [2, 26].
4. **Mediloque**: The Mediledger Project is a group effort between well-known drug companies like AmerisourceBergen, Pfizer, and Genentech. Blockchain technology is being used by the project to make the drug supply chain more efficient and safe. It makes it possible to track medicines in real time and works to make fake goods less likely.

5.8 Advantages, Problems, and Obstacles of Blockchain Technology in the Medical Supply Chain

5.8.1 Advantages

Blockchain can change the way healthcare is delivered, making it safer for patients and more efficient. It can do this by making things more open and easier to track. Let's take a closer look at a few of the ways that Blockchain can help the medical supply chain:

- **Loss of Control**: One of the best things about Blockchain-based medical supply chain management is that it is not centralised. Instead of having one central authority handle the supply chain, the Blockchain spreads it out over a network of nodes. This decentralised way makes things safer, makes it less likely that someone will cheat or lie, and makes sure that the supply chain keeps going even if one or more nodes stop working [3].
- **Even More Safety**: One of the best things about Blockchain in the medical supply chain is that it makes things safer. This is one reason why Blockchain-based software is becoming more popular. Using Blockchain technology, the medical supply chain's record can't be changed and is safe. This lowers the risk of fraud, forgery, and other criminal activity. Medical product makers, distributors, and patients can have more faith in the dependability and quality of medical things if they use Blockchain-based supply chain management [4].
- **Better Efficiency**: Using Blockchain in the healthcare supply chain management system can automate several tasks, such as keeping track of deals, keeping an eye on the movement of products, and making sure that regulations are being followed. This technology can make the supply chain work better and save time and money at the same time [5, 25].
- **Better Transparency**: In the Blockchain-based medical supply chain, everyone can see the full history of all transactions for any drug or medical gadget. This makes things more open and honest. This openness makes everyone more responsible and lessens the chance of fraud, which also keeps the supply chain running smoothly.
- **Better Patient Safety**: Blockchain-based medical supply chain management can improve patient safety by making sure that medical items are real, correct, and safe. Patients can make sure that the things they buy are real and legal, which lowers the risk of side effects or other harm. Because the Blockchain is decentralised, private data is not kept in one place. This means that there is less chance of data breaches or cyberattacks. Using encryption and other security measures also keeps patient data safe from people who shouldn't have access to it [6].
- **Better Trust**: All the people involved in the medical supply chain can trust each other now that Blockchain is used. By providing a safe, open, and effective system, Blockchain-based medical supply chain management can help build trust among manufacturers, wholesalers, regulators, and patients.

5.8.2 Problems and Obstacles on the Way to Adoption of Blockchain in Pharma

Blockchain was used in supply lines, which are very complicated areas. This caused a lot of problems and created new areas to study [7].

- **Technical Difficulty**: Adding Blockchain to current systems needs technical know-how and the allocation of resources. To get past this obstacle, tech experts and pharmaceutical workers will need to work together.
- **Regulatory Landscape**: Rules and laws are still changing to accommodate Blockchain technology [31]. To make sure Blockchain solutions follow the law, it's important to find a mix between new ideas and following the rules.
- **Data Privacy**: Blockchain makes things more clear, but privacy worries still exist. Finding the best mix between sharing data openly and protecting patient privacy is always hard [8].
- **Resistance to Change**: The pharmaceutical business has been slow to adopt new technologies in the past because they could cause problems. For Blockchain to become widely used, it's important to address worries and show how valuable it is.
- **Interoperability**: Making it possible for different Blockchain networks and old systems to share data without any problems is still a technology problem that needs to be solved. As we move towards a future powered by Blockchain, the pharmaceutical business is about to change [30]. By recognising and tackling these problems, everyone involved in the business can work together to create a future where openness, accountability, and patient-centredness are the norm [9].

5.9 Research Directions

The pharmaceutical industry is set to see Blockchain's role grow as its ability to revolutionise transparency and traceability is more and more apparent. Let us take a trip into the exciting world of future possibilities, where Blockchain will change the way pharmaceutical processes are done. The following is a list of some important problems that Blockchain experts need to research further before they can be widely used for supply chain tracking [10].

- **Analytics are built right into Blockchain**. At the moment, Blockchain data is just a record of events and can't be used with tools for processing large amounts of data at once, such as Dryad Spark, Flink, or MapReduce. The Blockchain data needs to be scanned before statistics can be run on it. Putting the input reader and the processing engine together could help the Blockchain keep track of data automatically. Add-ons for Edge Analytics are also possible.

It's still being looked into how to make this work with modern Blockchain systems so that built-in analytics can be used [12, 13].

- **Combining and analysing on-chain and off-chain data**. To add to the last job, analysis could be done on both on-chain and off-chain data systems. People are looking into new ways to combine and examine data from both on-chain and off-chain sources [29]. One of these is query federation, which is the processing of queries over federated data. It's also important to find and improve the best ways to check the methods that move data from the on-chain database to the off-chain database and use analytics. When you do analytics on both on-chain and off-chain data [14], another problem is making sure that the copied data can't be changed and is safe.
- **Making templates for smart contracts**. Most of the time, the logic that is put into Blockchain smart contracts is written by hand after reading papers on the subject. Aside from taking a long time, this method often gets things wrong. To make the whole process run by itself, a common semantic system needs to be set up for smart contracts. Another research challenge in this area is to make standard templates of smart contacts for different legal problems and tasks. So that this automated template development can work, legal papers need to have natural language processing algorithms that are developed enough to pull out relevant data and operational parameters and put them into smart contract templates [15].
- **Making tools for checking how safe smart contracts are**. If someone breaks into a smart contract, they can see both the programmed reasoning and the Blockchain data. There is a chance that this will go badly, and data could be taken out of the Blockchain through secret attacks. To do this, smart contract security research tools that are very good need to be made. You also need to think of ways to make sure that smart contracts between people are semantically reliable. We also need to learn more about how to find bugs in smart contracts, fix smart contracts that don't work right, and add the right code to them without stopping the network that's already up and running. All the security studies that have been done on smart contracts must be included to follow the rules set by groups and laws like HIPAA and GDPR [16, 17]. There must also be different levels of privacy, security, and confidentiality promises.
- **Making the government more uniform and automated**. Blockchain smart contracts could change how the government works and what it does. In turn, this could make the government and its services more open. This would make the government smarter and more trustworthy, as well as flatten its organisational processes and make the government's data safer [27]. Blockchain technology could help in these ways, but it also makes it hard for the government to make the right rules, laws, and ways to run things. The main idea behind Blockchain technology goes against how states usually work, which is a big plus. Blockchain is a decentralised system that doesn't need help from anyone else. Governments, on the other hand, count on a central authority. This has nothing to do with technology [18, 19].

- **Query execution system for encrypted data in Blockchain.** Most of the best data access technologies and methods from earlier tech trends don't work well with Blockchain because it is so complicated. We need a plan for how to access Web 3.0 info for Web 3.0. This issue is mainly brought on by decentralisation, lack of openness, and keeping data in a certain order. People want a way to do searches on Blockchain data that is encrypted [20].
- **Trusted electronic data management systems.** Electronic data management systems that can be trusted, with tools to make sure the data being entered is right. The fact that Blockchain can't be changed makes things harder and better at the same time. The problem is that mistakes can't be changed once the data is in the system. It has to be perfectly correct the first time it is put in. A lot of work is going into making sure that the information added to the Blockchain transaction repository is right [28]. Electronic data management tools that can be trusted are a big part of this study. Also, making sure that technologies like IoT, RFID, and gadgets that gather data are safe is a problem. Because a lot of research has already been done, the answers need to be looked at again using these technologies along with Blockchain.
- **Compatibility standards.** Businesses that want to move their current systems to Blockchain with trust need to set compatibility standards [11, 21].
- **Making it easier to increase throughput, storage, and network communication.** As Blockchain is added to more systems, issues like the amount of data, how to process and change that data, and how important it is to complete transactions on time are growing. What needs to be done and what can be done to make Blockchain more scalable are still very far apart [22].
- **Adding the "right-to-forget" choice to Blockchain.** People who ask must have their personal information wiped from all copies that have been shared in the past. This goes against the main idea behind Blockchain, which is that it can't be changed. The General Data Protection Regulation (GDPR) says that everyone has the "right to be forgotten." Blockchain has to be able to change or remove data when asked to, which makes following the rule hard, if not impossible. Some work has been done to meet these regulatory goals while keeping Blockchain safe, but there is still a long way to go and this is still a question for further study [23, 24].

5.10 Conclusion

According to the literature analysis and classification, SCM is a very popular area of study. Most studies and articles published in the SCM field focus on supply chain management strategies, frameworks, trends, and challenges; alliances and relationships; the World Wide Web and electronic commerce; and WWW and related topics. The purpose of this paper is to survey the research on supply chain management. A survey of the relevant literature shows that studies on SCM have recently seen a significant uptick. Supply Chain Management and Distribution Management are integrated and shared knowledge is shared. The idea of extended enterprise has emerged as a consequence of this integration, and the supply chain has taken on a new form as a collaborative supply chain that transcends borders and companies to optimise value across the board.

We are hopeful that this study can shed light on where SCM research is headed. Researchers have primarily relied on exploratory reviews, normative studies, methodological reviews, and literature reviews when it comes to their approaches. Moving forward, our research will focus on developing a simulation model that takes this scenario into account. This broadens the scope of the study to include dynamic design in addition to steady-state design. To keep inventory under control, the model will employ a periodic order-up-to strategy, which allows for some wiggle room by distinguishing between goods' "can" and "must" order levels (for details on this method, see the article "On a Basic Class of Multi-Item Inventory Problems," [78]). Delivery must revolve around many drops; therefore, transportation factors must also be considered while deciding what to replenish. A difficulty with inventory routing exists here. Improving customer service while minimising total distribution costs is the goal of the model. It will also be useful for estimating how much of a boost Vendor Managed Inventory (VMI) could be.

Chapter 6

A Comprehensive Review of the Advantages of Internet of Things-Integrated Blockchain-Based Supply Chain Management across Various Industries

6.1 Introduction

As supply lines become more fluid, they need to involve a lot of different people and depend on a lot of different outside partners. Blockchain has become a serious contender to untangle all the data, documents, and communication exchanges that happen in the supply chain network. A huge amount of data and information is always being sent back and forth between the different parts of a supply chain [1]. IoT and Blockchain can be used in the supply chain to handle huge amounts of data and keep it safe. This will help make the supply line safer, more productive, more efficient, and more profitable. The Internet of Things is a network of interconnected gadgets that work together to collect data and make smart decisions. However, IoT is open to security and privacy risks because it doesn't have built-in protections.

DOI: 10.1201/9781003520702-6

With its Safety by Design feature, Blockchain can help make IoT safer in important ways. Some of the problems with IoT's architecture can be fixed with Blockchain features like immutability, openness, traceability, data encryption, and organisational freedom. With IoT, it would be possible to keep an eye on both the health and safety of the workers and the technical state of the equipment. It can also give everyone in the supply chain more communication directions and make things easier to see while they're in transit [2].

1. IoT and Blockchain solutions are both very useful on their own, but when they work together, in what is called the Blockchain of Things (BIoT), they can be used in a cool way by businesses.
2. The report briefly discusses supply chain security issues due to data volume and complexity.

Information is often kept separate, hard to get to, organised in a way that doesn't make sense, or hard to analyse. It might be too much to think about how to drive creativity in any field. The good news is that even the simplest uses of Blockchain technology could make things much more productive, efficient, and profitable. The report shows how Blockchain technology and IoT can be added to the normal supply chain network and how different security problems can be fixed [3].

6.2 Literature Review

In publication [1], writers say that Blockchain technology is currently being used to work on shipping data. The writers suggest a way to connect things using a fresh way of dealing with digital identities. Their study finds important problems in maritime transportation that might cause wrong information. A digital identity framework and complete architecture for Blockchain-based maritime supply chain management systems are suggested to simplify things. Additionally, it suggests a plan that helps connect the real and virtual worlds, stops cargo from going missing and makes examining cargo easier.

The writers of paper [2] describe a significant method for automating and spreading out the management of the supply chain. With the proposed method, the whole supply chain tree would be a system, and everything in it would work together. The suggested system is a good and efficient replacement for the current supply chain. It cut down on mistakes at different points in the chain and made customer service better for everyone. It would make it possible to fully retrace and travel through the supply chain tree, which would help find problems at different levels of the tree. The current supply chain management systems will be a good and affordable alternative thanks to this system.

Authors of paper [10] state that it looks at how Blockchain can be used to solve some problems in the supply chain, like double marginalisation and information asymmetry. This study talks about how important it is to have a good supply line.

The study says that suppliers in the supply lines need to know a lot about it to grow it. The study advises focusing on the "strategic transaction" that will revolutionise the supply chain because so much data must be created and delivered to make goods. The writer talked about issues with incentives that come up when there are big differences in risk, like the risk of capacity. It is because of the imbalance that capacity risk has a bigger effect on the decentralised supply chain than on the vertically linked supply chain. Some people have suggested using Blockchain to solve this problem and stop people from being left out twice.

Authors of paper [15] state that it uses Blockchain technology to study and do research on how to handle the logistics supply chain for cross-border e-commerce. This paper starts by explaining what "decentralisation" means and then suggests three new ways that it could be used in logistics, cash flow, and information flow. It is shown in the paper that e-commerce has grown very quickly in China. It concludes that when Blockchain technology is used in China's cross-border transport supply chain, it will enter a new phase of growth.

Authors of paper [19] state that it discusses Blockchain IOT. Data added to the Blockchain can be stolen. This is "proof of work." Another approach to leak info is address search. To safeguard this, the study used knowledge zero proof. The use of smart contracts and zero-knowledge proof to secure data is the topic of this article. Information technology data held on a Blockchain can be accessed or altered by an unauthorised entity. Smart meters track how much power devices use and output. Smart meters have security flaws that compromise privacy. This study uses smart contracts and zero knowledge to argue data can be protected and transactions can happen.

Authors of paper [21] state that it talks about how SCM can be improved by using Blockchain technology. Blockchain is a public, digital, decentralised ledger of all cryptocurrency activities. To fight fake goods and protect companies, this can be used. The food, warehousing, and e-commerce businesses all need a more open and efficient supply chain. This technology improves transparency, risk minimisation, freedom, and speed. The customer requests and receives the product. The article talks about how early adopters of block technology used IoT, focusing on how widely Blockchain technology was used in different fields for verification, accountability, and tracking. After reviewing the literature for this research, we can conclude that the existing centralised supply chain management approach will delay e-cross-border commerce. Coordination, collaboration, and flow control are most difficult due to the sites' distance. Thus, Blockchain technology can help fix the problem. It records transactions between the parties in a permanent, verifiable fashion. Safely sending data, files, and money is a good defence. Blockchain is typically utilised to store transportation data. Blockchain, a network of methods, can work with the Internet of Things (IoT). The plan ensures that current supply chain management approaches operate properly and can compete.

This research will examine how the Internet of Things and Blockchain technologies might improve the security of the conventional supply chain. The conventional supply chain's security issues can be alleviated with this.

6.3 Blockchain Technology

6.3.1 A Quick Look

Satoshi Nakamoto came up with the idea of Blockchain in 2008 so that it could be used as a public record of Bitcoin activities [3, 4, 32, 33]. Blockchain is a decentralised, distributed ledger that timestamps peer-to-peer network events, so that none of the records involved can be changed after the fact. This lets people who use the Blockchain check and monitor transactions clearly and independently. Since "blocks" are records that are linked together using cryptography, the Blockchain can be thought of as a building stack of them. Every block needs to have the hash code of the block before it, the time, and a list of transactions that have been approved [5, 34]. A Blockchain is a made-up way to organise data in a decentralised way. The Blockchain is arranged like a book with infinite pages, and each page (block) has fresh transactions. Blockchain records ran on peer-to-peer networks and public time-stamping servers [6, 35]. The decentralised, open, and safe design of Blockchain makes it possible to track transactions. Double spending has been a problem for a long time [7, 21, 36], but this tool can fix it. Every Blockchain block has a unique hash number that tells other blocks its identity. The chain's first block is a "genesis block." As illustrated in Figure 6.1, it has no parent block. Figure 6.2 shows how each block is put together in a general way.

Every block unit has a title and body. Block headers have six parts:

- The block version number determines the consensus mechanism used by the software.
- The hash code that links all block transactions is validated by Markle Tree Root Hash. The description included a binary tree of hash codes in the shape of a circle.

Figure 6.1 Blockchain in the form of a chain of blocks hashed.

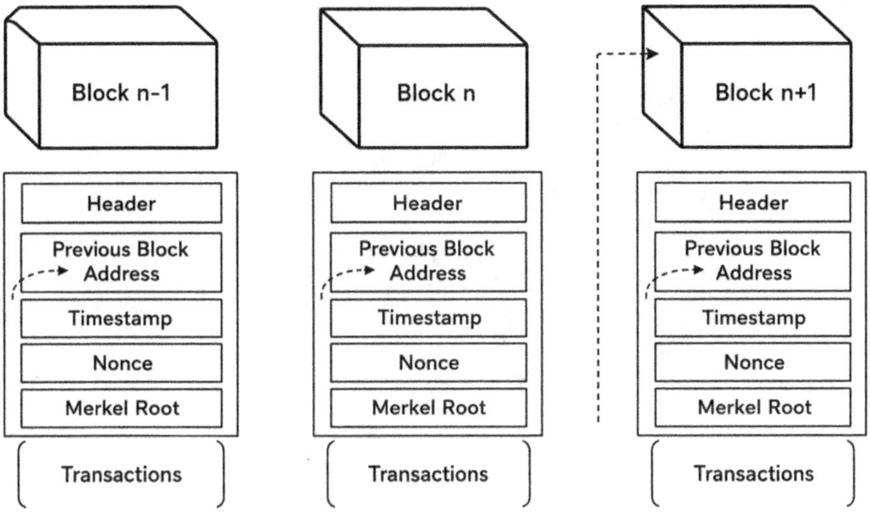

Figure 6.2 A high-level overview of Blockchain block architecture.

- The timestamp is reported in seconds since January 1, 1970. It records block creation and update times for block integrity guarantee.
- The objective hash code threshold is determined by N-Bits, which aids in identifying valid blocks.
- Once-created nonces are used in cryptography messaging. A new set of "0s" is appended to the 4-byte field with each hash calculation.
- A 256-bit code that refers to the block that came before it is called a Parent Block Hash. Connecting and displaying the order of blocks on the Blockchain would be impossible without this component.
- The block body, on the other hand, has all the transactions that have been approved and valid within the block.

Block Transaction Counter (BTC) tracks block activities. At one point, the block state displays who sent Bitcoin to whom. Only a block-level transaction between two nodes is known. The block is then added to the Blockchain after it has been checked for errors. A public record is required for this. Blockchain systems rely heavily on peer-to-peer networks [8, 22, 37]. In a P2P network, each node works together to update and safeguard the Blockchain. Each node stores the latest Blockchain. Using P2P network design in Blockchain offers three key benefits:

1. Users can always utilise a Blockchain browser to view the Blockchain without a third party.
2. To enter blocks, a malicious party must assault hundreds or millions of nodes simultaneously.
3. Blockchain cannot be removed since all P2P nodes must do so.

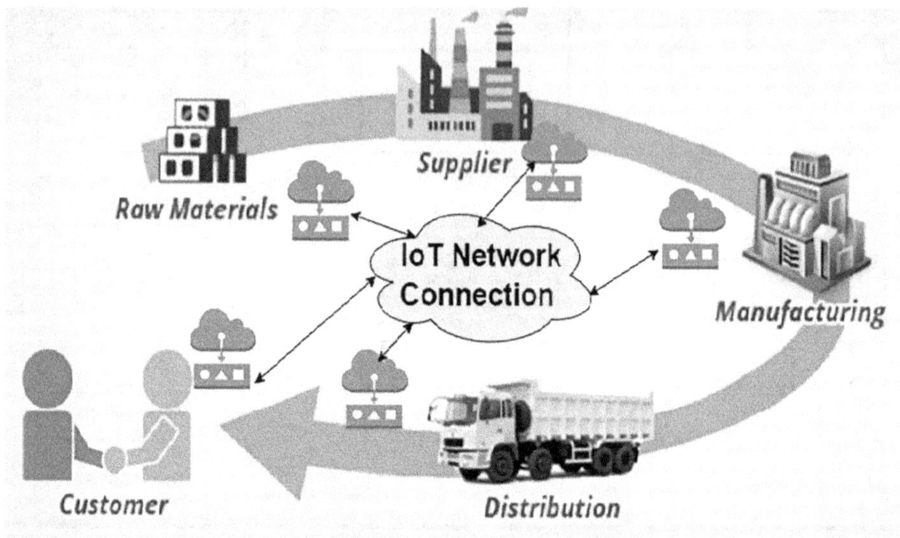

Figure 6.3 Supply chain with IoT.

6.3.2 Blockchain Features

Blockchain surpasses the majority of centralised database systems in four key ways, as illustrated in Figure 6.3.

Decentralisation: This means that the events in the Blockchain are handled and checked by a P2P network-based distributed ledger. For example, unlike the central bank, the Bitcoin Blockchain does not rely on a central authority. All nodes collaborate as peers to contribute and verify block events in the Blockchain.

Persistence: The addition of a transaction to a Blockchain block cannot be removed or altered once it has been persistent. Not to mention that invalid agreements could be located immediately.

Free Expression: Everyone can communicate with the Blockchain while keeping their true identity hidden behind a randomly generated virtual ID. Thus, this feature renders Blockchain transactions less private and secure [9, 23, 38].

Audibility: For a block to be auditable, it must have a secure connection to the block preceding it. With this layout, monitoring and checking progress are a breeze.

6.3.3 Processes in the Supply Chain

According to the usual supply chain process, raw materials are bought and then turned into a physical product that is sent to the customer. There are producers, dealers, distributors, logistics companies, distribution centres, and retailers in the supply chain. There is a network between a company and its producers that makes a product and sells it to a customer. This network is made up of different things, people, groups, knowledge, and resources. The steps that are taken to get the product or service from where it was made to the customer are shown in the supply chain. Getting goods to customers takes several steps. The process begins with sourcing raw ingredients and continues through manufacturing, packaging, shipping, and ultimately selling the final product to consumers. Because it allows processes and managers to make decisions and complete transactions, information is crucial to the supply chain's performance [10]. People at different points in the supply chain need to share what they know. Between the different parts of the production chain, information is the link. It helps them get their work organised, which is one of the best ways to increase the general productivity of the supply chain. Clear information improves supply chain asset use. It also improves supply chain coordination to reduce costs and increase response. Managers need information to know what customers desire and how much inventory they need. Current supply networks have several issues:

- A lack of openness from one end to the other leads to many problems, including theft and violations of rules and regulations.
- Not being able to adapt to sudden changes in demand and controlling running costs: demand is always shifting because of globalisation. Because of this, indirect increases in running costs happen.
- A lot of the tasks in supply chain management have to be done by hand, which takes a lot of time.
- Inefficient supply chain risk management: A system that isn't good at managing risk in the supply chain can't see danger coming and can't act on it.
- Not having enough high-tech stuff. The problem that came up because of globalisation's fast changes can't be solved by new technologies used in modern supply chain management.
- Not watching the system in real time, keeping an eye on how the goods move, where they are in storage, the shipment requests, payment processing, and other things.

6.4 IoT in the Supply Chain

A normal supply chain model is made up of links between all the people, groups, and tasks involved in the business process, from the provider to the final customer. In business areas like retail, manufacturing, logistics, and e-commerce, keeping an eye on supply lines is very important. However managing the supply chain can get harder as customer needs grow, the market changes, and delays happen out of the blue. Also, a lot of the tasks that are part of supply chain management have to be done by hand, which takes time. Business leaders are trying to figure out how much stock they have left and when they should buy, make, or ship more goods. A bad flow of information can make supply chain management more efficient, effective, and combined. Here are a few problems that the company may face because of it. Yet, as we saw earlier, there are several issues with the way the supply chain usually works [11, 24, 39]. As a result, it has to deal with a multitude of difficulties. Some of them are that the system isn't being watched in real time, so there's no way to keep track of the movement of goods, their location in storage, shipping requests, payment processing, and other very complicated things. Putting in place the IoT will fix these issues.

6.4.1 The Implications of the IoT on the Supply Chain

As a network, the physical devices that make up the Internet of Things may transmit and receive data, as well as detect and record occurrences. IoT devices usually link to computers that are part of a network through Wi-Fi or data networks. IoT devices use sensors to find out about their surroundings, like where they are, the temperature, the humidity, the amount of light, their ability to move, their speed, the ability to handle things, and other external factors. Products related to the Internet of Things can take numerous forms, including RFID readers, mobile phones, and portable sensors. Internet of Things systems use GPS and other technologies to monitor and confirm shipments and products in the supply chain. As a tool for supply chain quality management, IoT devices can keep an eye on equipment storage. Connected devices, networks, and applications make up the Internet of Things (IoT). Other examples include advancements in computer science and analytics, as well as in the fields of communication and information technology [12, 25, 40].

When IoT is used in the production chain, it can help in the following ways:

Data Collection: IoT monitors can be put in many things to find out how each person uses them. With this technology, the usage habits of different groups of people can be studied, and the information gathered can be used to create new products [13, 41].

Monitoring the Goods and Equipment: Businesses can agree on the minimum value of goods that need to be kept at certain temperatures and humidity levels, like food. IoT sensors can let the right people in the building know if the limit is pushed too far.

Product Lifecycle Management: Another significant aspect of supply chain management is product or material lifecycle management. Products are handled by a wide variety of parties, including manufacturers, distributors, retailers, suppliers, and business-to-business partners. Internet of Things sensors can track inventory levels and identify problems. Locating geologically suitable commercial sources could potentially be aided by IoT [14, 42].

Stock Management: IoT monitors can give businesses real-time stock information. IoT sensors will help business leaders estimate product demand.

Logistics: Ships, vehicles, and containers transport commodities and packages along the supply chain. Connecting these parts to IoT lets firms track delivery trucks in real time.

Building Maintenance: IoT in supply chain management lets enterprises maintain their tools and delivery trucks. Automotive, tool, item, retail shelf, and workshop floor sensors gather data in real time through the Internet of Things. Problems arise with supply chain IoT. The concerns at hand pertain to matters of privacy and security. Problems with interoperability, a dearth of legislation, legal challenges, rights concerns, the changing economics of the Internet of Things, and expansion are among the other barriers [15, 43].

Security Information: A big concern for any industrial network that is linked to the Internet is the safety of the information or data. It's becoming more normal for people to attack websites, and hackers may be interested in IoT technology as well. Vulnerabilities in data handling and storage can lead to attacks and leaks from outside the company, which can hurt its reputation and make failure more expensive.

Data Pools: The IoT creates enormous data pools for supply chain managers, among other benefits. With that much power comes the responsibility to ensure the server can store and analyse all the data [16, 26, 44].

Secure Internet Connectivity: Getting a safe Internet link is very important for IoT. It's not always safe to connect to the network because truck drivers are moving around. When adding IoT to the supply chain, you should also think about how fast the internet is.

- Also, supply lines go over thousands of kilometres all over the world. It can also be hard to fix problems with how IoT systems work together.
- Team that is knowledgeable: Even without IoT training, it's hard to get a team of people who know enough about the problem to come up with a strategy that works for the company.
- Putting together rules for how to use business networks and drawing up security policies takes a lot of time [17, 27, 45].

6.5 Implementing a Blockchain Supply Chain

The research demonstrated the typical flow of a company's supply chain and how the Internet of Things might improve and accelerate this process. The likelihood of data breaches is directly proportional to the proliferation of Internet of Things devices. However, incorporating Blockchain technology into its framework could mitigate these dangers. The Internet of Things provides precise data regarding materials and items in a supply chain by connecting the physical and digital worlds. The use of Blockchain technology to link Internet of Things devices in the supply chain facilitates the retrieval of data. This makes the flow of both real and digital goods safer, more reliable, clearer, and less expensive [46].

Step 1: Launch a custom Blockchain system. Private Blockchain networks can be enabled by Ethereum. It is a decentralised computing network that is built on open-source Blockchain technology. Each company needs a powerful computer to create an Ethereum Blockchain. This is an "Ethereum node." Use cross-platform programs like GoEthereum or "get" to set up an Ethereum server [47].

Step 2: Develop smart contracts. Smart contracts are Ethereum's sophisticated functionality. The software makes trading products, money, houses, shares, and other valuables easy. Smart contracts are computer programs that act when particular circumstances are satisfied. Which runs smoothly without being interrupted, restricted, hacked, or tampered with. All firm supply chain data is stored in a central repository and database in traditional intranet systems. Smart Contracts have one address that maintains the database for all nodes and serves as the network hub. Both C++ and JavaScript are capable of writing smart contracts. Smart contract compilers are available online for these programming languages. An Ethereum Blockchain can host the contract [48].

Step 3: Create a decentralised app. Smart contract ledgers are dynamic databases that distributed apps can access and update. You can access this Smart Contract ledger from any device, as it is mostly cloud-based. This worldwide Blockchain application may be made easily utilising HTML and CSS and Ethereum's Blockchain interface, Web3Js [49, 50].

Figure 6.4 shows Ethereum's distributed app development stack. The last three layers of the Ethereum stack must remain unchanged. To display a spread application on a web page instead of HTML or CSS, it can be transformed into any Web3J-supported scripting language.

Benefits of Blockchain-enabled Supply Chain IoT: Because our supply chains are intricate and unreliable, people are interested in how Blockchains can make the sector safer. Blockchain could prevent certain production chain issues:

- Inventory theft
- Information theft
- Smuggling and theft
- Third-party vendor data sharing
- Internet of Things sensor data exposure

Address all problems by compromising Blockchain.

Inventory Theft: Employee stock theft still threatens supply chains, especially in distribution facilities. It's hard to keep track of everything because so much flows through these hubs. This is why theft methods are confusing. Drivers and corporate employees work together to remove stolen goods from the distribution hub for resale. Each item in this inventory can be marked

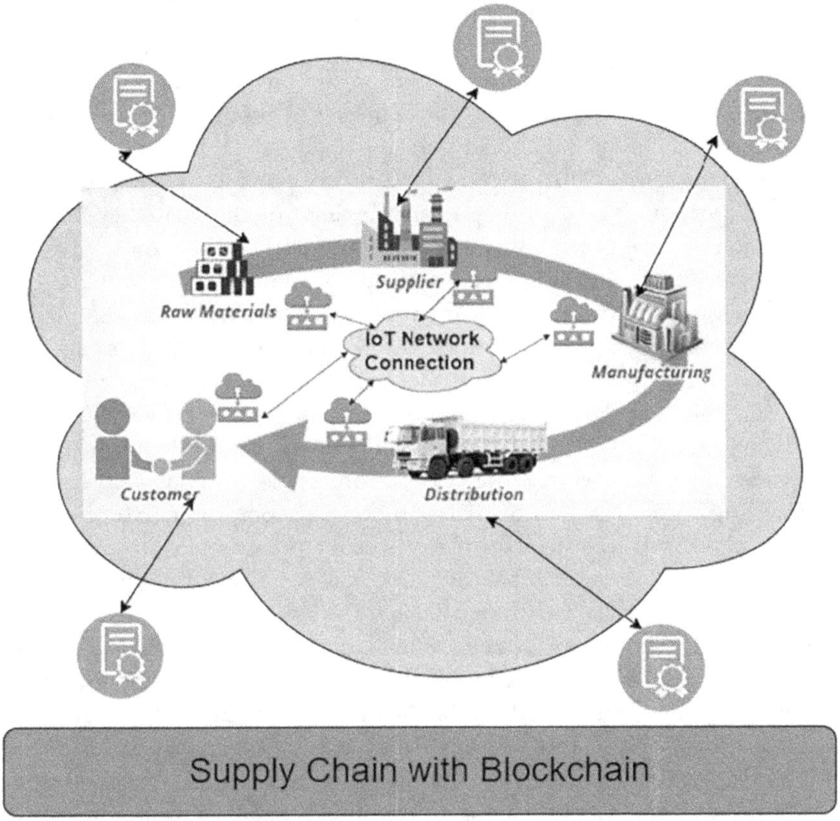

Figure 6.4 Integration of supply chain with Blockchain.

using IoT technology to follow its movement remotely. Inventory tags can be saved in the Blockchain, making inventory data, intended use, destination, and other private data safer.

Theft of Information: Data security in the cloud is becoming more important as more and more supply chain tools and storage systems migrate to the cloud. If you can't manage cloud access properly, you could end up with major IT risks, like giving users too many rights. This means that anyone who wants to can view the cloud data. Blockchain can also be used to deal with this safety issue. It is possible to do so with strong access control and permissions. This will make it safer for people to get to the cloud information. Safeguarding and storing this type of data is possible, as is randomly changing the access keys so that anyone can access them without concern for hackers [51, 52].

Crimes Like Smuggling and Piracy: Smuggling items can put the supply chain at risk. Products from the "grey market" and fake or stolen goods are moved across countries with the help of shipping companies. This affects both the location and the customers, as well as the supply chain because it stops it from moving smoothly. Blockchain makes it easier to keep an eye on and record every step. Things like the whereabouts and timing of shipments are meticulously recorded. No one involved in the transaction can alter, remove, or modify any record without the consent of all others thanks to the Blockchain feature. That puts a stop to the illicit transfer of goods and theft in the goods trade, which is a major concern [53].

Sharing Data with a Third Party: Cloud service providers invest much in website and reputation security. precisely because of this that they depend on their jobs. It makes sense that some businesses still don't want to give private information to third-party vendors. The risk goes up when you use a cloud tool that doesn't prioritise security. It's also important to hire companies that have handled private applications before and can pass strict safety checks. These groups also have to follow a lot more rules and protect their data more thoroughly than the companies whose data they store. It's very risky to give info to a third party. Still, a lot of businesses rely on third-party providers to protect their data because they can't afford to do it themselves. Sending or accessing data from a third-party vendor can compromise security. In this case, Blockchain can help make it easier for information to flow while still providing the best level of security. This makes the data movement happen in chunks. These blocks are what make it very safe because they are secured [54].

IoT Sensor: Compromise-IoT gadgets have internet-connected sensors. They are increasingly utilised to track supply line inventory. They are also used to guess when machines will break down before they happen. But hackers can use all of this sensor data to find out more about the supply chain, such as the number of orders, the ties between key suppliers, and other things. At every point in the IoT world, devices should be checked and tested for security and encryption. This is what Blockchain technology is used for. IoT devices can keep information in encrypted form, which makes it almost impossible for hackers to get or read that information [55, 56].

6.5.1 Supply Chain and Logistics Blockchain and IoT Applications

Here are some ways that Blockchain and IoT can be used in transportation and the supply chain.

Communication over Wireless: Huge steps forward have been made in wireless communication, which receives data from the sensor hub and sends it to the assigned client and base station. This lets devices talk to each other even if they are not physically linked. Wireless communication is helpful for smart tactics with IoT [57].

Inventory Management: IoT gives companies a clear picture of what their coordinate systems are doing, which encourages regular stock connection even more. Radio Frequency Identification (RFID) stickers and sensors also help logistics keep track of their stock and where and how they are right now [58].

Product Source: Blockchain and IoT make it possible for both the company and the customer to keep track of a product's full life cycle in the supply chain. All of the conversations between IoT devices are saved in the Blockchain. It gives businesses quick access to information about the product, such as the date it was made, registered, and sold—a full record [59].

Intelligent Insights: Blockchain and the IoT make it safe for partners and things in the supply chain to share information. Partners can use the most advanced AI techniques to find new pieces of information across their supply lines by putting this data together with data from other sources [60].

Route Management: A lot of people use IoT devices to keep track of their routes and locations. GPS tracking and truck beacons help keep track of where a vehicle is and what path it's taking to make sure deliveries happen on time and keep customers informed of the progress of their orders [61].

Smart Contracts: Blockchain and IoT can work together to make sure that shipped goods are safe, even when they are traded between countries. Smart contracts are like an online deal or arrangement between everyone interested in the trade. The rules of the contract are written in computer codes that make it possible for people who don't know each other to send money to each other without any problems [62].

How to Fix Documentation Issues in Container Shipping: The flow of documents in container shipping uses a lot of time and resources. Because there is a lot of paperwork, there is a chance of loss, fraud, tampering, and other problems with paper goods documents, especially when shipping goods between countries. Blockchain solutions can help connect large networks and set up a link between ports, shipping companies, and customs to make it easier to move documents around and make digitising paper records more efficient [63].

Tracking the Provenance of Goods: Buyers care most about where the goods came from and how original they are. Customers don't want to buy fake things and only want real ones. To get rid of the fear of fakes, Blockchain technology can help keep track of the product's supply line and paperwork.

6.5.2 Blockchain and IoT Benefits for Supply Chain and Logistics

Supply chain and logistics firms, manufacturers, and suppliers can all benefit greatly from the integration of Blockchain technology and the Internet of Things. Some of the most significant benefits of integrating the supply chain with Blockchain and the Internet of Things are as follows:

Insights Based on Data: Blockchain and IoT make it safe for all players in a supply chain ecosystem to share data. The dataset and third-party data sources can be used by stakeholders to learn more about their supply chain through machine learning methods [64].

Maximise Supply Chain Transparency: Digital Bill of Lading and smart contracts made by combining IoT and Blockchain can help you keep track of things and their whereabouts in the delivery process in real time, making sure that your obligations are met [65].

Regulated Reliability of Supply Chain: Goods must be moved within strict temperature limits and time frames in industries with a lot of rules, such as food and medicine. If that isn't done, the high-value package could be held up. With the Internet of Things (IoT), temperature feeds from onboard devices can be sent online to the Blockchain framework, which makes sure that the information sent and received is safe and correct [66].

Real-Time Visibility of the Entire Supply Chain: Because there are so many people involved, it can be hard to see the whole chain from beginning to end. Companies keep track of the problems in the supply chain by collecting data, but they need to check the data from different companies to make sure it is accurate. However, by connecting IoT devices to supply chain tracking systems and then sharing that data via a Blockchain-based system, everyone can access the data in real time [67].

Better Financing for the Global Supply Chain: The global supply chain includes deals that take place in different countries. It takes a lot of red tape and paperwork, which can slow down international payments because of local banking rules and the number of parties involved. Any mistake can cause the payment-clearing process to take longer than planned [68].

6.6 Supply Chain IoT and Blockchain Use Cases

Businesses can improve supply chain tracking and value with Blockchain and IoT. The digital supply network is now able to react autonomously to signals of supply and demand thanks to the Internet of Things and Blockchain technology. There will be less effort and better efficiency in global supply systems. Businesses can now monitor their products' whereabouts in real time thanks to sensors linked to the internet. Distributed Ledger Technology (DLT) enables all participants in a supplier network to have access to immutable product records. IoT and Blockchain can work together to make the whole supply chain more open, accountable, and transparent, with a single source of truth that everyone can use [17]. This can lead to better supply chain management. To get these kinds of results, CIOs and supply chain leaders can look into how these tools can be used in real life. Here are five main ways that IoT and Blockchain are used to help businesses improve their next-generation digital supply networks [69].

Tracking. Even though many businesses have put a lot of money into their supply chains, it's not always easy to track items as they move through global networks. This is a problem because customer safety, company profits, and reputation are all at risk. By using IoT and Blockchain in the following areas, businesses can collect useful data, gain deeper insights, and speed up the detection and resolution of incidents:

Tracking Where a Product Came From. With IoT, businesses can better keep track of where their goods (or parts of them) came from and share this information on the Blockchain. This makes things more open and could improve how people feel about and are loyal to a brand. For instance, food distributors could give grocery shops more information about allergens, ingredients, and other things that might help people feel better about buying [18].

Tracking the Progress of a Product. When things move around the world, they often run into problems with logistics. Delays in shipping, for example, can damage fragile items like medicines, wines, and veggies. Fake goods can get into supply lines without being caught [29, 71]. With IoT and Blockchain, businesses can share and track the exact location of their products much more accurately, even when there are problems or events.

Keeping Track of Changes in Ownership and Care. Many important people in the supply chain are involved in moving items around the world. Many more fall under this category, such as manufacturers, suppliers, banks, insurers, goods forwarders, and third-party logistics firms. IoT sensors keep track of where things are physically located, and smart contracts on the Blockchain can record when ownership and custody change hands [30, 72].

Electronic Paper. Shipping problems caused by paperwork, like fake documents or documents full of mistakes made by hand, can cause delays, losses, and other risks in the supply chain. This is a big problem for supplies of things like meat, medicines, and dairy that need to get there quickly. Uploading shipping data generated by IoT to the Blockchain can automate validation and verification processes and digitise paperwork [19, 73].

6.7 Challenges in Traditional Supply Chain

When using old methods, transportation, and supply chain workers have to deal with problems like these:

Depending on Brokers: The supply chain is complicated, and rules mean that customs brokers are needed to make sure that papers are real, keep delays to a minimum, lower risks, and keep people from getting fined [20]. There are also breaks and extra shipping costs because of this.

Inefficient Inventory Management: Not being able to see where and when packages are can cause problems with routing and inventory management, leading to shortages, higher costs, and unhappy customers because of late deliveries [21, 74].

Late Payment for Damaged Goods: When there are gaps in visibility, it's not only hard to keep track of assets, but it's also hard to find damaged goods, which means that payments are late [30].

Costly Letter-of-Credit Process: In foreign trade, banks use letters of credit as a way to guarantee that a buyer's payment will be received on time and for the right amount. However, they take a long time and cost more money [31, 75].

Poor Routing and Batching of Goods: When companies can't automate the batching of their goods, they often have to pay more for shipping and use their containers less efficiently.

6.8 Conclusion and Future Directions

This study talks about how a Blockchain-based supply chain that includes the Internet of Things is different from a normal one. This study looked at what new chances there might be for supply chain stability and operational efficiency if the Internet of Things and Blockchain came together. Blockchain and the Internet of Things could change the way supply chain management is done, which could completely change the industry. These technologies improve supply chain visibility, efficiency, security, and tracking by fixing some problems that plague traditional supply chain management systems. Blockchain makes it possible for a single, shared record to be created so that only authorised parties can safely record and retrieve connections and information. There is less need for agents, fraud is less likely to happen, and people are more accountable. Smart contracts on the Blockchain could be used to automate and execute agreements between parties. This would make things run more smoothly and save money on administrative costs. The Internet of Things (IoT), on the other hand, lets you connect real-world materials and objects to the internet. This creates new ways to collect data, keep track of it, and handle it. Internet of Things sensors in commodities, containers, and autos can give supply chain management vital information about location, humidity, and quality. Real-time data analysis enables proactive decision-making, predictive maintenance, and supply chain optimisation. These tools function well together and can transform SCM.

With the Internet of Things (IoT), you can see what's going on in the physical parts of the supply chain in real time. Blockchain also makes sure that data is safe and clear throughout the supply chain. This merger makes it possible to track a product from the time it is made to the time it is delivered, making it easier to make sure that it is real, that it meets quality standards, and that it follows all the rules. Adding Blockchain to the Internet of Things can cut down on the time it takes to ship goods across foreign borders and make the process safer, more efficient, and less expensive. All of this is possible because of the spread ledger that can't be changed and stops fraud. Smart contracts can be used to automatically carry out and enforce deals between two or more parties when certain events take place. The issues these industries are having because they still use old-fashioned supply lines have been discussed in this essay, along with how Blockchain- and Internet of Things-based solutions could help them fix these issues.

This paper solely outlines a Blockchain-based traceability plan. Some implementation details remain unexplored. Increasing device-to-network fault tolerance and reducing Blockchain code computational needs for low-configuration IoT edge devices. We will also look at ways to get everyone on the network to agree on something and simple network methods for getting devices to talk to each other and spread information.

Chapter 7

Empowering the Metaverse: Integrating Machine Learning and Blockchain Technologies

7.1 Introduction

The Metaverse is drawing the attention of technology specialists and laypersons globally. Over the next decade, empirical data forecasts substantial expansion in this industry, and various governments have commenced the implementation of Metaverse-based advanced services. To establish Metaverse services, technological, social, and economic obstacles must be surmounted [1, 23, 24]. The Metaverse amalgamates the physical and virtual realms, enabling user avatars to interact socially, participate in diverse events, and execute financial, commercial, and governmental activities. This concept facilitates the establishment of a parallel environment that offers services comparable to and more advanced than those in the actual realm. The Metaverse employs several contemporary technologies to enable users to fully immerse themselves in a three-dimensional environment and interact with both physical and virtual creatures. The Metaverse is not a novel concept. It originates from several decades ago. The social media conglomerate "Meta" declared its transition into virtual and augmented reality, hence popularising this term. Bear in mind that the Metaverse is not a singular domain. It employs Blockchain technology to construct a virtual environment from several digital landscapes [2, 25]. Digital avatars engage with friends and family within the Metaverse, a three-dimensional virtual environment.

 DOI: 10.1201/9781003520702-7

The Metaverse facilitates the acquisition and exchange of digital currency and assets. Virtually traverse several digital locales. Manifestations of the Metaverse encompass NFT galleries, virtual planets, digital thoroughfares, and additional elements. Stakeholders and developers engage in collaboration regarding the Metaverse. Consumers in the Metaverse purchase products and services with digital currency. Exploring the Metaverse transports you to another virtual realm [3, 26]. Technology has facilitated numerous procedures, producing vast quantities of electronic data. The 3D Metaverse will employ virtual reality, Blockchain technology, and artificial intelligence to generate a realistic digital experience for individuals and enterprises.

Blockchain is frequently seen as the foundational architecture of the Metaverse. Blockchain offers clear, accessible, efficient, and reliable regulations for the Metaverse by linking many tiny firms and creating a solid economic structure. Numerous advantages of Blockchain mitigate the aforementioned issues and concerns [4, 27]. The immutability and accounting features of Blockchain technology enhance the transparency of transactions within the Metaverse. Its distributed architecture facilitates low-latency data access from various places and safeguards stored information with sophisticated encryption. Blockchain connects the technologies of the Metaverse ecosystem, merging the physical and digital realms. The dynamic characteristics of the Metaverse may impede Blockchain consensus, block creation, and smart contracts. The rapid increase in simultaneous users can burden Blockchain capabilities, diminishing system performance. Consequently, sophisticated artificial intelligence methodologies ought to employ Blockchain to accommodate system modifications [5, 28–30]. Employing this strategy will enhance Blockchain performance. AI-driven techniques can enhance the scalability and security of Blockchain technology, minimising consensus latency and optimising smart contract performance. This position paper examines the role of AI in the development of intelligent Blockchain systems and its impact on the Metaverse. This work examines the function of Blockchain technology in the Metaverse and its associated issues. It subsequently presents AI-driven Blockchain technology. This article examines the incorporation of AI into Blockchain systems.

7.2 Background Work

The subsequent section succinctly examines Blockchain and artificial intelligence, highlighting how their integration enhances performance.

7.2.1 Blockchain Technology

Bitcoin has augmented the significance of Blockchain technology in academic circles. This milestone initiated a significant technological advancement, expanding Blockchain to encompass many distributed ledger systems. The aforementioned enhancements have facilitated the application of Blockchain technology in banking, healthcare, cybersecurity, and commerce [7, 31, 32]. The Blockchain network comprises about 2.4 million cryptocurrencies at different tiers, with a market capitalisation of US$2.66 trillion [3, 33]. Approximately 90% of organisations in the US, UK, India, and China utilise Blockchain technology to varying degrees within the corporate sector. Global governments are employing Blockchain technology to enhance public services, optimise administrative procedures, and increase public trust [2, 34]. The World Economic Forum indicates that 98% of countries contributing to global GDP are contemplating the use of Central Bank Digital Currencies (CBDCs) [5, 37, 38]. The data indicates a consistent increase in Blockchain adoption, generating global governmental and corporate opportunities. Bitcoin's Proof of Work (PoW) has been supplanted by earlier consensus algorithms such as Practical Byzantine Fault Tolerance (PBFT), leading to the emergence of other consensus frameworks [6, 35]. DLT technologies tackle scalability, energy efficiency, and transaction velocity, demonstrating their versatility [7, 36]. The research on scalability and interoperability emphasises the continuous advancements of Distributed Ledger Technology (DLT) to facilitate seamless integration across many frameworks and sectors [8]. In addition to technical advancements, these technologies influence social structures, governance frameworks, and the trust in digital transactions [9, 39]. The extensive development demonstrates the diverse potential of Blockchain and distributed ledger technologies, signalling a new era of technological progress and societal transformation.

Bitcoin transactions illustrate how Blockchain technology facilitates secure data management and rapid modifications in decentralised networks [10, 40]. Recognise that "secure" in a ledger indicates that the entries are unaltered, although it does not ensure their veracity at the time of recording. Blockchain enables users to connect and communicate updated information across a distributed network, wherein each participant maintains a copy of the ledger. Recognise that "participants" encompasses all entities inside the Bitcoin ecosystem, including the network, protocol, governance, and application layers. These actors require a reliable network of intermediaries, whose dimensions and trust framework are dictated by the consensus mechanism of the Blockchain system. Decentralisation in trust authenticates and documents transactions through a consensus process that requires the involvement of two or more participants. Blockchain technology enhances transaction security and transparency via cryptography, decentralisation, and consensus mechanisms, although it is contingent upon user trust. The Proof of Work (PoW) consensus of Bitcoin presupposes that trusted nodes possess significant computational capacity. This assumption safeguards ledger integrity against 51% attacks. Rather than diminishing trust, Blockchain technology emphasises its establishment, particularly in environments vulnerable to the 51% attack, software vulnerabilities, or collusion [11, 41]. Blockchain technology facilitates secure transactions devoid of intermediaries; nonetheless, the degree of trustlessness is contingent upon the design. Decentralised public Blockchains such as Bitcoin and Ethereum foster trust

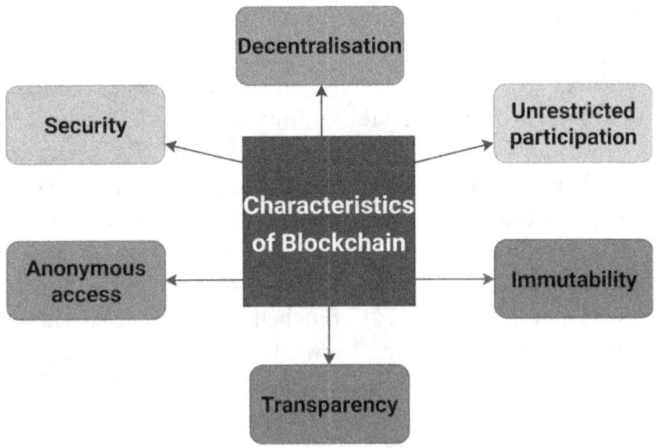

Figure 7.1 Essential characteristics of Blockchain.

when protocol regulations are adhered to and system vulnerabilities are mitigated. Conversely, private Blockchains necessitate trust from a restricted group of participants. Previous network modifications demonstrate that Blockchain operators and majority stakeholders can significantly influence Blockchain operations. The Ethereum DAO fork and Bitcoin's SegWit exemplify the adaptability of Blockchains to security and centralisation, illustrating the fluidity of the technology and the influence of major parties. Figure 7.1 illustrates the fundamental Blockchain components required for the operation of each distributed project.

1. **Decentralisation**: Blockchain is a distributed system engineered for Peer-to-Peer (P2P) communication. Decentralisation mitigates singular points of failure, enhancing system resilience [17]. Decentralised systems lack a central authority, while distributed systems disseminate data and processing among multiple nodes. Decentralisation guarantees that no singular body governs the network, while distribution disperses the ledger among multiple nodes for redundancy and security. Decentralised Blockchains, such as Bitcoin, exhibit greater resistance to censorship and control because to the unrestricted participation of whole nodes. Attack resistance is contingent upon the protocol and network configuration, threat model, and attack surface [42].
2. **Unrestricted participation**: Permissionless Blockchains exhibit resistance to censorship. A consensus mechanism employing a decentralised network of nodes documents transactions on the Blockchain, rendering it challenging for any singular entity to dominate or suppress transactions. Permissioned Blockchains, governed by a membership service that assesses participant eligibility, have reduced censorship resistance. They frequently withstand censorship more effectively than centralised databases. The permissioned character of

the Blockchain and its distributed control among authorised parties engender resistance [43].

3. **Immutability**: The consensus mechanisms and decentralised architecture of Blockchain technology establish immutability. Consensus mechanisms, such as Proof of Work (PoW) and Proof of Stake (PoS), ensure the ledger's security and immutability. The decentralised consensus mechanism renders Blockchain data immutable without network agreement, hence enhancing its resistance to modification and tampering [44].
4. **Transparency**: Blockchain enhances transparency by allowing all nodes to access transaction data [14]. Blockchain technology enables participation from all nodes within the network, in contrast to centralised systems where a singular server governs all data. These nodes have the capability to access and evaluate transaction data. Each node possesses an individual ledger that records all transactions, ensuring synchronisation with the most recent Blockchain updates [45].
5. **Anonymous access**: Blockchain networks enable users to create several access addresses, safeguarding their personal information from dissemination on external platforms. This strategy provides substantial anonymity, however not flawless privacy due to technological constraints [16, 46].
6. **Security**: Blockchain technology provides robust record-keeping and transaction tracking. Merkle trees safeguard data integrity and immutability by effectively and verifiably connecting transaction blocks [17, 47]. These attributes also ensure robust data integrity protection, particularly for medical records [8] and financial transactions [9]. Blockchain technologies can be tailored for specific applications or used with artificial intelligence algorithms for data analysis to enhance security and thwart unauthorised access.

7.2.2 Artificial Intelligence

Artificial intelligence enables machines to reason and resolve issues akin to human capabilities. AI autonomy refers to the capacity of artificial intelligence to function independently of human intervention or supervision. AI can be classified into four categories: human-like cognition, rational cognition, human-like behaviour, and rational behaviour [12, 48]. Artificial intelligence encompasses the examination of algorithms that facilitate perception, cognition, and action, as well as techniques that enable computers to execute jobs often performed by humans. Adaptability and learning differentiate AI methodologies from conventional programs that employ clearly defined algorithms. In contrast to traditional programming techniques, artificial intelligence algorithms can manage intricate and dynamic environments owing to their non-deterministic nature.

Artificial intelligence, particularly Large Language Models (LLMs) such as GPT, Massive Multitask Language Understanding (MMLU) techniques in Gemini, and other AI-powered autonomous agents, possess the capability to analyse and interpret

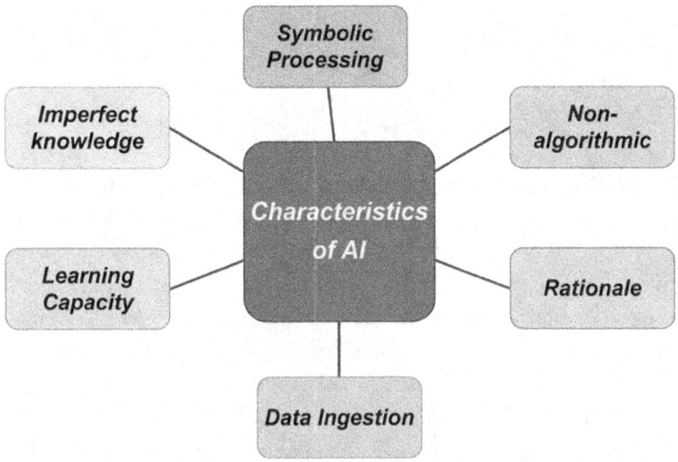

Figure 7.2 Principles of artificial intelligence.

extensive datasets. These sophisticated AI models demonstrate proficiency in natural language comprehension and production following rigorous training on enormous datasets. These models eschew conventional information storage techniques; nonetheless, their intricate topologies facilitate swift retrieval and modification of extensive models. Contemporary techniques such as fine-tuning, temporal engineering, and reinforcement learning do this. These strategies enhance system resilience and effectiveness in fluctuating environments. Artificial Intelligence (AI) synthesises knowledge from various disciplines, including nature, neuroscience, psychology, philosophy, linguistics, electrical engineering, and computer science [13, 49]. Figure 7.2 depicts the fundamental characteristics of AI.

1. **Symbolic Processing**: AI algorithms favour symbols rather than numerical or alphabetical representations. Strings signify modified real-world entities, occurrences, and settings. Subsequently, the strings are converted into symbols and organised into lists or hierarchies [14, 50] to illustrate their connections. Robots can identify tangible objects, occurrences, and environments through artificial intelligence algorithms.
2. **Non-algorithmic**: Conventional computer programs adhere to established algorithms and necessitate human intervention at every stage. Conversely, AI systems autonomously resolve issues. AI's ability to adapt to evolving conditions without human intervention enhances autonomy, hence streamlining solutions and augmenting adaptability [15, 51].
3. **Rationale**: AI is capable of processing knowledge instead of just data, facilitating deductive or inductive reasoning. This is essential for enhancing machine cognition. Consequently, numerous methodologies such as case-based reasoning, case-based judgements, and analogical reasoning [16, 52] have been

suggested to enhance machine cognition. Through these logical methodologies, artificial intelligence systems effectively identify solutions, emulating human cognitive functions.

4. **Data Ingestion**: In data ingestion, Artificial Intelligence (AI) uses statistical techniques and Machine Learning (ML) to manage extensive datasets from several sources. Autonomous data input minimises human errors, accelerates processes, and mitigates data management inaccuracies. The advantages include improved efficiency and precision in data processing [18, 53].
5. **Learning Capacity**: The learning capacity of AI seeks to replicate human cognition by assimilating past experiences, adapting to novel circumstances, and performing tasks that require intelligence. Artificial intelligence is employed in chess, stock market forecasting, and autonomous vehicles. Data integration is essential for AI models to execute specific tasks, enhance their learning capabilities, and replicate human intelligence [19, 54].
6. **Imperfect Knowledge**: Conventional applications necessitate exact information, but AI systems can handle unstructured and ambiguous data. Contemporary techniques such as fuzzy set theory, formal logic, and mathematical morphology assist artificial intelligence in managing faulty data. The adaptability of artificial intelligence renders it beneficial in practical applications where precision may be challenging [20, 55].

7.2.3 A Synopsis of Metaverse Economics

The economy supports the Metaverse. Optimal Metaverse interoperability would enable users to exchange virtual assets like as clothing and automobiles across different platforms. As illustrated in the diagram. We shall initially delineate the economic underpinnings of the Metaverse using prominent games and empirical studies [21, 56]. The economic system of the Metaverse comprises digital innovation, assets, markets, and currency. The traditional economy will transform through the efficient utilisation of these elements. Digital creation is fundamental to the Metaverse. This manufacturing technique is analogous to concrete. Creator engagement propels the expansion of the Metaverse economy. Consequently, digital production necessitates a fundamental authoring tool to enhance and tailor development [6, 7, 57]. The SDK and the Builder are two writing tools for creating interactive applications offered by the gaming platform Decentraland. The Builder employs a drag-and-drop interface for application creation without coding, whereas the SDK provides users with significant flexibility. Article [9] provides a summary of studies in Metaverse computational arts. Immersive and robotic arts are integrated with virtual-physical realms [22, 58]. An undisclosed characteristic of a Digital Asset is necessary for transaction. Players can add "skins" to their weapons in *Counter-Strike: Global Offensive* that display their unique traits. These "skins" are tradable, sellable, or purchasable on BUFF and Steam. Nonetheless, these trading platforms are required to disclose usernames publicly, potentially leading to privacy concerns due to the absence of a robust security solution for the digital asset and platform. Consequently, the value of Blockchain and encryption derives from the individual verification of digital assets. Consensus techniques authenticate transactions, while encryption algorithms safeguard data.

Avatars are exchanged in digital marketplaces for profit. The advanced Metaverse market, which enables product creation and authentic transactions within the Metaverse, must be differentiated from the digital market. The evolution of retail from traditional methods to digital platforms and, finally, to Metaverse retailing is examined in Article [3], which also emphasises the influence of the Metaverse on this shift. An academic study that uses machine learning and artificial intelligence to separately discover, apply, and improve adaptive automated trading methods in financial markets is examined in Article [1]. Users can sell on-chain assets, such as physical goods, on the Decentraland marketplace.

Avatars engage in transactions utilising digital currency within the Metaverse. The exorbitant expenses associated with legal tender hinder fiat currency's ability to satisfy the requirements of Metaverse development. Moreover, fiat currency is derived from tangible assets like as gold and silver, in contrast to Metaverse currency. Roblox enables players to purchase stuff with real currency, a premium allowance, or by creating and selling virtual goods online. The Diem payment system supports Multi-Currency Coin (XDX) as well as USD, EUR, and GBP stablecoins (Figure 7.3).

The Wealth of Nations demonstrates that traditional economics is predicated on assumptions such as resource scarcity and self-interest. Users of the Metaverse exhibit altruistic and illogical behaviours. The individuals prioritise the articulation of their feelings, including joy and achievement. This situation arises from the absence of agrarian and industrial civilisations, as well as traditional industrial organisation in the virtual realm. The economic operations of the Metaverse will be founded on the conceptual economy. Financial currency today employs digital social money in lieu

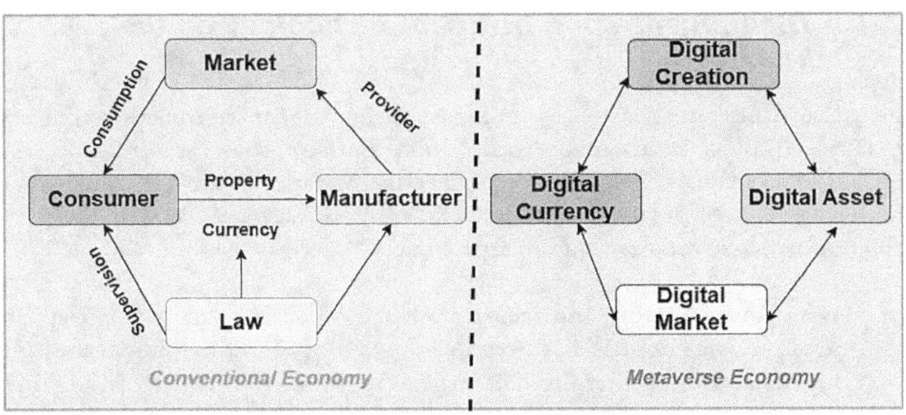

Figure 7.3 Conventional and virtual economies.

of precious metals. A method to delineate the Metaverse economy in contrast to the traditional economy is as follows:

- The valuing of the Metaverse is predicated on identification rather than on indistinct labour.
- As the marginal advantages of physical production diminish, the marginal benefits of the Metaverse will increase.
- Items will incur reduced marginal costs compared to the physical realm.
- Transactions within the Metaverse occur often owing to minimal transaction fees.

Since the Metaverse economic system is still in its infancy, there are few opportunities to implement and evaluate digital economy innovations like inclusive finance, digital currencies, collaborative economies, and sharing economies. To guarantee a complex and safe environment, we support integrating Blockchain and artificial intelligence into the Metaverse's infrastructure. Consequently, we will assess pertinent studies that may offer insights in the subsequent sections.

7.3 Blockchain in the Metaverse

Numerous Metaverse services will get advantages from the integration of Blockchain technology's ecosystem. Blockchain technology is adept at arranging and linking vast quantities of data from both physical and virtual platforms. Blockchain and cryptocurrencies can streamline commercial and financial transactions in both digital and physical realms. All processed and real-time data from the ecosystem can be securely saved and safeguarded on the Blockchain. This section examines the primary advantages and disadvantages of integrating Blockchain technology into the Metaverse.

7.3.1 The Influence of Blockchain Technology on the Metaverse

Blockchain is essential to the Metaverse. As a fundamental element, it connects enablers and provides advantages to all. Smart contracts, consensus protocols, and various Blockchain methodologies influence the Metaverse ecosystem and several technologies. The primary advantages include data privacy and security, interoperability, distributed topology, and smart contracts.

1. **Data confidentiality and security**: Altered Metaverse data may encompass sensitive user information susceptible to novel threats. The computers within the Metaverse can alter this data to generate counterfeit avatars, raising trust issues due to their difficulty in detection. Privacy and security are paramount in the Metaverse. The Blockchain architecture enables users to possess their

data solely. These tools authenticate users and regulate data access. Blockchain data is secured by encryption and hashing algorithms. Data security and confidentiality are inherent to the Blockchain [59, 60].

2. **Data interoperability**: The Metaverse depends on data interoperability facilitated by sophisticated technologies. The exchange of data among Metaverse ecosystem modules and activities supports this collaboration. Integrating data across many applications, algorithms, stakeholders, and models of both the actual and virtual realms is crucial to the Metaverse. Blockchain technology facilitates transparent integration. Block validation, consensus processes, and various Blockchain protocols enhance data integrity. Enhancing data integrity and transparency fosters collaboration in Metaverse technologies [61].
3. **Distributed topology**: The Blockchain's distributed architecture provides the Metaverse with data immutability and accessibility. Redundant data complicates data modification. Data can be rapidly and seamlessly sent from any proximate facility [62].
4. **Smart contracts**: These are autonomously generated agreements facilitated by the decentralised architecture of Blockchain technology. Consequently, transactions can be validated distinctly and unequivocally without the necessity of a third party. This can enhance decision-making in the Metaverse, particularly for physical-digital interactions, and augment system reliability [63].

Digital trust is essential, particularly for the dependability of information. Many question the authenticity of converting the physical environment into virtual data. Blockchain independently and securely stores data through decentralised and encrypted trust technology. Blockchain technology facilitates user access to the Metaverse. Blockchain technology fosters trust in transactions. Blockchains are decentralised data storage systems composed of interlinked blocks. Only a single block is acknowledged and connected to the preceding block. Consensus algorithms are fundamental to Blockchain technology. Each Blockchain employs a consensus process for network decision-making. The security, decentralisation, immutability, and speed of Blockchain substantiate its integration into the Metaverse architecture. Advancements in technology are expected to augment the number of users in the Metaverse. This necessitates substantial development of Metaverse data, which holds significant value. Increased Metaverse data is associated with greater value. Consequently, security and reliability are of utmost importance. Blockchain technology is capable of authenticating Metaverse data. Virtual currencies supported by Blockchain technology are utilised in the Metaverse. Blockchain-based digital currency will facilitate transactions in virtual shopfronts and avatar customisation for Metaverse inhabitants. Blockchain technology can authenticate identities through reliable third parties, enhancing communication and collaboration, particularly in the Metaverse, while also enabling transactions. Valuing Metaverse resources and commodities will be challenging without Blockchain technology, particularly if these virtual elements merge economic activity with the physical economy.

Consequently, examining Blockchain technology within the Metaverse is advantageous. This section addresses Blockchain-enabled Metaverse applications across four primary domains: cryptocurrencies, transaction attributes, authentication, and market and business dynamics.

7.3.2 Metaverse Cryptocurrency

What is the role of cryptocurrencies within the Metaverse? In what manner might Metaverse cryptocurrencies be generated and utilised? This text evaluates the Metaverse's significance in relation to the traditional coin issuance standard. Blockchain is predominantly utilised for cryptocurrency. It enhances the allure of Blockchain technology. The confidence and dependence of diverse users underpin the fundamental principles of cryptocurrencies and promote their circulation and trade. The global issuance of virtual currencies exceeds 12,000, with new currencies being generated daily. Market-leading cryptocurrencies attain unprecedented valuations. The conversion rate of USD to BTC is 50,000:1. The tangible world depends on fiat currencies, whereas the forthcoming Metaverse will require cryptocurrencies for circulation, payment, and settlement. Blockchain systems have generated, documented, and exchanged coins. Every one of these processes is crucial for the Metaverse. Bitcoin has utilised the UTXO transaction framework to oversee its transactions. Tools such as Etherscan for Ethereum datasets enable immediate access to account balances. Recall that UTXO and Ethereum utilise Proof of Work. Miners generate new blocks through the process of coin minting. Nonetheless, block production incurs expenses for them. Miners resolve intricate hash puzzles to extract blocks in a Proof of Work (PoW) consensus mechanism, necessitating substantial computational resources. In Ethereum 2.0's Proof of Stake (PoS) consensus mechanism, validators are selected based on the age of their currency holdings to produce blocks. Blockchain technology facilitates many approaches for managing Bitcoin transactions. Most Bitcoin transactions are facilitated by centralised exchanges like OK Exchange (OKEx). Low latency transactions, user-friendly interfaces, and improved security are made possible via centralised exchanges. Centralised markets present challenges, including incidences of insider pricing manipulation that exploit informational asymmetries. Decentralised cryptocurrency exchanges utilise smart contracts or peer-to-peer networks to automate transactions. Smart contracts such as IDex and Paradex maintain continuous-limited order books off-chain. The exchange or counterparty aligns orders and transmits them to the smart contract for execution. In Uniswap and Bancor, smart contracts engage in direct transactions with users. A future featuring numerous corporate Metaverses is probable. Consequently, smaller Metaverses must convert their various currencies like to fiat currencies. Numerous cryptocurrencies are anticipated in the forthcoming Metaverse. Users of the Metaverse must be capable of exchanging cryptocurrency through an identical mechanism [3, 64].

7.3.3 Characterisation of Metaverse Transactions

Financial transactions like as property sales, rental agreements, and service purchases are anticipated in the Metaverse, reflecting the majority of physical activity. Consequently, Metaverse transactions extend beyond mere token transfers and interactions within the Metaverse. Conventional Blockchain transactions are initially disseminated to miners and subsequently retained in their local transaction pools. Upon selecting a series of transactions, the miner performs hash-based consensus. The consensus chain and all miners will get the block produced by the initial miner who resolves the problem at the designated difficulty level. The extensive user base of the Metaverse, engaging in virtual settings via intra- and inter-Metaverse applications, suggests that Blockchain nodes will process numerous transactions. Complete Blockchain nodes in the Metaverse are required to retain the entirety of historical transactions, incurring substantial costs. Minimum confirmation delay constitutes an additional concern regarding transactions in the Metaverse. Internet applications designed for human interaction exhibit end-to-end latency ranging from tens to hundreds of milliseconds. Three-dimensional Metaverse applications require a latency of 10 milliseconds or less to prevent dizziness. Transactions within the Metaverse require little confirmation latency for applications demanding low latency [13, 65, 66]. Current Blockchain consensus mechanisms have considerable limitations that hinder Metaverse applications. To reach consensus on transaction data, the Proof of Work (PoW) system leverages the hashing power of miners. Resources for Proof of Work (PoW) consensus mining are required because of the substantial data volume in the Metaverse. Proof of Stake (PoS) utilises the coin holdings and ages of miner nodes to achieve consensus on transactions. The Metaverse's pronounced Matthew effect complicates the ability of Proof of Stake (PoS) to ensure equity among miners. Consequently, the Metaverse requires innovative consensus algorithms and Blockchain techniques to establish rigorous transaction rules.

7.3.4 Blockchain-Enabled Metaverse Market

Prior to Ethereum, Bitcoin and other Blockchains permitted only token transactions. Ethereum facilitated Turing-complete programming within smart contracts. Smart contract codes facilitate intricate activities within virtual machines. Ethereum makes the shift from cryptocurrency to crypto-business easier for Blockchain applications. Various market and commercial Blockchain reorganisations are possible. Blockchain technology-driven Decentralised Finance (DeFi) has the potential to enhance Metaverse markets and commerce. This study encompasses numerous leading DeFi market and industry analyses. The cryptocurrency market's arbitrage bots are analysed in [67, 68]. Arbitrage robots observe and execute risk-free arbitrage operations within the transaction pool. They also advocate for a collaborative approach to enhance the profitability of arbitrage robots and observe that miners can function as arbitrage robots. The Minier Extractable Value (MEV) may incentivise forking attacks. The concept employs collaborative bidding to optimise earnings. Their research indicates that the monthly MEV surpasses 25 times the expense of a 51% attack against Ethereum. Decentralised Finance (DeFi) use smart contracts and Fungible Tokens (FTs) to transform Metaverse economies. Efficient alternatives such as Uniswap, an Ethereum-based decentralised exchange, provide consumers with automatic liquidity for token deposits. A Decentralised Exchange (DEX) is an innovative platform for secure, direct trading of crypto-asset tokens. A Decentralised Exchange (DEX) utilises an atomic swap to facilitate direct trading of tokens or crypto-assets between two parties. Cybex, a decentralised application built on a decentralised exchange, offers a peer-to-peer token trading platform. Cybex possesses its token, CYB. CYB is exclusively authorised for use within the Cybex market for token exchange, staking to acquire crypto-asset tokens, and transaction fees. A connected network of validator nodes underpins the Diem Blockchain, the technology underlying the payment system. Users can tailor the Blockchain software to align with their financial requirements [14, 69].

7.3.5 Authentication with Metaverse Blockchain

Economic activity inside the Metaverse encompass land auctions, unique item transactions, valuable real estate dealings, land development and leasing, gaming rewards, and cryptocurrency investment returns. The Metaverse provides an innovative funding mechanism that integrates physical and digital components. NFTs are primarily utilised to commemorate events or accumulate digital assets. The integration with the Metaverse has broadened its scope to encompass a novel digital content enterprise. Non-Fungible Tokens (NFTs) preserve encrypted Blockchain transaction records to maintain the uniqueness of digital assets. Every token possesses a distinct value, facilitating the verification of digital asset ownership. Blockchain-based Non-Fungible Tokens (NFTs) exhibit the distinctiveness of Metaverse avatars and artefacts [15, 70, 71].

7.4 The Artificial Intelligence Metaverse

Science fiction author Neal Stephenson coined the word "Metaverse" in the early 1990s, and subsequent developments have included Microsoft, Second Life, Mana, Gala, Shibverse, and Meta (previously Facebook). Facebook's AI algorithms and innovations are well known. The business does AI research in a variety of fields, including computer vision, whole-body position estimation, text analysis, and self-supervised voice processing. The aforementioned factors may influence Meta's future and activities [16]. While virtual reality environments can exist independently of artificial intelligence, their integration enhances realism. The subsequent three use cases may be impacted:

1. **Avatar Creation**: The Metaverse centres on users, and the precision of avatars significantly influences interactive experiences for individuals and others. An advanced AI system can generate a realistic virtual representation from 2D or 3D user images or scans. The avatar can then exhibit a range of facial expressions, emotional states, hairstyles, age-related characteristics, and additional attributes to enhance dynamism. AI is assisting Ready Player Me in the creation of Metaverse avatars, whereas Meta is formulating its own [16, 72].
2. **AI Robots**: AI robots possess the capability to comprehend user visual and auditory inputs. They can also replicate human conversations through verbal and nonverbal communication. Metaverse chatbots are three-dimensional artificial intelligence entities that react to user interactions within virtual reality. Non-Player Characters (NPCs) are digital entities in gaming or virtual environments that adhere to predetermined scripts or regulations instead of being operated by a player. Artificial intelligence robots, which are entirely synthetic, are crucial to the advancement of the Metaverse. The virtual reality workplace may employ non-player characters or automated helpers [3, 73].
3. **Language Functions**: AI models digital humans through language processing. Artificial intelligence can interpret natural languages such as English, transform them into a machine-readable format, assess the content, develop a response, and translate the results back into English for user display. A complete conversational exchange can occur in an instant. The AI's training facilitates the translation of outcomes into any language, so providing global access to the Metaverse. The collection of data is essential for machine learning and artificial intelligence. A model utilises historical data to integrate prior outcomes and propose new results. As the model acquires additional data and human feedback, its outputs enhance. This technique increases the probability that artificial intelligence will execute tasks and yield precise results akin to humans. The Metaverse ought to exhibit improved scalability as human participation diminishes [11, 74, 75].

In summary, artificial intelligence enhances human–computer interaction. The sensors of sophisticated, AI-integrated virtual reality headgear identify and predict your electrical and muscle patterns, discerning your movement preferences within the Metaverse. Artificial intelligence can enhance the haptic experience of virtual reality. It enables voice-activated navigation through interaction with virtual elements without the use of controllers.

7.5 Application of AI in the Metaverse

The science of artificial intelligence posits that all facets of learning can be sufficiently encapsulated in theory [5]. Artificial intelligence forecasts by employing learning and pattern recognition on extensive data sets. Artificial intelligence assists individuals and organisations in minimising human errors and alleviating monotonous repetitive jobs. The Metaverse will encompass extensive AI-generated data. A range of artificial intelligence systems can collect and analyse data, learn from historical trends, and generate innovative processes and applications [3]. The integration of AI with AR, VR, and Blockchain can enhance trust, accountability, privacy, and decision-making. In a conference or gathering, the most vocal or influential individual typically prevails. Artificial intelligence can effectively assess meeting participants based on their subject knowledge, expertise, and prior performance. It can evaluate perspectives and select the optimal one, irrespective of status or authority. Artificial intelligence and Blockchain technology can determine optimal Metaverse solutions. A cooperative approach can facilitate success, unlike the actions of deceptive individuals. In the fields of computer vision, decision-making, and natural language processing, machine learning, deep learning, and reinforcement learning have recently been the focus of artificial intelligence research. Artificial intelligence's practical use inspires ideas for the Metaverse. Machine learning is essential for Metaverse technology to acquire knowledge akin to human learning. It will significantly impact Metaverse intelligence and efficacy. Metaverse users have precise technical support from advanced speech services, encompassing voice recognition and dialogue capabilities.

7.5.1 Exemplary AI Applications

Linear regression, random forest, and singular value decomposition enable robots to acquire knowledge from experience and data, thereby emulating human behaviour. Support Vector Machines (SVMs) were developed for pattern classification, regression analysis, and learning ranking functions. Machine learning approaches are constrained in their use due to dependence on manual feature selection and substantial quantities of labelled data. Convolutional Neural Networks (CNNs), sometimes referred to as ConvNets, are deep neural networks inspired by biological neural networks. Traditional CNNs employ convolutional kernels or filters with shared weights to vertically traverse input features and construct translation-equivariant feature maps. Convolutional Neural Networks (CNNs) consistently incorporate convolutional, pooling, and fully connected layers [4]. Weight sharing among neurones results in a substantial reduction in Convolutional Neural Networks (CNNs). Convolutional Neural Networks (CNNs) are proficient supervised learning techniques for facial recognition, image retrieval, and augmented reality applications. An agent must acquire knowledge through trial and error in a dynamic environment to make successive decisions in reinforcement learning [10]. Deep neural networks in deep reinforcement learning and Markov Decision Processes (MDPs) can improve Artificial Intelligence (AI) and make it easier to create autonomous systems that can assess visual settings. Reinforcement learning relies on two main strategies: value functions and policy optimisation. Value function approaches evaluate a condition's worth or expected return. There are established reinforcement learning techniques like asynchronous advantage actor-critic, Trust Region Policy Optimisation (TRPO), and Deep Q-Network (DQN). Deep Reinforcement Learning (DRL) systems can surpass human performance in various domains [14].

7.5.2 Synthesis of Metaverse Simulation Environments

Together with tangible objects or entities, Metaverse users interact with the Metaverse, developing to precisely replicate the composition, actions, and settings of certain physical assets (such parts, people, or procedures) in the virtual world. Recent advancements in digital transformation have resulted in the extensive development of Digital Twins across several industries for utilisation throughout asset lifecycles using real-time data. Digital Twins are essential for conceptual planning, prototyping, testing, design optimisation, and operation. In the Metaverse, organised and unstructured data are produced in substantial amounts, diverse forms, and rapid rates. Fundamental Digital Twin (DT) technologies employ deep learning. Virtual reality and data sciences enhance the visibility of fundamental mechanics to stakeholders [8].

7.5.3 Creation of Metaverse Objects

Following the discourse on AI-driven virtual world construction, the focus will shift to Metaverse authoring tools. These technologies enable all systems and occupations to learn beyond human capabilities. Authoring tools will significantly influence the operational efficiency and cognitive processes within the Metaverse.

7.5.3.1 Synopsis of NPCs and Avatars

Sanskrit provided the term avatar. It delineates the terrestrial manifestations of Vishnu. Nonetheless, virtual player avatar technology was revolutionary. Avatars are utilised in gaming, e-commerce, virtual social environments, and remote business meetings [7]. Utilising reinforcement learning [6] trains a virtual figure to guide participants to a destination. A head-tracked stereo HMD with a wide-angle view simulates an alleyway. This technology facilitates the deployment of applications in which the virtual environment adapts to human responses to attain objectives. AI-driven Non-Player Characters (NPCs) confront, assist, and enrich the narrative as adversaries, companions, and supportive entities. Most human-like Non-Player Characters (NPCs) lack the cognitive ability to interact with players in real-time strategy or first-person shooter games, which require tactical decision-making.

7.5.3.2 Application of AI in the Metaverse

Games explicitly elucidate and exemplify the principles of the Metaverse. Nonetheless, no game possesses an impeccable Metaverse. Regulations, goals, and limitations delineate a game's gameplay experience. However, the Metaverse does not require specialist gameplay features. The Metaverse is exemplified in online social games such as *The Sims*. The Metaverse distinguishes itself from video games by incorporating non-entertainment activities. Refer to the reviewed samples in the following. The Metaverse enables users to participate in concerts, virtual exhibitions, remote education, and collaborative meetings without the need for travel. The Metaverse evolves concurrently, regardless of individuals departing the virtual realm, due to its symbiotic nature. By differentiating video games from the Metaverse, we may implement the Metaverse concept across various sectors, including industry, education, innovation, entertainment, and social interactions.

7.6 Convergence of Blockchain Technology and Artificial Intelligence within the Metaverse

Establishing the Metaverse economy necessitates Blockchain technology. A central authority will ultimately govern the Metaverse economy in the absence of Blockchain technology. The absence of Blockchain support complicates the valuation of Metaverse assets or commodities and hinders the development of economic transactions akin to those in the physical economy. NFT-driven Blockchain technology has propelled the Metaverse forward. WEB 3.0 and Blockchain 3.0 have enabled the Metaverse to fulfil its potential. In the Metaverse, individuals manifest as avatars or undergo three-dimensional scanning. In the Metaverse, individuals are seen as beings akin to clones, rather than mere virtual characters. In the Metaverse, individuals construct avatars and preserve artefacts that reflect their individuality. This assertion is substantiated by Blockchain-based NFT technology.

7.6.1 Superior Learning Data

Artificial intelligence in the Metaverse can address temporal, labour, and financial challenges. Newscasting necessitates the employment of an announcer, studio recording, and editing. In virtual reality, an AI announcer may rapidly and consistently disseminate critical and time-sensitive information. To disseminate news in the Metaverse, one must comprehend broadcasters' facial expressions, muscular movements, vocal characteristics, nuances, and gestures. To produce an artificial intelligence announcement video from a broadcaster's lengthy news piece, we isolate the excerpt utilising an alternative reporter's voice and noise-free audio. We employ specific identification detection techniques to render the announcer's face and voice perceptible to the camera. Blockchain meta-information during data retrieval facilitates the selection of only the essential, unadulterated material for educational purposes, hence enhancing the quality of learning. Metadata within the Blockchain block selectively permits access to essential high-quality data. Precise Metaverse data expands the user base.

7.6.2 Reutilisation of Data

Recently, creative endeavours within the Metaverse have increasingly relied on artificial intelligence rather than human input. Artificial intelligence artists acquire knowledge of contemporary trends and styles while creating art. Historically, style analysis included extensive data sets. Artists utilising artificial intelligence archive data in a distributed ledger for selection and reutilisation. Collecting additional data and engaging in practice diminishes the likelihood of selecting erroneous data, hence decreasing validation time.

7.6.3 Robust Decentralised Network

The Metaverse, a three-dimensional digital realm, necessitates substantial data and server capacity. Overseeing operations with a centralised computer system might be expensive. A network architecture that combines the Metaverse environment with individual user devices is essential to use the distributed system of Blockchain technology. Personal autonomy about the Metaverse environment utilised or accessed mitigates the difficulties associated with the centralised management of extensive data sets. It may also inhibit large technical corporations from monopolising the Metaverse.

7.6.4 Confidentiality

A regulatory framework is necessary to mitigate ethical concerns about Metaverse participants. Only information that is publicly accessible regarding real and virtual individuals should be revealed. Privacy necessitates safeguarding through a personal information security system. Nonetheless, digital virtual entities lack legal protection, rendering them more susceptible to image manipulation than actual individuals. A flawed algorithm may result in significant racial and gender bias. Blockchain technology safeguards personal data against external cyberattacks. An auditable method that is time-stamped can effectively manage inadvertently modified personal data.

7.6.5 Distinction between Virtual and Real

A device capable of differentiating between artificial intelligence and humans is essential for stabilising the Metaverse and preventing user confusion. Metaverse literary characters have become so complex that distinguishing between them is challenging for humans. A robust data construction system is essential for comparing and assessing actual and fictitious individuals. Data transparency and descriptiveness facilitate the identification of fraudulent news and images. Data must be recorded on a Blockchain to guarantee precise comprehension of artificial intelligence data and provide access to historical records when necessary. Blockchain technology facilitates the interpretation of AI data [8].

7.6.6 Abundant Substance

Artificial intelligence emulates and substitutes human behaviour. An artificial intelligence system forecasts a Metaverse user's personality, intellect, and affluence based on their verbal and written communications. The Metaverse employs artificial intelligence to generate human-like voices and customised content. Data may be effortlessly transformed into games, YouTube videos, news articles, advertising, and educational content by inputting basic information. Artificial intelligence can utilise Metaverse data to create pattern material that emulates human behaviour. Blockchain technology safeguards personal information and facilitates diverse content development [9].

7.6.7 Economic Virtue Cycle

In banking and commerce, AI can determine the optimal data to utilise. Enhanced data reliability is essential for precise forecast modification. The historical handling of Blockchain data enhances the credibility of corporate estimates. Cryptographic payments employing Blockchain tokens and currency facilitate the Metaverse Marketplace.

7.7 Challenges and Unresolved Matters

Previous research indicates that the Metaverse requires artificial intelligence and Blockchain technology. These technologies have the capacity to create a scalable, dependable, and efficient Metaverse; yet the Metaverse remains under development. The difficulties, problems, and suggestions pertaining to the combination of Blockchain and Metaverse AI are covered in this section.

7.7.1 Issues in the Metaverse Digital Economy

The potential for limitless innovation characterises virtual digital creation. The value of digital things is established by identification, in contrast to traditional economic labour. Authoring tools that enable users to efficiently and economically produce distinctive content are essential in digital production. These technologies may enhance interaction among Metaverse content creators. In the Metaverse, marginal production advantages are anticipated to increase, in contrast to the physical realm. Reconciling the marginal benefits of the physical and virtual realms necessitates value transformation. In the forthcoming Metaverse, individuals will utilise their virtual wardrobes to select digital outfits, while enterprises will impose substantial costs for virtual skins, apparel, and properties, so eliminating numerous players. Global enterprises must unite to offer specific governance measures. The establishment of a digital currency system for the exchange between Metaverse and conventional currency remains ambiguous. The Metaverse will facilitate many more transactions than the physical realm. Consequently, enabling substantial and frequent transactions in the forthcoming Metaverse presents challenges. The proliferation of cryptocurrencies inside a decentralised economic structure reliant on Blockchain and AI technology may precipitate inflation in the future Metaverse [13].

7.7.2 Challenges of Artificial Intelligence

Advanced artificial intelligence technologies, particularly deep learning, have propelled Metaverse automation and development beyond traditional methods. Artificial intelligence is employed to rapidly create realistic digital avatars for conversational virtual assistants in the Metaverse [8]. Contemporary deep learning models possess significant depth and parameterisation, complicating the implementation of learning-based applications on resource-constrained mobile devices. AI systems necessitate human intervention to guide the machine in certain tasks instead of allowing autonomous learning. Numerous learning tasks perform effectively in fixed static environments; nonetheless, they exhibit deficiencies in resilience and interpretability, rendering them inappropriate for open and dynamic situations [14]. A promising paradigm that makes it possible to compare machine learning techniques empirically across a range of learning tasks is meta-learning. By utilising this expertise, meta-data can pick up new responsibilities faster than previous approaches. Meta-learning accelerates and enhances machine learning pipelines and neural networks, enabling the substitution of manually crafted algorithms with data-driven learning techniques. Meta-learning posed a significant challenge to autonomous machine learning in the forthcoming years.

7.7.3 Blockchain Challenges

The incorporation of Blockchain into the Metaverse continues to pose challenges, notwithstanding recent progress in Blockchain technology. The next section poses enquiries designed to motivate readers to engage with technical research. Are current NFT systems capable of accommodating Metaverse transaction volumes? Non-Fungible Tokens (NFTs) based on Blockchain technology are distinct cryptographic tokens. NFTs digitise art and real estate owing to their distinctive characteristics. Nonetheless, contemporary NFT systems remain in a state of evolution. Addressing the substantial demands of forthcoming Metaverse applications necessitates research and engineering to enhance NFT platform service standards. What criteria must the Metaverse fulfil to establish a robust Blockchain-enabled market and enterprise? Decentralisation and regulation may be effective for the Blockchain-enabled economy. The Decentralised Autonomous Organisation (DAO) is an effective and promising concept that unites individuals with shared interests globally. DAO members possess intrinsic treasuries that cannot be accessed without community approval. Smart contracts facilitate DAOs, which are characterised by transparency and verifiability. Consequently, DAOs can regulate decisions via proposals and voting, guaranteeing that each Metaverse inhabitant possesses a validated vote. Can the practical application model of Blockchain be utilised in the Metaverse? Recent Bitcoin speculations and a fraudulent ICO have undermined confidence in the Metaverse. Blockchain-based application models are inadequate for the Metaverse's demands for low latency and high throughput [15]. Consequently, forthcoming Metaverse applications require a secure Blockchain-based application framework. Is there a necessity for novel Blockchain and consensus mechanisms in the Metaverse? Blockchain employs Proof of Work and Proof of Stake consensus mechanisms. Cryptographic computations and security challenges afflict contemporary consensus systems. Future decentralised applications necessitate a Blockchain platform characterised by low latency, high throughput, efficient transaction sequencing, offline transaction payment capabilities, minimal transaction costs, and a contemporary free internet business model. Innovative Blockchain systems and consensus methodologies are anticipated for the Metaverse.

7.7.4 Governance of the Metaverse

The Metaverse is predominantly utilised and endorsed by Roblox and Meta (formerly Facebook). Major businesses construct and manage the most prevalent ecosystems. Limited applications are present in the tiny Metaverse. Conversely, the macro Metaverse would encompass all user-specified conditions. Prominent corporations must collaborate to establish a vast interconnected Metaverse to achieve this objective. Encouraging significant organisations to cooperate is challenging. In what manner can coherent regulations govern the unified Metaverse once it is established? Conversely, market manipulation and money laundering will afflict the future Metaverse. Consequently, market governance will become increasingly essential in the jurisdiction of the Metaverse [16].

7.7.5 Blockchain Applications Transforming the Metaverse

The virtual economy of the Metaverse will expand through Blockchain-integrated office applications, social networks, NFT marketplaces, and game funding. Axie Infinity, a Blockchain-based game, enables players to combat, breed, and exchange Axies. Ronin Bridge enables users to transfer Ethereum funds to Ronin wallets. The game facilitates currency conversion between fiat and cryptocurrency. Ethereum can be purchased on Binance, Coinbase, or Ronin using fiat currency. As cryptocurrency is permitted in certain jurisdictions, individuals can transfer funds to their respective addresses. Implementing Blockchain-based game financing may pose challenges in certain countries; nonetheless, the forthcoming Metaverse is anticipated to be more transparent, equitable, and just.

7.7.6 Security and Privacy in the Metaverse

Security and privacy within the Metaverse provide significant challenges for organisations, developers, and individuals. Privacy infringements, identity theft, and fraud may ensue [9]. Digital assets, virtual item identifiers, cryptocurrency transaction records, and other sensitive user information must be safeguarded in the Metaverse. Cryptography designed for the Metaverse can safeguard privacy within that environment.

7.8 Conclusion

A multitude of Metaverse users produce substantial quantities of secondary and tertiary data. The data within the Blockchain-based Metaverse is labelled and verifiable. Data is increasingly valuable to Metaverse AI. The Metaverse employs artificial intelligence and Blockchain technology to provide a secure and liberated digital environment for human social and economic activities outside the physical realm. The rapid implementation of these novel technologies is anticipated. Artificial intelligence and Blockchain will be essential for the expansion of the Metaverse. We examine pertinent literature on Metaverse elements, digital currencies, artificial intelligence technologies and applications in the virtual realm, and Blockchain-enabled technology to furnish academic and industry professionals with a comprehensive assessment. We also anticipated considerable challenges to the advancement of the Metaverse's fundamental components via artificial intelligence and Blockchain technology. Academics and industry must collaborate to establish a transparent, equitable, and rational Metaverse through multidisciplinary research and inquiry.

Chapter 8

Blockchain-Driven Agricultural Supply Chains: The Role of AI and IoT in Smart Farming

8.1 Introduction

Effective management of logistics and agricultural product growth within the supply chain is essential for ensuring food safety. The increasing number of reports on food contamination has heightened the need for robust traceability systems that can monitor the flow of resources, including energy, throughout the supply chain [1, 43, 44]. Additionally, as agricultural products are frequently traded across international borders, accurate tracking mechanisms are necessary to comply with diverse regulatory standards in different countries. In the agricultural sector, traceability involves the systematic collection, sharing, and documentation of data related to a product's origin and every point it passes through in the logistics network [2, 45]. However, the dynamic and fragmented nature of the agri-food supply chain where goods are produced, processed, and distributed through multiple intermediaries poses significant challenges to effective tracking. Contaminated products and their associated health risks underscore the critical role of traceability as a policy tool for ensuring food safety and quality [3, 46]. Current traceability systems in agriculture are hindered by siloed data structures and centralised control mechanisms, which

DOI: 10.1201/9781003520702-8

increase the risk of data manipulation and reduce the transparency needed for swift action in the event of contamination [4, 47]. When contamination does occur, the ability to isolate affected products and identify the source quickly is essential to mitigating harm.

The modern supply chain has become increasingly complex, involving numerous stakeholders at various stages [5, 48]. For effective management, collaboration among these stakeholders is vital. Growing concerns about food safety and supply chain disruptions have pushed the food industry towards greater customer focus and faster response mechanisms. Comprehensive traceability systems can significantly reduce the likelihood of distributing unsafe or substandard products, thus minimising the risks of false advertising, legal disputes, and product recalls [6, 50]. The adoption of traceability solutions in the agri-food sector is growing, improving food safety and boosting consumer confidence in product quality [3, 49]. Organisations like the FAO and ITU promote the use of advanced ICTs in agriculture to support farmers and enhance traceability systems [7, 51]. As food supply chains become global, reliable identification and tracking methods are essential to maintain product quality and safety for consumers [8, 52]. Blockchain for Supply Chain is a natural combination of two technologies that were made to work together for activities on a shared ledger. In many cases, a supply chain shows how goods move between businesses and between countries. Where food comes from is one of Forest Stewardship Council's (FSC's) toughest problems [9, 53]. Companies have to deal with this problem right now. End-to-end food tracking is not a big deal in the food business because there is a global supply chain network with different rules and procedures for different countries [10, 54].

Distributed ledger/Blockchain is a very important tool that can have a big effect on how the supply chain is managed. This essay discusses how Blockchain technology could be used in the supply chain for both manufacturing and products that go bad quickly [11, 55]. There is a fast adoption of the Blockchain system in the food supply chain. Blockchain can be used to give people access to a lot of detailed information about food products, like those sold by Carrefour. This makes it easier to know about the quality and ingredients of the food. China has been very worried about food safety for a few years now. Traditional agri-food logistics methods aren't meeting customer needs anymore, so it's getting more and more important to create a traceability framework for agri-food supply.

Several aspects of farming can be monitored in real time by farmers using IoT devices, including weather, soil moisture levels, humidity, and temperature [12, 56, 57]. Data is the foundation of intelligent agriculture. The created data, regardless of its accuracy, must be recorded in the Blockchain as a record. To do this, Machine Learning algorithms add structure to the generated data. There are a lot of different ways to track food from start to finish, and different countries have different rules about how food can be handled [13, 58].

Distributed ledger and Blockchain technology are crucial to supply chain management. Blockchain technology can be used in supply chains to create and track perishable agriculture items [8–10]. Blockchain allows businesses like small-town merchants to provide customers with a lot of food product information, so they don't have to guess about quality or ingredients. China has been very worried about food safety in the last few years. Because the old ways of moving food and agricultural goods will not matter in the future [14, 59].

The word "artificial" lets us make a system that can work like a person or copy the brain [15, 60]. A lot of real-time data has been collected by new technologies like IoT and gadgets with sensors built in. Artificial intelligence technologies use this data to come up with new solutions for businesses [5, 61]. Another thing that has helped AI grow is this. Blockchain is increasingly considered as a secure method to store the massive amounts of data used by AI [16, 63]. At the moment, AI-enabled Blockchain is seeing a lot of use [17, 62]. Maximise the use of AI in the supply chain. But if you use smart contracts to code business logic with Blockchain technology, you can make things move much more efficiently and prevent dishonest people from wasting money [18, 64].

8.1.1 Contribution

This work makes the following key contributions to the field of agricultural supply chain management:

- It presents a comprehensive discussion on the transformative roles of Artificial Intelligence (AI), the Internet of Things (IoT), and Blockchain technologies in enhancing transparency, efficiency, and trust within the food supply chain.
- It explores the opportunities offered by AI in the agricultural sector, including predictive analytics, automation, demand forecasting, and intelligent decision-making.
- It demonstrates how IoT technologies can improve supply chain operations by enabling real-time monitoring of agricultural products through sensors that track environmental conditions, location, and product quality.
- It examines how Blockchain technology can enhance the supply chain by providing a secure, immutable, and decentralised platform for recording transactions, improving traceability, reducing fraud, and ensuring fair compensation for farmers.
- It proposes and discusses a novel AI- and IoT-enabled Blockchain-based application framework tailored for agricultural supply chains, aimed at addressing current inefficiencies and ensuring data integrity across the network.
- It includes a case study that illustrates the practical implementation of the proposed model and highlights the potential outcomes and benefits of adopting such an integrated ecosystem.

8.2 Literature Survey

8.2.1 Supply Chain Management

Agricultural supply chains have shifted from local, decentralised setups to complex global networks involving many stakeholders: farmers, manufacturers, transporters, distributors, retailers, and consumers, who all impact the production and delivery of goods. According to the authors of [19, 65, 66], the lack of full transparency in these supply chains raises the risk of fraud, often causing financial losses for producers, especially farmers, who face challenges in receiving fair payment. Furthermore, the complexity of the supply chain makes it difficult to trace products accurately, thereby making food fraud harder to detect and prevent. This growing challenge underscores the urgent need for more transparent and traceable supply chain solutions. To establish a reliable and effective trading system, paper [20] argues that significant changes are necessary to the present supply chain structure. For this reason, we keep track of all transactions using Blockchain technology so that all parties in the supply chain can see them. So that all parties involved in the project can access the information about the events, it is stored in a block. Every block in the chain is connected to every other block in the chain in this scenario [17–20]. Once data is saved on a decentralised platform, no one with a stake in the data may alter it. What gets things done on the Ethereum network is known as the EVM node. In addition to smart contracts, the EVM stores information about all linked accounts. All the details of the transaction are contained in a smart contract, similar to the one that exists between the buyer and the farmer [21–23]. The execution of a smart contract's program initiates a transaction. Any agreement that requires signatures will have conditions to explain them. When specific conditions are met, a transaction is added to a corresponding block on the Blockchain. A miner (referred to here metaphorically as a "child") is responsible for validating and appending this transaction to the block. Once a miner successfully solves the required computational puzzle, they broadcast the solution to other miners. This mechanism is known as Proof of Work (PoW) a consensus protocol that verifies and validates transactions before appending them to the Blockchain. As the Blockchain grows with each validated block, the overall security and immutability of the transaction records are strengthened. According to the study in [21], transaction data on the Blockchain can only be altered by the involved parties, and even then, only with mutual agreement typically requiring 51% consensus. This decentralised control ensures data integrity and makes unauthorised alterations nearly impossible. In the context of food safety, Blockchain applications aim to improve traceability within the food supply chain. Technologies such as Radio Frequency Identification (RFID) have been integrated into Blockchain systems to track and trace food products at each stage of the supply chain. The authors of the referenced study addressed scalability issues associated with traditional Blockchain databases like BigchainDB. This approach aligns with initiatives by major corporations; for example, IBM is currently developing Blockchain-based food traceability solutions to enhance food safety, transparency, and accountability [22].

8.2.2 The Part of Machine Learning Models

Artificial Intelligence (AI) enables the development of systems that can learn autonomously by adapting to new information using previously acquired knowledge. Similarly, in Machine Learning (ML), large volumes of existing data are used to train algorithms, allowing them to construct models that can analyse patterns and generate useful insights [23, 67]. These models can then be refined to predict additional attributes or future trends based on newly received data [8]. Traditional algorithms are often inadequate for making accurate predictions in complex agricultural environments. To address this, machine learning methods are categorised into three primary types: supervised learning, unsupervised learning, and reinforcement learning [24, 68]. The ML process typically begins by feeding input data into an algorithm, which then processes the data to produce predictive outputs. This predictive capability is especially valuable in agriculture. By applying ML-based predictive analytics, farmers can analyse data from diverse sources, simulate different scenarios, and uncover insights even in uncertain or challenging conditions. This technology supports smarter decision-making by taking into account variables such as geographic conditions, soil nutrient levels, rainfall patterns, and local socio-economic factors. As a result, AI and ML empower farmers to plan more effectively and optimise their agricultural practices for improved productivity and sustainability. In paper [10], the authors say that the field of gardening has many sensors, such as sensors for sunlight, moisture, water level, and motors [25]. Because of IoT devices that can give farmers information about their farms, the idea of "smart farming" is still very new. Each farming field is run by its owner, who uses a computer or a cell phone. The owner decides who can see the data that is made in the agricultural field. Data mining, sensor data, and other sorts of data are all examples of the types The first step in any Machine Learning (ML) pipeline is data collection. Once collected, the data undergoes *preprocessing*, which includes scaling, handling missing values, and either imputing or removing incomplete entries. The cleaned dataset is divided into training and testing sets for model evaluation. As noted in [27], feature selection is key to enhancing model accuracy, with methods like Principal Component Analysis (PCA) and Linear Discriminant Analysis (LDA) used to identify the most important features. Machine learning algorithms such as Naïve Bayes, Random Forest, and K-Nearest Neighbours (KNNs) are trained on these features. Model performance is then assessed on the test data using metrics like accuracy, Root Mean Square Error (RMSE), precision, recall, and cross-validation scores. The best-performing model is selected to perform tasks like *crop classification and recommendation generation*. These insights are delivered to end-users via an application server's monitoring interface, which provides real-time forecasts [28]. Once developed, the ML model is deployed using a *Machine Learning Runner* through a *Model Server* and stored in the cloud to support ongoing development and scalability. According to [29], autonomous learning mechanisms can generate control signals that are sent to an integrated controller, which then manages devices like sprinklers, heaters, windows, and coolers. As the system continues to collect and store data in the cloud, model accuracy and performance improve over time.

8.2.3 Artificial Intelligence in Supply Chain Management

Artificial Intelligence (AI) is revolutionising *Supply Chain Management (SCM)* by enhancing operational efficiency, improving decision-making, and increasing profitability [30, 69]. In warehousing, AI helps companies monitor inventory levels, optimise storage, and streamline distribution through intelligent data collection and analysis. Key applications include *demand forecasting, order modification*, and *dynamic rerouting* of in-transit goods. Major technology firms like *Google* and *Amazon* have heavily invested in AI to refine their supply chain operations [31, 70]. Among the many AI techniques employed, *Artificial Neural Networks (ANNs)* stand out for their ability to process large datasets and detect patterns, trends, and relationships. ANNs are often based on *mathematical regression models* that map input sources to output variables across various processing units [32, 71]. In SCM, ANNs are applied in a variety of areas including the following:

- *Sales forecasting*
- *Supplier selection*
- *Demand and consumption prediction*
- *Pricing strategies*
- *Marketing decision support* [33]

Due to their ability to model complex and nonlinear relationships, ANNs have become widely popular in handling large-scale supply chain data. This is illustrated in Figure 8.1 (as referenced). Other promising techniques include *Fuzzy Logic (FL) modelling*, which handles imprecise information well, making it suitable for uncertain or ambiguous scenarios in SCM [17, 72]. Additionally, *Natural Language Processing (NLP)* is emerging as a powerful tool for improving SCM by enabling systems to interpret and respond to textual data, such as customer feedback or supplier communications [34, 73].

8.2.4 AI in Agriculture

Various aspects of agriculture require improvement to enhance efficiency and productivity. Recent advancements in technologies such as Artificial Intelligence (AI) have made this transformation possible [19, 75]. Machine learning, natural

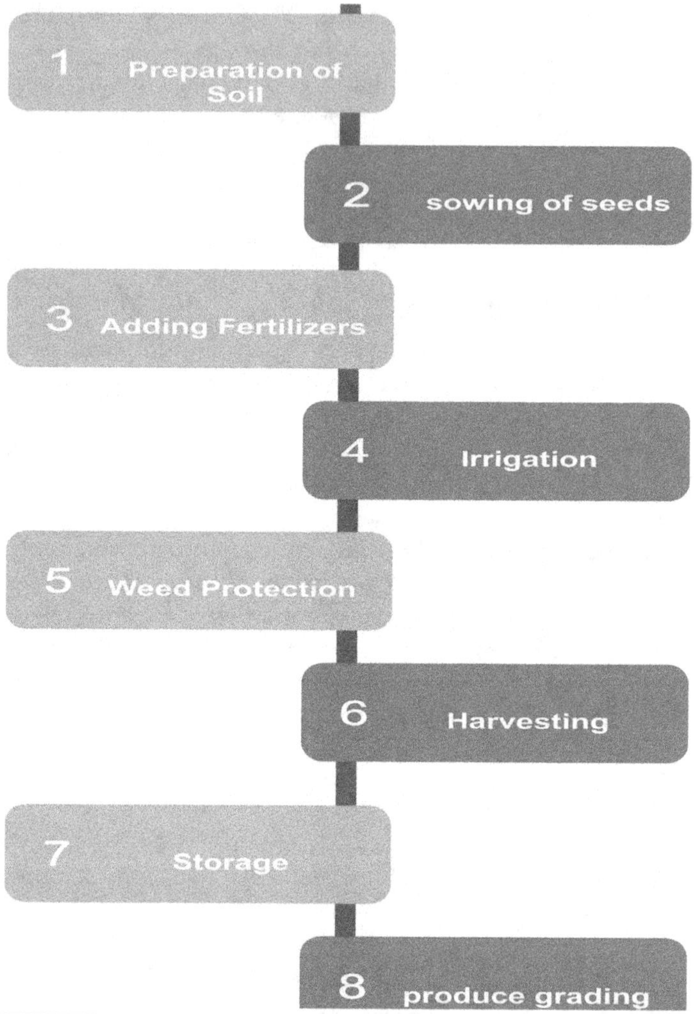

Figure 8.1 Several steps in the process of farming with AI.

language processing, and deep learning have been extensively applied across multiple stages of the farming process [35, 74]. As illustrated in Figure 8.2, AI has significantly impacted and transformed several key farming operations [36]. AI technologies are utilised for monitoring crops and soil health, determining optimal harvest times, performing precision spraying, enabling automated weeding, conducting aerial surveys and imaging, as well as grading and sorting agricultural products. A prominent subset of AI, machine learning, is specifically employed to predict crop yields, assess crop quality, and detect diseases and weeds, among other applications. Figure 8.2 highlights various domains within agriculture, where AI can be effectively implemented to optimise tasks and decision-making [37].

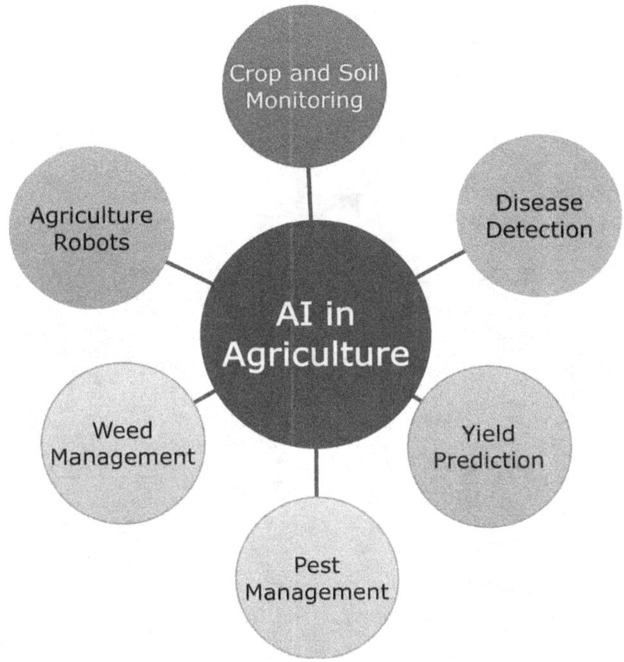

Figure 8.2 Application of AI in agriculture.

8.2.5 Supply Chain Management with Blockchain Technology

Blockchain technology holds tremendous promise for enhancing supply chain management [38]. As illustrated in Figure 8.3, its benefits include real-time tracking, faster transaction processing, improved traceability, enhanced customer engagement, higher return on investment, and streamlined trade operations [24]. By decentralising control, increasing transparency, and enabling real-time monitoring, Blockchain addresses many limitations of traditional supply chain systems. Conventional supply chains rely heavily on paper-based records and manual processes, which often cause delays and inefficiencies. In contrast, Blockchain technology eliminates these intermediaries, automates record-keeping, and significantly accelerates the entire supply chain workflow [39].

8.2.6 Blockchain in the Supply Chain for Farm Products

In this study, article [40] analyses the potential dangers to human health and the pollution of agricultural products that are transported all over the world through our distribution chain. There is a lack of food product tracking and approval within this one-of-a-kind agri-food supply chain. Ensure that the safety of the product is

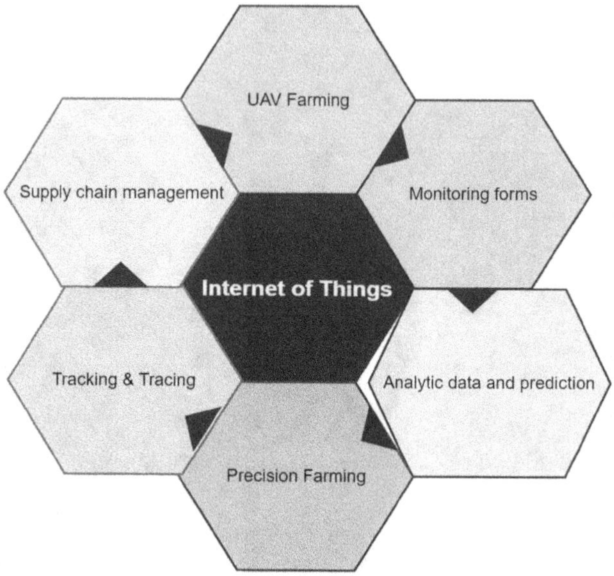

Figure 8.3 IoT applications for smart agriculture.

maintained by constructing an efficient traceability system that can be used as a quality control tool in the agricultural supply chain. Blockchain could make farm supply chains more transparent [40]. This study advocates using the Blockchain to complete economic transactions along the agri-food supply chain to track crop pricing and transparency. This paper describes the method by naming each database section a "block." The progression of the transactive state is reflected in the addition of a block to the block series in sequence flow. This block has a connection to another block. Following that, the new block is replicated throughout the network. This makes sure that the Blockchain is the same in all store areas. Each person who takes part in this transaction gets a copy of the Blockchain [41]. In this way, the move can be confirmed by both parties. Blockchain technology is versatile and open to new ideas. The customer can then put down exact prices. Fair prices for farmers' goods are possible. The government can track agricultural costs and broker misconduct. They used smart technologies and Blockchain to monitor, track, and manage agricultural supply chain business processes. This would get rid of middlemen and the most important places where food prices are set in traceability. This would be good for the government, buyers, and most importantly, farmers. It is a good choice for all three key providers [42]. Transaction is important when there is a link between the buyer and the seller. Blockchain gives encryption when two people start a transaction. Blockchain checks the transaction and adds it to the chain. The new block is added to the Blockchain, and the record for the future is changed. Figure 8.4 displays different Blockchain-based transaction processes in the supply chain management system.

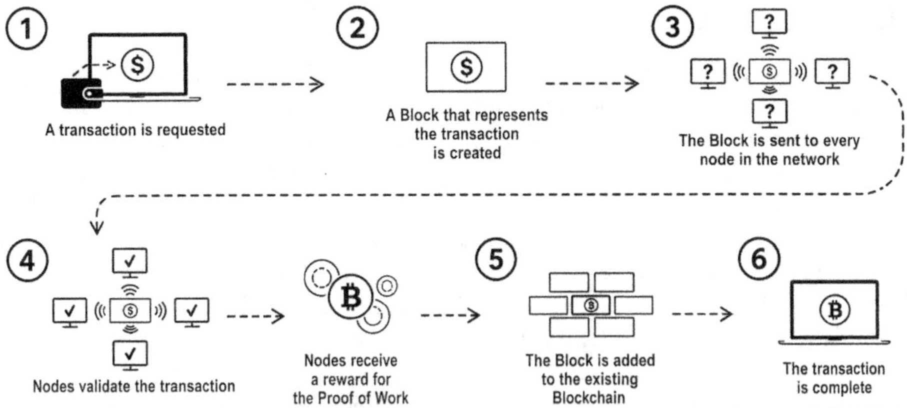

Figure 8.4 Blockchain-based transaction process in the supply chain.

8.2.7 How to Use IoT

The Internet of Things (IoT) refers to a network of intelligent devices that can operate individually or as interconnected components within a distributed system. According to the author in [7], IoT represents a key technology of the Fourth Industrial Revolution and is being widely adopted across various sectors including business, energy, housing, agriculture, and environmental management to enhance automation and intelligence in industries. Agriculture plays a vital role in the economic development of every country, and modern farming is increasingly recognised as a smart approach to maximise productivity and efficiency. One of the primary challenges in agriculture is effective irrigation and crop monitoring. There is growing interest in generating and managing data tailored to specific agricultural needs. The integration of IoT with advanced data collection and analysis techniques enables smarter farming practices that significantly boost productivity [11]. Figure 8.3 illustrates several applications of IoT technology in smart agriculture.

Scientific organisations, study centres, and businesses are all competing to offer a wider range of Internet of Things (IoT) products to people involved in the agricultural business. By doing this, they are laying the groundwork for a clear purpose when IoT becomes a standard medium. It's hard for the IoT creator to make sure that the data they collect is safe and private [12]. In this case, Blockchain technology has a lot to give. There are makers, sellers, traders, and buyers in the complicated supply network for agriculture. Management of the supply chain is needed to cut down on waste and losses and make sure that food is safe and efficient. IoT and Blockchain technologies have a huge impact on how well, efficiently, and honestly the supply chain works. The Internet of Things could be used to keep an eye on goods and movement in real time, which would make stock management better and lower the risk of food going bad or going to waste [13]. Temperature monitors, for example, can be used to keep track of how goods that go bad quickly are moved and stored, making sure that the right temperatures and levels of humidity are kept.

8.3 System Design

The agricultural food supply chain consists of many interconnected components, making it challenging to track the entire process from farm to table, covering production through delivery. To ensure effective traceability, detailed records are maintained at each stage. Each food item is assigned a unique ID and lot number, which are recorded with every new transaction. Additionally, a hash value is generated to verify the authenticity of each transaction. In this system, a batch refers to a group of food items stored together in a warehouse, identified by a unique batch number. To manage large data volumes, Hyperledger stores data hash values while the InterPlanetary File System (IPFS) holds the actual transaction details. This hybrid method overcomes Blockchain's storage limits and IPFS constraints. Access control policies restrict read/write permissions to authorised users only, boosting data security. Similarly, smart contracts restrict execution rights to specific organisations, enabling automated and secure interactions between entities and devices within the supply chain. Figure 8.5 illustrates the processing of each component in the agricultural food supply chain, with detailed explanations provided in the following.

1. **Bureau of Agriculture**: Manages farmers by maintaining accurate records of farmers, seeds, plots, and yields. Data is stored in IPFS, with hash values recorded on the Blockchain for verification.
2. **Farmer**: Plants and monitors crops using sensors tracking water, air, sunlight, and soil. Stores related data (photos, videos) in IPFS and records data hashes on the Blockchain. Creates smart contracts.
3. **Processor**: Transforms harvested crops into consumable food. Stores batch, quantity, and inspection data in IPFS, with hashes saved on the Blockchain. Generates and attaches product labels.
4. **Quality Supervision Bureau**: Conducts regular quality inspections and enforces standards. Stores inspection data in IPFS and records hashes on the Blockchain to ensure compliance, prevent counterfeiting, and stop illegal sales.
5. **Distributor**: Processed farm products may pass through multiple distribution levels before reaching retail stores. Distributors store and sell these products in bulk to retailers. Information about the distributor, sale timing, pricing, and

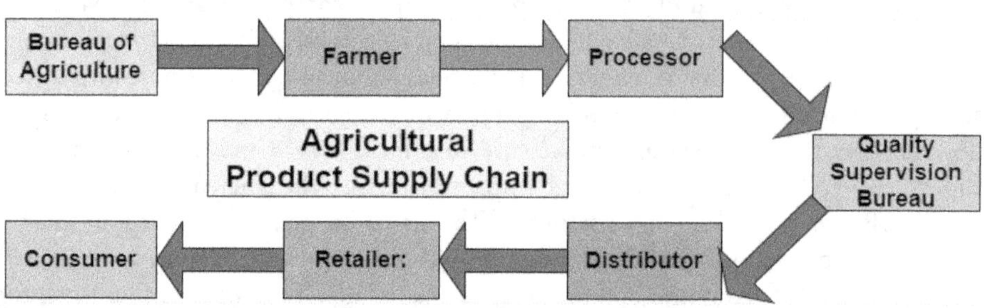

Figure 8.5 A simple agricultural food process in the supply chain.

other relevant data is saved in IPFS, with corresponding hash values maintained on the Blockchain to guarantee data integrity.

6. **Retailer**: Retailers sell smaller quantities of processed food products to consumers. Data such as store details, sales times, and amounts sold are stored in IPFS, with the Blockchain keeping the hash values for verification.
7. **Consumer**: The end consumer purchases and consumes the agricultural products. Thanks to traceability features enabled by technologies like barcodes, RFID tags, or QR codes on product packaging, consumers can access detailed information about the entire supply chain of the food item.

8.4 Implementation

The AI-IoT-Enabled Blockchain Ecosystem uses IoT sensors like moisture and temperature sensors to gather real-time field data. Drones capture images to train machine learning models for early disease detection. Blockchain ensures food safety and prevents fraud through transparent, real-time supply chain monitoring, boosting consumer trust. This traceable, open system helps reduce food waste and improves resource management in agriculture. Figure 8.6 illustrates this AI-IoT-Blockchain ecosystem for supply chain management.

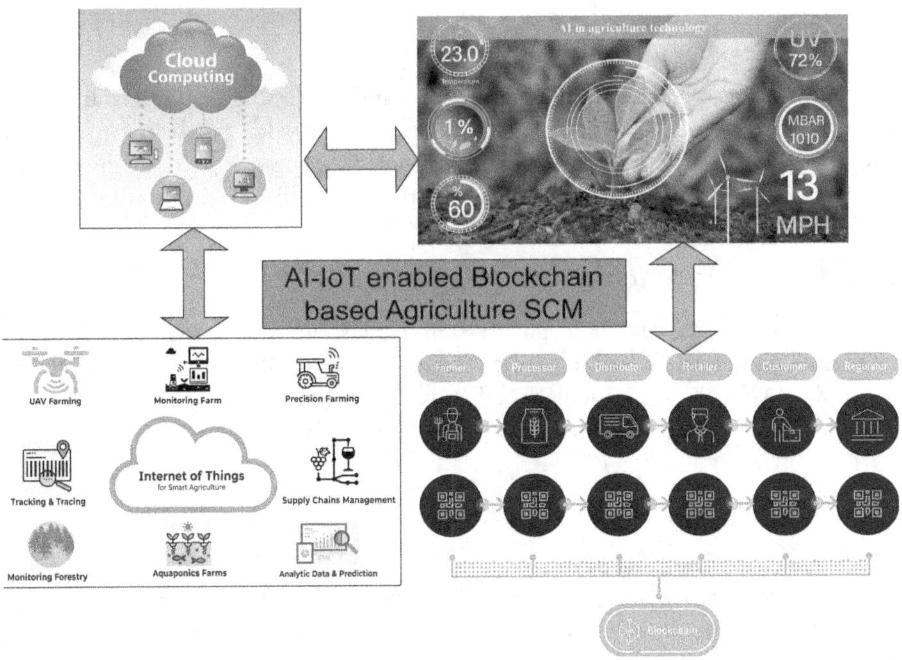

Figure 8.6 AI-IoT-enabled Blockchain-based supply chain management system.

8.4.1 Step-by-Step Approach for Effective Supply Chain Management

8.4.1.1 Data Collection

Various devices are employed to gather crucial information, including the following:

- Location sensors
- Soil sensors
- Electrochemical sensors
- Dielectric sensors for soil moisture

These sensors collect real-time data on crop growth, humidity, sunlight, soil conditions, and other environmental factors that impact crop quality and development. This data is securely stored on a Blockchain network, creating a permanent and transparent record of the crop's health and progress.

8.4.1.2 Data Preparation

Raw data from IoT sensors often contains noise or missing values. To ensure accuracy, the data is cleaned and pre-processed using machine learning techniques before analysis.

8.4.1.3 Insurance Claims Automation

Smart contracts can automate the verification and processing of farmers' insurance claims. For example, if meteorological data or crop yields fall below predefined thresholds, the smart contract triggers an automatic insurance payout. This reduces fraud and accelerates claim settlements by verifying conditions on the Blockchain.

8.4.1.4 Training Machine Learning Models

Machine learning models such as regression, time series forecasting, and clustering are trained on historical data to predict future demands and trends. Artificial Neural Networks (ANNs) are particularly effective in modelling complex relationships, such as estimating soil moisture from various input parameters.

8.4.1.5 Smart Contracts with RFID Integration

Smart contracts streamline payment and settlement by automatically releasing funds to farmers once crops are delivered and verified. Every transaction is immutably recorded on the Blockchain, enabling end-to-end traceability, preventing fraud, and ensuring product authenticity and regulatory compliance.

8.4.1.6 Quality Monitoring

IoT sensors track the quantity and freshness of agricultural products during storage and transportation. Storing this data on the Blockchain assures all stakeholders of the product's quality and reliability throughout the supply chain.

8.4.1.7 Supply Chain Coordination

Smart contracts integrate with the supply chain system to automate order processing, inventory management, and delivery scheduling. This reduces intermediary reliance, improves operational efficiency, and ensures compliance with food safety and environmental regulations by securely storing critical data on the Blockchain.

8.5 Future Research Work

When there aren't information security and privacy, stakeholders like farms worry that information will get leaked when it's sent to other external systems, which hurts the accuracy of the process. An open system would also mean that people in the agri-supply chain don't want to share their information with competitors. For Blockchain-based farming, different data security and privacy methods have been used, such as ring signatures. However, there are no ways to hide the transaction data, which includes the source and recipient's names and the amount of the transaction. In IoT and Blockchain-based agriculture, this means that information security and control are very important. Future research should focus on how to hide the knowledge about transactions involving more than one party in both hypothetical testing and real-world situations. It's also important to look at what governments can do to support these new technological advances. Also, it's important to look at how users act to improve information security and figure out how to get people to share information more freely in Blockchain-based agriculture. Both IoT and Blockchain-based agri-sector research have problems with scalability. The Blockchain-based farm supply chain doesn't look into the important issues of latency and scalability enough. For sustainability reasons, both science and business have already looked into how different technologies, like IoT and AI, can work together in the Blockchain. Then, the results of the studies can be used to help the agriculture business grow sustainably.

Concerns have been raised by farmers about the risk of losing money they have invested in these new tools. The "theory of inventive problem-solving" should be used in the future to come up with solutions that cut costs. Political scientists need to study how to effectively push lawmakers to create the right policies to support technological progress. High carbon dioxide emissions and energy use are the main problems that go against the goal of a sustainable world. To find and support eco-friendly and green technologies, more research needs to be done on comparing the growth of the agri-sector based on different IoT and Blockchain applications. The main problem with rules and guidelines that everyone can follow is that there aren't any uniform standards. These standards make the market more stable by controlling how people act, which increases public trust and the use of new technologies. Policies and standards in the agriculture sector can be looked into in the future. However, putting the same standards into action depends on many people in the supply chain who control the growth of hardware, software, equipment, and systems. To set standards at different points in the supply chain, future studies need to look at the roles and duties of the government. Researchers should look into how managers combine resources, make sure they work together, handle conflicts, and come up with more ways to make these tools have a bigger effect on the agricultural sector.

8.6 Conclusion

Our study offers a comprehensive overview of AI-, IoT-, and Blockchain-based platforms for agricultural supply chains, emphasising the vital role of automation. We detail the use of Blockchain (including Bitcoin), AI in agriculture, and supply chain systems. To implement the proposed framework, IoT infrastructure must minimise memory, power, bandwidth, and computing needs, addressing device limitations and security challenges. Given the many stakeholders involved, a trustworthy, Blockchain-based cross-chain SCM system is essential. This smart, secure platform should be user-friendly, resource-efficient, interoperable, easy to deploy, and reliable without human intervention. Our literature review not only shows rapid growth in Blockchain, AI, and IoT in agriculture but also highlights significant challenges and research gaps. Blockchain can transform food and farm supply chains by enabling secure, transparent tracking, building trust, reducing fraud, and improving efficiency. Smart contracts and distributed ledgers allow real-time monitoring and immutable recordkeeping accessible to all stakeholders. Our farming case study demonstrates how integrating AI and Blockchain benefits buyers, sellers, and others by creating safer, more efficient ecosystems. We also plan to develop a mobile app to support practical adoption. We hope this work advances understanding of smart supply chain management and inspires further research and real-world applications of these technologies.

Chapter 9

Next-Gen Connectivity for the Metaverse: Network Slicing and Multi-Access Edge Computing

9.1 Introduction

The integration of the physical and digital realms through the Metaverse has become one of the most revolutionary technological phenomena of the 21st century [1, 36, 37]. The Metaverse is conceived as an expansive, linked, and immersive virtual realm that surpasses conventional definitions of cyberspace by facilitating real-time, interactive encounters across social, economic, and industrial sectors. The Metaverse presents limitless prospects for innovation and expansion, encompassing Virtual Reality (VR) games, Augmented Reality (AR) applications, Digital Twin cities, and virtual workspaces. The establishment of a fully functional and scalable Metaverse requires sophisticated communication infrastructures that provide ultra-low-latency, high-bandwidth, and uninterrupted connectivity [2, 38]. Network slicing and Multi-Access Edge Computing (MEC) are necessary for solving the Metaverse's complex technical difficulties. Network slicing, enabled by 5G technology, lets operators create many virtual networks on a single physical infrastructure with different performance criteria. This is especially crucial for the Metaverse, where a singular infrastructure must accommodate a wide array of services, ranging from high-speed data streaming for entertainment to mission-critical applications like remote operations and autonomous vehicles. Every application

DOI: 10.1201/9781003520702-9

possesses distinct latency, reliability, and bandwidth requirements, and network slicing offers the adaptability to simultaneously meet these varied demands [3, 39].

Concurrently, MEC enhances cloud computing accessibility for the end user by decentralising computational resources to the network periphery. This minimises the distance data must traverse, leading to markedly reduced latency and expedited reaction times. In the Metaverse, where real-time interaction is essential for user experience, MEC facilitates data processing in proximity to people, hence enabling seamless and immersive encounters in virtual environments. MEC facilitates extensive data processing necessary for applications like virtual reality, augmented reality, and real-time simulation, hence alleviating the burden on central cloud data centres [4, 40].

The amalgamation of network slicing and MEC within the Metaverse tackles several critical issues in actualising this digital frontier. These technologies facilitate uninterrupted connectivity and immediate responsiveness while also being crucial for optimising resource allocation, improving security, and minimising operational expenses. The dynamic and developing characteristics of the Metaverse necessitate adaptable, scalable, and secure network designs, with network slicing and MEC leading the way in fulfilling these requirements [5, 41, 42].

This study examines the architectural frameworks, applications, and problems associated with the integration of network slicing and MEC inside the Metaverse. The discussion initiates with an exploration of the fundamental principles underlying network slicing and MEC, thereafter analysing their contributions to the development of Metaverse infrastructure. The study further explores practical applications of these technologies in several Metaverse settings, emphasising significant use cases across various industries. The talk ultimately focuses on the essential technological and legislative difficulties that must be surmounted to realise the complete potential of network slicing and MEC within the Metaverse [6, 43, 44].

This study seeks to elucidate how network slicing and MEC facilitate the next development of the internet and establish the technological groundwork for the Metaverse, placing these technologies as crucial catalysts for future digital ecosystems.

9.2 Background Work

Background information regarding the Metaverse, network slicing, and edge computing is presented in this article.

9.2.1 Edge Computing

Edge computing is a distributed computing paradigm that brings computation and data storage closer to the location where it is needed, rather than relying on a centralised cloud-based data centre [7, 45]. This approach addresses various challenges associated with traditional cloud computing, particularly in scenarios where low latency, real-time processing, and bandwidth efficiency are critical. Some of the background work of edge computing are as follows:

- **Data Proximity**: Edge computing minimises the distance data must travel between devices and processing units. By processing data closer to the source, it reduces latency, which is essential for applications like autonomous vehicles, smart cities, and real-time analytics [8, 46].
- **Decentralisation**: Traditional cloud architectures centralise resources, which can lead to bottlenecks. Edge computing decentralises processing by distributing workloads across numerous edge nodes, such as routers, gateways, and local servers [47].
- **Improved Bandwidth Utilisation**: With the rise of IoT devices generating vast amounts of data, sending all that data to the cloud can overwhelm bandwidth. Edge computing allows for local processing and filtering of data, transmitting only relevant information to the cloud, thus conserving bandwidth [48].
- **Real-Time Analytics**: Many applications require real-time data analysis to function effectively. Edge computing enables immediate processing of data as it is generated, which is critical for applications like video surveillance, industrial automation, and healthcare monitoring [49].
- **Reliability and Resilience**: Edge computing can improve system reliability by enabling local processing even when cloud connectivity is lost. This is particularly important for critical applications in sectors like healthcare and manufacturing [50].
- **Scalability**: Edge computing supports scalable architectures by allowing additional edge nodes to be added easily as demand grows, thus accommodating an increasing number of connected devices without overwhelming central resources [9, 51, 52].

9.2.2 Network Slicing

Network slicing is a technology that allows multiple virtual networks to be created on a shared physical infrastructure. This approach is particularly relevant in 5G networks, where it enables the customisation of network resources for different applications or services, ensuring optimised performance and efficiency [10, 53, 54]. The major use case is *IoT applications*. Some of the key features of network slicing are as follows:

- **Isolation**: Each network slice operates independently, providing isolation between different services. This ensures that performance issues or security breaches in one slice do not affect others [55].
- **Customisation**: Slices can be tailored to meet specific requirements, such as bandwidth, latency, and reliability, making it suitable for diverse use cases like IoT, augmented reality, or mission-critical applications [56].

- **Resource Efficiency**: By sharing physical infrastructure while providing dedicated resources for each slice, network slicing optimises resource utilisation and reduces operational costs [57].
- **Dynamic Management**: Network slices can be dynamically created, modified, or terminated based on demand, allowing for real-time adjustments to network resources [58, 59].
- **Enhanced User Experience**: Different slices can prioritise traffic based on user needs, improving overall service quality and user satisfaction [11, 60].

In essence, network slicing enhances flexibility and efficiency in network management, making it a cornerstone of next-generation telecommunications.

9.2.3 Metaverse

The Metaverse is a collective virtual space created by the convergence of virtually enhanced physical reality and physically persistent virtual reality. It encompasses immersive digital environments where users can interact, socialise, and participate in various activities, often through avatars. The concept has gained popularity as a vision for the future of the internet, combining elements of Virtual Reality (VR), Augmented Reality (AR), and social interactions. Some of the key technologies used in Metaverse are as follows:

- **AI**: AI plays a key role in the Metaverse by enhancing user experiences and interactions. It powers intelligent avatars that can mimic human behaviours and emotions, making virtual interactions more lifelike. AI also facilitates content creation, enabling dynamic environments and personalised experiences tailored to individual preferences. Additionally, it can analyse user data to improve recommendations and optimise gameplay or social interactions. AI-driven algorithms help in moderating content and ensuring safety within virtual spaces [12, 61, 62].
- **Blockchain**: Blockchain plays a vital role in the Metaverse by enabling decentralised ownership of digital assets, such as NFTs and virtual real estate. It ensures secure transactions through smart contracts, allowing users to automate agreements. Additionally, Blockchain enhances identity verification, fostering trust among users. Its interoperability facilitates asset movement between different virtual environments, while enabling the creation of virtual economies with digital currencies [13, 63, 64].
- **Computer Vision**: Computer vision is essential in the Metaverse as it enables real-time interaction between the digital and physical worlds. It allows for facial recognition and motion tracking, enhancing avatars' realism and responsiveness. Through spatial mapping, computer vision helps create immersive environments by accurately rendering objects and scenes. Additionally, it

supports Augmented Reality (AR) experiences, blending digital content with the physical environment [31, 65–67].

- **Networking**: Networking is essential in the Metaverse to ensure seamless, real-time interactions and immersive experiences. High bandwidth supports 3D content and video streams, while low latency enables responsive virtual environments, critical for gaming and augmented reality. Multi-Access Edge Computing (MEC) brings processing closer to users, reducing delays, and network slicing provides dedicated virtual networks optimised for specific applications. Reliable and scalable networks are needed to accommodate millions of concurrent users, and interoperability ensures smooth connectivity across platforms and devices, creating a unified and persistent Metaverse experience [14, 68, 69].
- **Edge Computing**: Edge computing plays a crucial role in the Metaverse by processing data closer to the source, reducing latency and enhancing real-time interactions. This is vital for applications like Virtual Reality (VR) and Augmented Reality (AR), where low latency is essential for a smooth user experience. By offloading data processing from centralised cloud servers to local devices, edge computing improves responsiveness and can handle the high volume of data generated in immersive environments. Additionally, it enhances privacy and security by keeping sensitive data closer to the user [32, 70].
- **Extended Reality (XR)**: It refers to computing technologies such as augmented, virtual, and mixed reality. Future XR and Metaverse predictions include an interactive data transfer collaboration in education and business [71].
- **Internet of Things and Robotics**: 5G and B5G networks enable significant IoT and robotics connections. Data from the physical world can be sent to the Metaverse by the Internet of Things (IoT). Robotics are essential for automating Metaverse-connected real-world operations [35, 72].
- **AR/VR**: In virtual reality, people stay in a digital environment and do not interact with the physical world. Augmented Reality (AR) adds computer-generated interactive elements to the real world. Both solutions provide device-based Metaverse access with high QoE. Advancements in the Metaverse create new use cases. There are several use scenarios in the following [73].
- **Gaming**: Regularly published interactive games have a growing audience. Metaverse immersion enhances experience sophisticatedly [15, 74].
- **Immersive Commerce**: Virtual reality-based shopping in virtual real estate presents promising Metaverse applications.

Remote schooling enables interactive classroom instruction and simulation-based learning. Additional skill-oriented self-education is possible. Standards are lacking since the Metaverse is new and poorly integrated into existing ecosystems [33, 75]. To hasten acceptance and the creation of open standards, the Metaverse Standards Forum collaborates with numerous businesses that have invested in the Metaverse and associated services [16]. Because of the sophisticated features and delicate user interaction, rules and laws must be developed to avoid unlawful and unfair use. There are three types of Metaverse systems: closed, hybrid, and open. A synopsis of each format is as follows.

- **Open Metaverse:** A decentralised, community environment for consumers and service providers. A distributed solution reduces censorship and distributes ownership to increase variation [17]. Internal architecture, code, and network components must be open source, and data flows must be transparent on this platform. Users and service providers can generate content and perform related actions in accordance with the code of ethics. The Metaverse should have more functionality and enabling technology than present networks [34]. The open Metaverse paradigm may allow users to develop services, create content, and access the network without restrictions. These features may improve deployment, but the regulatory framework must be adopted across all levels, service functions, and openness to promote network sustainability [18].
- **Closed Metaverse:** A closed Metaverse is centralised and has more limited functionality than an open Metaverse. Only a few stakeholders own the virtual platform, while users own little. Users can only access the platform's unique architecture, code, and core components for application-level output. The closed Metaverse owners set limits and limitations for content development and user activities [31, 35].
- **Hybrid Metaverse:** This model has elements from both the open and closed Metaverse. Certain characteristics proposed for the open Metaverse are rather idealistic for practical implementation. User access to the Metaverse requires monitoring or proper governance. Ownership may be allocated among the community; however, few central authorities are associated with that group, necessitating regulation for decision-making. Maintaining this platform incurs significant expenses, particularly for optimisation, partnerships, network infrastructure, and various other factors. A closed Metaverse can effectively manage resources and infrastructure due to concentrated ownership among a limited number of stakeholders. Nonetheless, in an open Metaverse, the absence of a designated governing authority or accountable entity complicates this job. It is imperative to delineate the framework and regulatory entities for an open Metaverse [9].

9.3 Applications of the Metaverse throughout Several Industries

As mentioned, the Metaverse is vast. Everything from education to gaming to tourism to healthcare is watched for Metaverse applications. Over 40% of AR/VR trends are based on the Metaverse framework. Here are some basic Metaverse instances and applications from various fields.

Playing Video Games: The game industry invests heavily on Metaverse technology. Players can communicate inside a single, compatible area thanks to this technology. Three popular online games in the Metaverse include Sandbox, Sorare, and Axie Infinity. Approximately 3 million people use Axie Infinity every month, and 350,000 use it every day. Additionally, Metaverse games have features that improve the player experience. Some examples are as follows:

- A connected social ecosystem for all users [32]. Metaverse games differ from VR games.
- Metaverse games offer play-to-earn Bitcoin, enhancing economic conditions.
- Metaverse architecture supports in-game NFT assets for permanent ownership.
- Metaverse provides a hybrid reality experience, allowing users to smoothly switch between virtual communication modes.

Travel and Tourism: Virtual tourism is a cutting-edge Metaverse application. The technology allows virtual globe travel, which benefits people who cannot travel far. Experts say the Metaverse's immersive augmented and virtual reality experiences are the travel industry's biggest advancement. The 360-degree virtual tour lets you see the recorded location and immerse yourself in it with realistic effects. Thomas Cook's Virtual Reality Holiday "Try before you Fly," lets prospective tourists virtually visit their chosen destinations [20].

Pedagogy and Cognition: The Metaverse has fascinating capabilities for education and learning. VR and Metaverse impacts have improved learning. Live experiments and better educational tools are now available to students. A recent video from New York showcases pupils studying astronomy in a virtual spaceship instead of a traditional classroom. This marks the commencement of a novel educational epoch. Metaverse eliminates language barriers, allowing students from different countries to learn in a single digital environment without social or linguistic barriers. Microsoft Mesh, a mixed reality technology, lets professors, staff, and students engage via 3D avatars. Microsoft Hololens, a wearable AI, can use Mesh for video conferencing and live meetings [33].

Telecommuting: Traditional business models have changed due to the Metaverse. The Metaverse virtual business structure houses several companies. Nike, Intel, YouTube, McDonald's, Gravity Sketch, and Upland are virtual office companies. A further application of the Metaverse in remote work is VR training, when employees undergo instruction through a virtual experience [34]. Virtual reality training is a principal advantage of the Metaverse, integrating corporate training with experiential learning, providing the workforce access to movies, manuals, audio materials, and diverse digital environments. Training, remote work in virtual environments, VR workforce communication and collaboration, and 3D avatar-based remote meetings are among the most common digital workspace trends [21].

Property Market: A fundamental characteristic of the Metaverse is its capacity to provide users with an unparalleled virtual reality experience. The real estate industry segment within the Metaverse might undoubtedly be lucrative. Metaverse property tour features eliminate the necessity for realtors to visit the site and allow clients to avoid the time-consuming process of travelling to multiple properties. A Metaverse real estate tour lets buyers see all possible options in real time. The Metaverse virtual tour can also be modified to the client's scale, preferences, and design aesthetic. The real estate market is anticipating investments in Metaverse application development tailored to the specific demands and requirements of realtors [35].

Medical Care: The Metaverse presents applications in healthcare, facilitating the delivery of treatments at reduced costs while enhancing outcomes. The Metaverse drives post-pandemic telemedicine and telehealth, enabling patient-doctor interactions in virtual 3D clinics. Therapy uses Metaverse technology to immerse patients in a relaxing digital world to reduce stress. Recent Metaverse applications incorporate virtual exercises and workouts to encourage users' well-being. Another example is Digital Twin technology, which is made possible by the Metaverse and enables the digital depiction of a patient for the purpose of assessing drugs and treatments [22].

Banking and Finance: The Metaverse drives post-pandemic telemedicine and telehealth, enabling patient-doctor interactions in virtual 3D clinics. Therapy uses Metaverse technology to immerse patients in a relaxing digital world to reduce stress. Access to Metaverse banking is available via your laptop or mobile device, even in the absence of a VR headset. The Metaverse represents a significant benefit for banking in terms of Blockchain, NFT marketplace development, and other DeFi cryptocurrency assets. Experts assert that Metaverse banking surpasses online banking by offering users identical services with enhanced personalisation and data visualisation.

Social Media and Entertainment: Longstanding concept of the Metaverse for social media has changed online entertainment for viewers. Digital avatars and replicas are used for communication. Facebook's rebranding as Meta suggests promising digital media opportunities. Metaverse applications are also used in sportswear, fashion, eCommerce, and the sports business, and they are expected to spread into Manufacturing IoT and supply chain soon.

9.4 A Comprehensive Framework for Network Slicing and Edge Computing-Enabled Metaverse

In this section, we create the foundation for the Metaverse using network slicing and edge computing. To actualise the Metaverse and integrate Metaverse apps into a functional network, an appropriate framework is required. The richness of the Metaverse necessitates unique network properties. As mentioned, the Metaverse cannot be realised using Long Term Evolution Advanced (LTE-A), previous network specifications, or QoE. Applications specific to the Metaverse can be deployed on 5G and B5G networks. The mobile network's core network layer, aggregation layer, and access layer must all adhere to network and quality of service requirements. Edge management is defined at the host and system levels via the ETSI MEC framework [23]. The host provides virtualisation infrastructure and application capabilities. MEC system abstraction and third-party access are managed at the system level. Edge service orchestration events concentrate on application lifecycle management and start-up and shutdown [2]. Figure 9.1 shows that network slicing and edge computing have lifecycles. Service deployment and Metaverse application QoS issues can be avoided by synchronising the steps. The suggested approach makes use of a resource manager to internally synchronise the requirements of Metaverse applications with edge computing and network slicing life cycle stages. Life cycle event management automation and programmability must be examined in this framework. End-to-end operations need to be automated in order to meet the QoS and network requirements of numerous Metaverse and

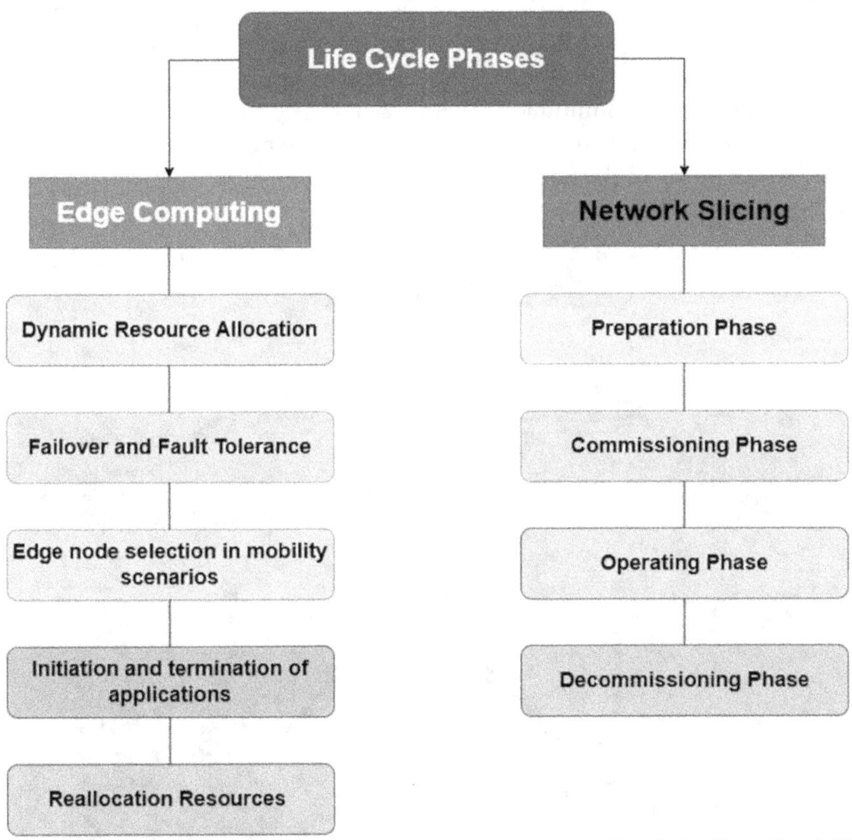

Figure 9.1 Life cycle synchronisation in between edge computing and network slicing.

non-Metaverse services on a commercial network. Network resources, the length of resource allocation, service migrations, and operational functionality all require optimisation [24].

Metaverse privacy problems are resolved by network slicing. Metaverse application slices can be customised with many security levels and policies. Core and radio access are the two primary kinds of a network slice [3]. In the network slicing design, the slice manager oversees and pairs the slices, while the slice pairing function pairs them. Metaverse implementation must address network ownership and orchestration goals. Infrastructure can also exchange resources between operators. Since application providers may install edge devices like cache servers, edge network deployment must be considered.

For bidirectional communication to be possible, a core network slice needs to work with a lot of radio network slices. All network slices are connected to on-premises or cloud-based application servers in order to support their services and data transmission.

Figure 9.2 illustrates this suggested structure. Metaverse applications are made possible via network slicing and edge computing. Slice up the physical network to accommodate both Metaverse and non-Metaverse applications by virtualising it. Metaverse slices can communicate with each other and non-Metaverse slices. An access device lets users use Metaverse programs like medicine, sports, and transportation, according to the framework.

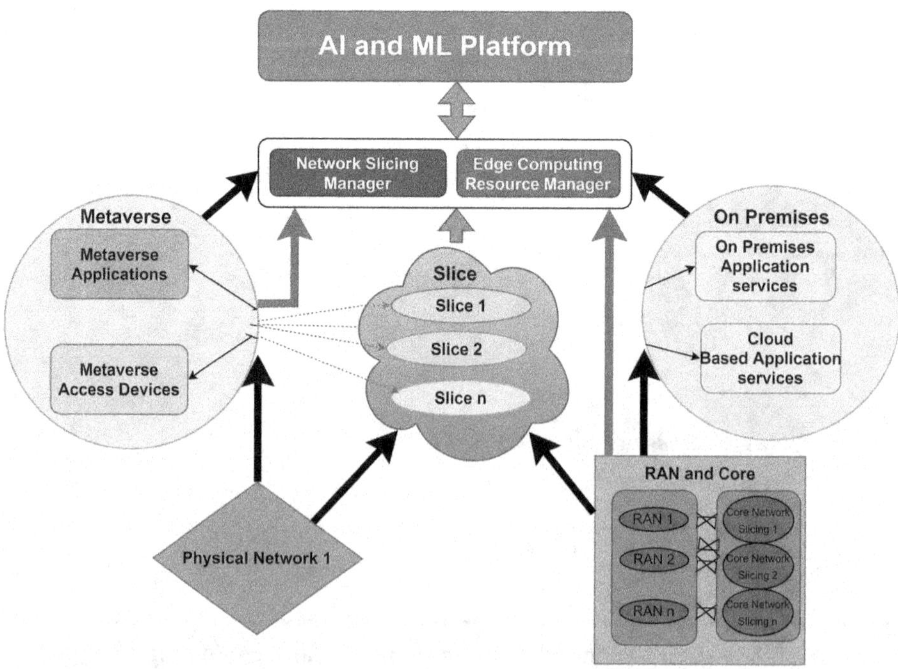

Figure 9.2 Simple Metaverse realisation network.

An edge computing resource manager controls edge computing resources in response to modifications made by the networking slicing manager, while the slicing manager oversees the upkeep of slice management. Based on previous data, an AI and ML platform coupled with resource management predicts future changes like user surges and emergencies. The resource management and the AI and ML platform should be integrated since slicing and edge computing are intricate and dynamic fields that require forecasting and analysis of resource allocation. This platform may predict Metaverse network behaviour using strong optimised algorithms and predictive methodologies. It can also feed Metaverse application user behaviour data to AI and ML platforms for better results. For services and data transmission, this topology connects all network slices to on-site or cloud-based application servers [25]. This approach emphasises end-to-end slice isolation because of data flows between the core and access slices. To maintain network resource thresholds, preconfigure network slice settings with various values. This framework may face many challenges, which are listed in the following.

- Greenfield development, network operator interconnection.
- Integration with already-existing networks under the same operator.
- Framework optimisation and vulnerabilities.

9.5 Deployment Obstacles

The implementation of the Metaverse is a multifaceted endeavour due to its numerous areas and features. This discussion addresses several deployment problems associated with Metaverse implementation, namely focusing on network slicing and edge computing methodologies [26]. As previously indicated, numerous methods can be executed utilising edge computing and network slicing. Nonetheless, numerous obstacles remain to be addressed in real implementations.

9.5.1 Network Slicing

Network slice communication can be divided into two categories: intra-slice communication and inter-slice communication. Due to slice configurations for different services, interslice communication is much harder than intraslice communication. It might be necessary for a single Metaverse application slice to interact with multiple Metaverse and non-Metaverse slices in the same or different regions. For example, a health application segment provides the personal health data required for a Metaverse application. Inter-slice Metaverse interaction. interactivity with the health application network slice. For example, a user of one Metaverse gaming application may purchase or rent clothing from another Metaverse application located on a separate network slice. Two slices share a virtual resource or service, and a financial transaction takes place between them. To have the optimum experience, the slices must interact multiple times. A mathematical model for 5G inter-slice communication that incorporates network slice security is presented [6]. For inter-slice communication events, article [7] provides network slicing activities as well as a queuing and graph theory-based solution. Application slices for the Metaverse must communicate with other Metaverse or non-Metaverse slices in a comparable way. Depending on the number of contacts, more resources need to be assigned when network slices exchange data. It is necessary to allow inter-slice communication while maintaining SLAs and QoS within a slice. Malware distribution and DoS attacks can stem from poor inter-slice communication [8]. The provider must validate the requester before communicating via a virtual secure link between slices. Access control lists can also improve security.

9.5.2 Cross-Domain Slice Extension

The Cross-Domain Slice Extension acknowledges that not every internet-based application is accessible everywhere in the globe. Nonetheless, it is feasible to augment or diminish according to the requirements and the availability of network infrastructure. Likewise, Metaverse apps must be able to disseminate services over the anticipated locations utilising feasible networking methodologies. When access devices become available and the apps are deployed appropriately, the user base of Metaverse applications could grow considerably. It is crucial to evaluate the capacity for expansion across all users within a constrained timeframe. Some network providers employ cutting-edge technologies, but others remain outdated. Creating a slice expansion framework for expected geographies is difficult. The possibility of extending a global slice under service extension must be assessed. The extension of this service slice needs consideration of ownership distribution, global slice management, continuity across numerous operators, slice characteristics, and end-to-end service architecture. The low requirements on a mobile network make public cloud networks practical.

9.5.3 Global Charging Model

All Metaverse ecosystem stakeholders must evaluate and price services. Network service providers and application and content providers are the two primary providers of Metaverse services. Network service providers provide network slices for the installation of Metaverse applications [20]. The process of slice creation and the provision of on-demand resources, along with service quality, network value enhancements such as optimisation systems, regulatory frameworks, governmental taxes, vendor types, and various other factors can result in varying charges for Metaverse applications across different operators and regions. Metaverse users must pay for their services. The payment options include monthly membership, pay-as-you-go, or other invoicing methods. The following fee situations are summarised in the following.

- **Scenario 1**: Billing service providers and network operators separately for Metaverse-related services and infrastructure. Since users pay separately for services, this technique reduces the operator's Metaverse application requirement. Operators can supply services based on usage and QoS.
- **Scenario 2**: Only the Metaverse service providers are subject to fees from the network operator, which pays them based on overall usage. This approach gives the operator more control over network services and Metaverse apps. Charging must be delineated by taking into account the user's individual status regarding inbound and outgoing roamers. Network slices may have capacity and resource constraints. Network slices may need to be created based on demand, contingent upon the user count and the resource requirements of the serving user. The user's subscription must be charged for this. Prepaid, postpaid, and pay-as-you-go subscriptions are available from operators [27].

9.5.4 Various Privacy Requirements

The Metaverse must comply with local laws and regulations while providing services to users. The content and certain services within the Metaverse application can be filtered in accordance with regional restrictions. Consequently, Metaverse users can only access permitted user content within a certain application. Network slicing is crucial as certain applications and services are implemented in accordance with regional legislation. Other content and services may need limited access. An effective system must pre-identify relevant content to restrict or filter. According to regional regulatory authority directives, content restriction should be possible. A Metaverse app's virtual world material violates national privacy laws [28]. The regulatory authority requests application content limitation or removal. Terminate deployed network slices or restrict their content by changing service slice properties.

9.5.5 Dynamic Slice Deployment

With network slicing, which allows network slices to be created and terminated on demand, several applications can host Metaverse services globally. As demonstrated in the following, different actions rely on the deployment and termination times of network slices.

- Because Metaverse apps are immersive and have complicated features, users are more sensitive to delay. The application's minimal delay standards must be met.
- Operating costs are impacted by delays in slice generation and termination. In order to save costs and satisfy user and application requirements, large-scale deployments must optimise slice deployment time.

9.5.6 Edge Computing

9.5.6.1 Aggregated Bandwidth

For instance, envision a situation in which extensive background synchronisation and data transfers occur on every internet-connected device to maintain the pertinent programs. Likewise, augmented bandwidth is necessary for Metaverse applications due to the frequent synchronisation of devices and background processes. A single Metaverse application can interact with several Metaverse and non-Metaverse applications. Thus, this connection may require bandwidth beyond the application's needs. This must be handled while implementing edge network entities [29]. Metaverse application, network bandwidth, and transport backbone network configuration are also needed. It is essential to identify the activities necessitating more bandwidth and the potential methods to mitigate that excess bandwidth.

- **Data Compression Methodologies**: Substantial bandwidth savings can be anticipated through enhancements in picture and video compression techniques. However, additional aspects, such as delay influenced by compression, must be considered. Latency varies with the type of compression for a specified bandwidth [13].
- **Data Synchronisation and Optimisation**: Data synchronisation uses updates, configuration modifications, and data exchange to synchronise data with Metaverse apps and services as well as the current application. Set this as the top priority so that the total bandwidth is restricted and user-prioritised programs can be supported in a user-configurable preference option that they can adjust as needed. It should show application priority and user impact. Devices and edge nodes can do this before forwarding traffic to the transmission network, which connects the edge node to the core network. Application bandwidths for Metaverse and non-Metaverse must be taken into account for optimisation.

9.5.6.2 Metaverse Service Assurances Caused Congestion on Priority Access Channels

Although resources are limited, it is possible to distribute edge resources for every service channel. Building a large-scale data centre infrastructure for resource allocation at the periphery is not viable due to the numerous nodes in a given area. Most operators and service providers struggle to appropriately size the network to accommodate future demand. Designing edge networks for Metaverse applications presents similar challenges. Due to their high bandwidth requirements, Metaverse apps might congest other application channels in instances of elevated utilisation. Traffic patterns may fluctuate due to several conditions, including emergencies, particular events, and ongoing subscriber growth. It is challenging to forecast patterns in subscriber growth, particularly in light of Metaverse apps and anticipated service network needs [30]. Consider a famous global event where people can freely use a Metaverse application. New and existing app users may desire to participate in the event within a particular window. The application may need more network slices from available resources owing to increased traffic. Congestion may result, lowering the amount of resources available for usage by other programs. Adaptive resource distribution based on traffic projections can be beneficial.

To reduce 5G network congestion, [7] highlights clever video acceleration technologies with edge servers. This strategy works for video and other data kinds in Metaverse applications. Predictive congestion techniques must be used alongside congestion avoidance measures. Machine learning-based traffic pattern detection helps identify temporal traffic fluctuations caused by events and trends. Machine learning is used to determine mobile traffic trends in a metropolitan area [4]. Analogous techniques can be applied to data analytics to forecast traffic changes based on external causes and situations with high traffic. User or virtual machine transfer to a less busy node is another option. Mobile edge computing-based virtual machine migration [14] improves application quality of service. This can be added to the success prediction. Service Level Agreements are provided for Metaverse and non-Metaverse apps on the edge network. This classification allows a worst-case resource allocation strategy that prioritises apps.

9.5.6.3 Dual Autonomy

Manual operations are complicated by the Metaverse's dynamic nature. Automate edge platform and Metaverse operations to improve performance. Self-sustaining ecosystems and network services are difficult to deploy. Robotic automation, machine learning, and AI may enable this autonomy without human involvement. Automation should cover resource allocation, application operation, regulation, protection, and transactions. Bots can use computer vision to understand visual spatial features and interactions [12]. Edge computing nodes and the Metaverse engine's AI-analytic platforms examine every function and procedure for automation. Bots and other processes can receive automation choices via the Metaverse platform. Automation is increased by integrating these AI platforms with the edge platform, Metaverse administration, and orchestration.

9.6 Interconnection between Metaverse and Edge Computing Virtualisation

Define the Metaverse's virtual entities' communication with edge computing. Although the architectures may differ, intercommunication must occur inside a unified operational architectural framework. The majority of network virtualisation standards utilised for edge computing virtualisation have already been established. Common standards and models for the Metaverse are currently under development. Meta has created a closed Metaverse to exist within the open Metaverse. Creating an end-to-end service provider network is difficult due to their deployment architecture [20]. An edge-enabled Metaverse requires a sophisticated model for communication with the Metaverse engine and infrastructure, not only application-level connection.

9.6.1 Sophisticated Orchestration

In contrast to the internet, ownership is more widely spread among users of the Metaverse. Despite the Metaverse being decentralised in terms of infrastructure and ownership, it requires sophisticated orchestration for effective management. It is essential to explicitly identify the provider of regulating directives and the organisation within the edge network that collaborates with those directives. The absence of a defined ownership structure complicates the identification of the Metaverse's ruling body. Standardising all Metaverse functions is crucial first. All service providers, including access devices, will be able to comply with standards upon standardisation. The Metaverse Standards Forum and other standardisation bodies are openly standardising, allowing any organisation to participate for free. The Metaverse functionality should operate autonomously to the highest degree, as previously described. The fundamental features of the Metaverse must be explicitly delineated, applicable across all ecosystems within the Metaverse. Furthermore, regulations and policies should be established according to specific countries or regions. Multi-country areas may have various network operators and their networks. The policy and regulatory manager for each area controls the region's countries and works with the senior manager. Initial automated laws and functions can include region-specific policies and functions. The regulatory authorities of the nations responsible for governance can define regional policies and functionality [23]. A designated technical committee can conduct a manual assessment of the automated manager's functionality. Contingent upon success, it may be permitted to operate entirely automated, with the option to implement manual modifications as necessary. Ultimately, it synchronises all locations and automates extensively to ensure service continuity.

9.6.2 Standard for Explainable Artificial Intelligence

AI may aid Metaverse application creation and execution. Edge intelligence applies to infrastructure and applications. Edge infrastructure can optimise communication, computing, networking, and storage resources and processes using AI [6]. Object creation, deletion, policy enforcement, content filtering, edge caching, and user identification for numerous virtual users are all requirements for a large-scale system. Artificial intelligence is the ideal solution for automating such performance, as previously discussed. Models of Explainable Artificial Intelligence (XAI) can be understood by humans. This is used by several functions to enhance user experience and results [3]. XAI clarifies, supposing the user believes the suggestions or conclusions. The explanation is contingent upon the task, expectations, and capabilities of the user [4]. The goal of every Metaverse application is to offer a more authentic experience.

XAI outputs increase transparency and user authenticity. Metaverse realisation through slicing and edge-based approaches concentrates intelligence at the edge, making Explainable Artificial Intelligence (XAI) techniques easier to apply. XAI standards are being developed by IEEE to assure system interoperability [15]. Varied applications use Metaverse implementations with varied specificities and sophistication. All deployments must follow one standard. For a particular application user, avatar management, including all avatar-related issues, should be consistent regardless of location, service provider, or other limitations. After standardisation, apps, devices, operators, and others can improve processes with accessible interfaces.

9.7 Conclusion

The Metaverse is emerging as the next trend in the technology sector due to its significant potential to deliver improved services to customers. Numerous technology firms are currently concentrating on and developing Metaverse implementations while tackling the issues of Metaverse adaptability. The realisation process may accelerate because to advancements in Metaverse access technology and rapid developments in telecommunications. As prospective telecommunications technologies for Metaverse implementation, edge computing and network slicing are thoroughly examined in this study. We first studied the Metaverse, its ecology, and its components, as well as relevant literature. Next, we outlined the key components of the Metaverse, network slicing, and edge computing. In addition, we designed an architecture for network slicing and edge computing and examined high-level execution. We also examined potential applications of edge computing and network slicing in the Metaverse. We looked at how network slicing and edge computing can address the technical needs for a Metaverse. After that, we looked into the problems and solutions related to the implementation of edge computing and network slicing. In order to support further research, we have finally emphasised the findings and prospective study directions. This research will improve Metaverse research and applications.

Chapter 10

Metaverse Health Revolution: Unlocking the Secrets of Ageing

10.1 Introduction

The typical physiological activities of living organisms progressively diminish with age, frequently governed by epigenetic mechanisms that affect the initiation and advancement of age-associated disorders [1, 39]. The change of the epigenetic system has propelled scientific progress and resulted in several anti-ageing medicinal treatments. Most anti-ageing pharmaceuticals address menopausal and ropausal symptoms, which are persistent hormonal alterations, rendering them challenging to manage. This underscores the necessity for alternative therapies [3, 40]. Digital Anti-Ageing Healthcare (DAAH) encompasses many medical and psychological interventions aimed at decelerating or reversing the ageing process. Anti-ageing healthcare requires nutrition, frequent medical exams, physical activity, skincare, and stress management [4, 41]. The global population is ageing, with projections indicating that the elderly generation will surpass the younger demographic in 35 years. Robust policies that tackle the intricate dimensions of ageing and emphasise preventive measures are essential [2, 42].

By reducing age-related physical changes, conventional methods have promoted healthy ageing. These practises improve health. A balanced diet rich in water, carbohydrates, fats, proteins, vitamins, minerals, and phytochemicals that improve cellular health is one of the best ways to maintain health and promote good ageing. Assessing an individual's usual dietary consumption may necessitate

DOI: 10.1201/9781003520702-10

professional guidance. Nutrition and dietetics specialists are frequently sought for personalised guidance. Regular exercise may facilitate healthy ageing. Aerobic, resistance, and flexibility training improve mood, stress, and cardiovascular health. Smoking and alcohol abuse accelerate ageing, while sugar and processed foods cause inflammation and oxidative stress [3, 43]. Thus, regular health checks can identify abnormalities and aid treatment. Stress management, sleep, and hydration accelerate ageing. While not guaranteed to fight ageing, the previously mentioned measures are beneficial.

Anti-ageing therapies alter appearance, particularly skin condition, while skincare products primarily preserve skin hydration and diminish wrinkles, hence lessening the visual effects of chronological ageing. Advanced techniques have been established to oversee the aforementioned routines, ensuring optimal compliance and extending biological longevity. The majority of prosperous enterprises utilise digital technologies. Digital anti-ageing methods are gaining popularity because to their non-invasiveness, diversity, and efficiency. Digital anti-ageing employs technological advancements to reverse or postpone ageing and enhance healthy ageing processes. Advancing anti-ageing healthcare necessitates digital technologies [4, 44]. These technologies enable AI-driven diagnostics, personalised diagnosis and treatment, telemedicine and remote monitoring, efficient data collection, and health information accessibility [5, 45]. Digital technology allows people to track their health, progress, and receive immediate feedback.

Information technology in anti-ageing methods can empower people, promote healthy habits, and detect and cure age-related health issues. For anti-ageing healthcare, artificial intelligence, Blockchain, the Internet of Things, immersive technologies, and Digital Twins have great potential [6, 46]. The contemporary Metaverse, a medium for immersive engagement, has the potential to transform anti-ageing and foster healthy ageing [7, 47]. Digital anti-ageing healthcare employs technology to enhance patient outcomes, decrease costs, and develop personalised therapy protocols to maximise anti-ageing efficacy. Digital technologies serve as potent instruments for the surveillance and administration of health and well-being. This study examines digital technology with anti-ageing therapeutic dietary management. This study analyses how digital technology affects diet and good ageing.

The study suggests that digital technologies can regulate diets and enhance the ageing process. Introductions describe research objectives, intentions, and contributions. The second segment addresses the importance of nutrition in ageing heath. Digital anti-ageing healthcare and food monitoring and administration are discussed in the final section. The next section discusses how digital diet management affects anti-ageing healthcare after discussing technology options, user experience, and legal compliance. The study concludes with limitations, challenges, and prospective directions [8, 48].

10.2 Utilisation of the Medical and Healthcare Metaverse

1. **Telemedicine Consultations**: Virtual consultations between physicians and patients via Skype, Teams, or Facetime are not novel. The patient may have a sense of detachment from the physician when utilising this equipment. The immersive nature of VR enhances communication, diminishing the perceived distance between participants. Healthcare virtual reality prototypes like the Virtual Health Consultation program have existed for years. Article [9] used Mixed Reality (MR) software for virtual consultations and other applications to enable real-time physical-virtual interaction. The VR spatial psychological treatment service platform [10, 49, 50] lets customers design and interact with avatars while facilitators interact in virtual spaces. This software may use a Metaverse to give patients home medical advice. Virtual consultations save doctors' time and help mobility-impaired patients. They can be combined with digital technology to allow patients and doctors to evaluate a visual representation of the patient during health consultations, improving patient comprehension.
2. **Medical Training**: The Metaverse could enable healthcare practitioners to train without endangering patients through virtual training and simulation. Virtual reality surgical simulations were suggested a century ago [20, 51]. Numerous virtual reality technologies facilitate training and simulation. Surgical Theatre's Precision VR technology creates patient-specific 360-degree VR models from volumetric scans like CT and MRI that can be modified and viewed from any angle on a touchscreen monitor or VR headset with controls [21, 52]. Medical workers, including nurses and surgeons, can get training in virtual reality using MetaMedicsVR [22, 53]. These VR instructional systems provide students with prompt, tailored feedback [23, 54]. In several medical disciplines and preclinical and clinical education, Metaverse games with avatars have improved learning outcomes and increased medical students' engagement, participation, and collaboration in a risk-free decision-making context [24, 55]. "Immersive learning" technology is evolving rapidly and could change medical education [25, 56]. Academic students prefer cyber-physical institutions to traditional ones, according to study [26, 57]. VR reference resources coexist with training and simulation. Medical Augmented Intelligence (MAI) startup created "BodyMap," a medically accurate 3D virtual reality body model for medical education.
3. **Instructions for the Patient**: The Metaverse may offer patients virtual health and illness prevention education [28, 58]. They could assist the patient in visualising the surgical or laboratory research results. Preoperative patient counselling services aim to alleviate patient anxiety by elucidating anaesthesia, surgical procedures, and postoperative challenges, while familiarising them with the operating room environment. Virtual therapy reduces language barriers, physician time, and the need for physically disabled patients to leave

home. HealthBlocks uses Blockchain to incentivise user engagement, while Healthify established a sports and health Metaverse. Digital Twins (DTs) facilitate patients' comprehension of their ailments by providing a digital representation of their conditions [27, 59, 60].

4. **Biomedical Investigation**: Researchers can utilise the Metaverse to replicate medical procedures and therapies for the purpose of testing and enhancing novel medicines. This aids in addressing mental disorders such as ADHD, AD, and Parkinson's disease. Immersive games with tailored training regimens improved mobility and autobiographical memory in virtual reality therapy [29, 61, 62]. When combined with standard therapy, virtual reality rehabilitation improves Parkinson's gait and balance. Metaverse can speed up clinical studies by removing physical and geographical barriers between clinicians and volunteers. Article [30] demonstrates that Blockchain technology facilitates secure and transparent data management in clinical studies. This technology enhances medical data security, fosters trust, and mitigates regulatory challenges, thereby increasing the efficiency and efficacy of clinical studies. Blockchain can safeguard Electronic Health Records (EHRs), enabling researchers to utilise their data securely. DTs can mimic human behaviour and medical devices, allowing researchers to test without patients [31]. Article [11] calls the healthcare Metaverse "MeTAI" ("medical technology and AI") and claims that it can improve AI-driven medical practices, notably imaging-guided diagnosis and treatment.
5. **Pharmaceutical Advancement**: The Metaverse can accelerate medical research, enhance drug safety and efficacy, and decrease the expenses associated with introducing new pharmaceuticals to the market. Pharmaceutical developers can simulate drug effects in virtual environments utilising the Metaverse. These models enable researchers to identify novel therapeutic safety and efficacy concerns prior to human clinical trials, thereby decreasing the duration and expense of medical development. Virtual Reality (VR) facilitates "interactive molecular dynamics in VR" (IMD-VR) simulations, allowing for the visualisation and interaction with molecular Drug Targets (DTs) in drug discovery [12, 63]. Virtual reality drug development tools such as UCSF ChimeraX and YASARA facilitate docking and the simulation of molecular interactions. Narupa iMD [13] facilitates user cooperation inside a cohesive virtual reality environment and enables interaction with real-time molecular simulations. These revolutionary methods allow pharmaceutical companies to undertake clinical investigations in weeks rather than months or years at lower costs [14, 64]. Along with molecular drug targets, organ-derived (e.g., liver [15]) or model organism-derived (e.g., mouse [16]) drug targets can improve drug development. The Metaverse can improve clinical trial design and recruitment for novel drug safety and efficacy testing. Virtual simulations and environments can improve clinical trial design and participant recruitment. Researchers can pool their resources and skills to find new

drugs by improving collaboration and data exchange. Internet platforms allow researchers worldwide to share data, discuss findings, and collaborate on medication development and bioinformatics.

6. **Psychotherapy and Assistance**: Individuals with agoraphobia, acrophobia, aviophobia, and PTSD may find "exposure treatment" beneficial, as it involves confronting anxiety-provoking scenarios. This happens "in vivo" when the patient faces their fear in real life or in a virtual reality setting that simulates the "threatening" occurrence. Virtual Reality Exposure Therapy (VRET) outperforms "in vivo" VR exposure therapy in safety, convenience, regulation, and cost. Virtual reality realism now uses multisensory integration to create a "embodiment illusion" that lets patients feel like they're in their "avatar" [17, 65]. Immersive Virtual Reality (IVR) helps Mild to Borderline Intellectual Disability (MBID) [18, 66]. The Metaverse could offer remote physical therapy and rehabilitation. Patients can improve movement and coordination at home with VR. This may help rural or distant residents or mobility-challenged people receive healthcare. The Metaverse may provide virtual support groups and therapy for chronic illness and mental health. Individuals without in-person support can find community in virtual support groups.
7. **Clinical Laboratory Science**: The educational and training uses of the Metaverse can enhance collaboration among students, scientists, and technicians in medical laboratories. Nonetheless, each of the three Metaverse components possesses applications peculiar to laboratories [19, 67]. Digital Twins of laboratories and their apparatus provide intelligent manufacturing, in-silico modelling, preliminary evaluation, and assay and device simulation [20]. Telepresence and virtual reality enable three-dimensional tours of virtual clinical laboratories and digital representations of lab activities [31, 68]. A Blockchain-based remote laboratory management system secures data interchange between lab equipment, staff, and students [12, 69]. Virtual reality helps bioinformatics and genomics researchers integrate and visualise biological data. VR allows molecular modelling, multi-omics analysis, mesoscopic rigid body modelling, and 3D cell imaging [20]. Bioinformatics employs Blockchain technology to securely send DNA sequencing data [21, 70].

10.3 Metaverse Virtual Anti-Ageing Healthcare

The Metaverse may enable digital anti-ageing healthcare research and engagement. Users can interact with avatars to see how diet and exercise affect their appearance and health. Metaverse technology for digital anti-ageing in healthcare is promising and will be exciting to watch. Modern healthcare relies on digital anti-ageing to promote healthy ageing, reduce chronic diseases, reduce signs of ageing, boost self-esteem, encourage lifestyle changes, and more [17, 71]. Metaverse technology for digital anti-ageing in healthcare is promising and will be exciting to watch.

10.3.1 Management of Chronic Diseases in the Metaverse

Chronic diseases necessitate ongoing medical intervention or restrict everyday activities. Chronic difficulties last at least a year and are linked to tobacco, second-hand smoke, poor nutrition, inactivity, and alcohol abuse. Chronic diseases include cardiovascular disease, stroke, cancer, diabetes, Alzheimer's, Parkinson's, arthritis, COPD, and obesity. Article [18] delineates four essential phases for the development of the medical Metaverse and the integration of technological solutions. The four stages are as follows:

- **Holographic Manufacturing**: This phase necessitates a static geometric representation of the virtual environment. This encompasses virtual hospitals, medical personnel, and apparatus. There are three sorts of environmental elements: landscapes, occurrences, and individuals. The equipment in an operating room is the setting, while patients and medical personnel represent the individuals, and the interactions among them signify the event [72].
- **Holographic Simulation**: Physical environments will be replicated and integrated into the virtual realm. To perpetually enhance physical execution, include and utilise all accessible technologies. Integrating medical data with contemporary data technologies should optimise the immersive process. Multi-sensor and real-time motion capture technologies expedite the operation using patient and physician avatars [73].
- **Integration of Virtual and Physical Elements**: Our objective is to render the virtual realm authentic. Mixed Reality (MR) integrates the virtual and physical realms in medicine, providing a fully immersive experience. The quest for a wholly immersive experience is propelled by digital technologies. XR devices facilitate communication between patients and clinicians in virtual settings, irrespective of their geographical locations. The virtual environment will utilise patient data in real time [19, 74].
- **Interplay between Virtual and Physical Environments**: Artificial Intelligence, Internet of Things, Brain-Computer Interface, and additional technologies will be employed to create medical simulation apparatus and methodologies. Technological advancements are anticipated to enhance execution and integrate physical and virtual medical procedures. Medical solutions can be incorporated into the Metaverse through the aforementioned four methods [75].

10.3.2 Utilising Metaverse Entertainment for Anti-Ageing

Entertainment holds greater significance. As individuals age, their social interactions diminish. Interacting with others is crucial for psychological well-being and contentment. The entertainment program is appropriate for elders and may encompass several components. Examples include puzzles, card games, coffee, gaming, and jewellery creation. Gaming is the foremost information technology entertainment medium for individuals of all ages. The great interaction and immersive worlds of 2D and 3D games have had a positive impact on users' well-being and perspective, alleviating stress. The Metaverse employs AI, Blockchain, and IoT, utilising VR devices to extend entertainment beyond gaming and foster a novel social milieu for interaction and exploration [20]. The Metaverse will facilitate meetings, collaborations, friendships, transactions for physical and digital products, virtual gaming, and participation in concerts, trade exhibits, and educational activities.

10.3.3 Metaverse-Enhanced Wellness and Anti-Ageing Fitness

Wellness and physical activity mitigate the effects of ageing. The Metaverse provides virtual reality-based potential in this domain. The gaming sector enhances human health. Studies indicate that virtual reality technology enhances cerebral activity, particularly in individuals with dementia. Individuals with dementia can utilise the Metaverse to explore various locations, reconstruct memories, and interact with family members. The Metaverse provides numerous exercise options [21]. Animoca Brands, a global leader, and OliveX have enhanced the Sandbox Metaverse to create Gamified Fitness, an interoperable fitness game ecosystem. Fortnite served as a paradigm, while fitness streaming is a preferred activity. While some may not consider the fitness Metaverse revolutionary, it is now one of the most exciting and disruptive fitness options.

10.3.4 Digital Dermatology for Anti-Ageing

Another aspect of anti-ageing is skin appearance. Anti-ageing medicines are thought to target physical youth only. Delaying ageing to attain youthfulness constitutes a facet of the anti-ageing process; nonetheless, the preceding sections addressed numerous more elements. Anti-ageing tactics emphasise skincare items such as sunscreen, moisturiser, and anti-wrinkle treatments from Dream E and Neutrogena to maintain youthful skin. The products contain vitamin A, C, peptides, coenzyme Q10, tea extracts, grape seed extract, and niacinamide. Users can find suitable skincare items using AI-enhanced VR/AR. Monitor product performance and make educated decisions. Cosmopolitan US Skin Analysis Face App evaluates selfies' flaws, wrinkles, texture, and dark circles using a composite model of many photos [22].

10.3.5 Mental Health and Metaverse

Healthcare depends on mental health, which affects ageing. Strong mental health reduces premature death. Technology in the Metaverse could change consciousness. Metaverse mental health therapy is possible. Patients engage in the Metaverse to obtain mental health or medical rehabilitation training. The Metaverse facilitates hospital education and virtual medical consultations. As an increasing number of organisations explore its potential, this technology may progress [23]. Virtual, augmented, and mixed reality are the primary technologies employed in this treatment, and they are progressively utilised to diagnose mental health conditions. Diagnosis of specific mental health disorders may possess uses within the Metaverse, including the following:

- Attention Deficit Hyperactivity Disorder (ADHD) diagnosis
- Eating disorders characterised by maladaptive eating behaviours
- Post-Traumatic Stress Disorder, anxiety disorders, and phobias
- Having autism
- Parkinson's disease
- Medications for the treatment of stress and discomfort
- Syndromes of psychosis, schizophrenia, and delusions

Numerous leading technology companies utilise Metaverse games to address mental health concerns. Bump Galaxy, a mental health application, was prototyped within Minecraft VR. It serves as a "game world treatment," providing patients with social support and safety while assisting them in overcoming sadness, anxiety, and trauma in Bump Galaxy. Community mental resilience and well-being can be enhanced by grassroots deep hypnosis visualisations [24].

10.3.6 Virtual Support for Critical Patients in the Metaverse

Digital anti-ageing necessitates continuous monitoring of patient health. The Metaverse is utilised for therapeutic purposes and monitoring to expedite health without risk. It therapeutically addresses numerous conditions. The healthcare provider can elucidate the treatment's objective and gather patient information. A three-dimensional virtual environment is generated with diverse software and hardware. The optimal approach creates and identifies the Metaverse's virtual and augmented reality for medical information. This approach facilitates treatment planning and implementation [25]. Figure 10.1 illustrates the workflow of a Metaverse Virtual Clinic. It provides an overview of how patients and doctors interact with each other through a virtual environment powered by data analytics, sensor technologies, and expert collaboration.

10.3.6.1 Key Features of the Metaverse Virtual Clinic

- **Remote Monitoring**: Patients can receive healthcare services without visiting physical clinics.
- **Collaborative Healthcare**: Experts from various fields can work together seamlessly, thanks to the Metaverse's immersive environment.

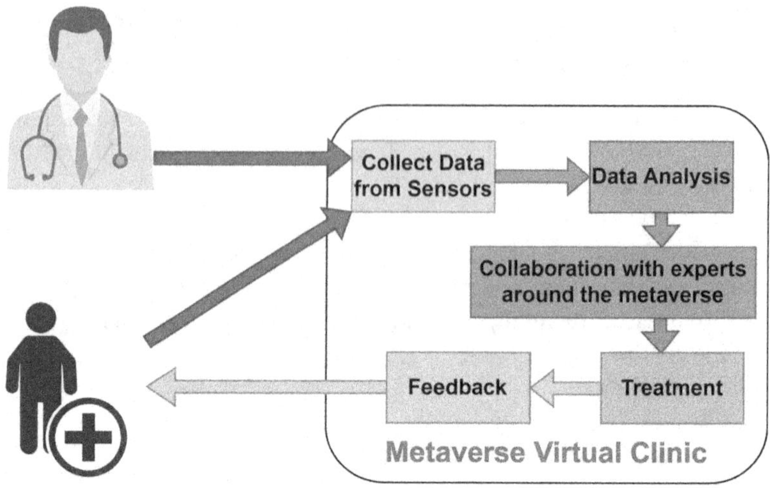

Figure 10.1 Monitoring patients in the Metaverse.

- **Real-Time Feedback Loop**: Continuous monitoring and real-time feedback ensure that treatment plans remain dynamic and responsive to patient needs.
- **Data-Driven Decisions**: The use of sensor data and advanced analytics enables more accurate and personalised treatment approaches.

10.4 Metaverse Technologies for Digital Anti-Ageing Healthcare Solutions

Alternative Metaverse healthcare technologies enhance accessibility and reduce expenses. Patients can obtain care remotely, hence diminishing transportation and healthcare expenses. Through this technology, healthcare practitioners can deliver more efficient and personalised care.

10.4.1 Artificial Intelligence

Artificial Intelligence (AI) is a subfield of computer science that focuses on the development of computer systems that are capable of doing tasks that are similar to those performed by humans, such as speech recognition, visual perception, and decision-making. Machine learning, deep learning, computer vision, and natural language processing are some of the subfields that fall under the umbrella of technology known as artificial intelligence. When it comes to the operation of the Metaverse, each and every subset of artificial intelligence is necessary, depending on the application domain. Textual and verbal communication are both made possible through the use of Natural Language Processing in the Metaverse. For the purpose of making therapy more accessible, medical data can be obtained through patient-physician avatar conversations [26]. In order to create and train accurate models for practical applications, various artificial intelligence technologies, including computer vision, machine learning (including supervised, unsupervised, and reinforcement learning), deep learning (including ANN, CNN, LSTM, RNN, and others), transfer learning, and others, are combined. This allows medical professionals to forecast Metaverse diseases while they are being treated.

10.4.2 Distributed Ledger Technology

Distributed Ledger Technology (DLT) refers to a decentralised system of recording, sharing, and maintaining data across multiple nodes or participants, without a central authority. Unlike traditional databases, which rely on a single administrator or central server, DLT ensures that all network participants have synchronised copies of the ledger. This technology offers increased transparency, security, and resilience, as updates to the ledger must be verified by consensus mechanisms, such as Proof of Work (PoW) or Proof of Stake (PoS). Blockchain is a popular example of DLT, where data is stored in blocks linked sequentially [27]. DLT is gaining traction across various industries, including finance, supply chain management, healthcare, and government, as it enables trust, reduces operational costs, and minimises the risks of single points of failure. The Metaverse healthcare Blockchain manages patient data, medical resources, safe transactions, and more.

10.4.3 IoT

Internet-connected physical devices that share data are called IoT. IoT greatly impacts telemedicine breakthroughs. Mobility constraints have led several tech companies to focus on IoT for remote applications. IoT devices improve healthcare Metaverse service customisation and efficiency. Healthcare practitioners can receive heart rate, blood pressure, and oxygen saturation data from wearable IoT devices. Remote patient monitoring enables healthcare professionals to identify problems prior to their escalation and administer expedited remedies.

10.4.4 Cloud and Edge Computing

Edge computing securely stores and processes large data sets, enabling healthcare Metaverse services. Healthcare applications can employ machine learning and artificial intelligence methodologies in conjunction with cloud computing. These algorithms evaluate extensive data sets to uncover illness patterns and treatment results, enhancing diagnostic and therapeutic accuracy [28].

10.4.5 Sixth Generation (6G) Network

High-speed, low-latency, and high-capacity 5G and 6G networks facilitate immersive and responsive experiences. The Metaverse requires connectivity to achieve complete immersion. Mischa Dohler, Chief Architect of Ericsson Silicon Valley, discusses the significance of 5G in the development of the Metaverse. 5G and 6G networks provide essential attributes such as speed, coverage, reliability, and low latency, which are crucial for healthcare, particularly within the Metaverse. This link would facilitate online consultations through avatars of patients and doctors, Metaverse medical training, and assisted Metaverse telesurgery, among other applications [29].

10.4.6 Immersive Technology

Immersive technology envelops users in a Metaverse, integrating physical and virtual realms. Contemporary immersive technologies are used in healthcare. VR, AR, and XR help doctors practise and simulate surgeries. Interactive visualisation in XR allows VR sufferers to receive drug-free treatment without touch. Medical professionals are employing VR, AR, and XR to develop three-dimensional simulations of their sophisticated operating rooms, facilitating real-time input from various institutions and international expert surgeons, as well as demonstrating surgical procedures to patients' families. The physician's avatar engages with the patient's avatar to provide healthcare solutions in a virtual Metaverse. Virtual reality technology assists physicians in administering treatment to patients within Metaverse environments. A virtual lecture conducted by medical personnel from Seoul National University Bundang Hospital featured Metaverse-based training for lung cancer surgery within a smart operating room [30].

10.4.7 Digital Twins

Digital Twins (DTs) are virtual representations of tangible entities. DT technology helps create patient and medical device digital therapies. Personalised medicine and the pharmaceutical industry require customised pharmaceuticals, and this technology provides novel and precise solutions for patient evaluation and adherence. DT employs IoT, XR, AI, and Cloud technologies to generate visual representations, as well as to gather, store, analyse, and provide intelligent data. These applications utilise Digital Twins to enhance medical diagnosis and treatment. In the Digital Twin methodology, physicians employ wearable sensors to identify early indicators. In the design and optimisation of medical devices, a Digital Twin (DT) symbolises the physical entity, such as humans. DT can establish a digital cohort of diverse patients to assess new pharmaceuticals in order to identify the most effective and suitable prescriptions. Digital Twins can forecast outcomes prior to therapy by modelling an invasive therapeutic procedure [31].

10.4.8 Human–Computer Interaction

HCI covers human-system interaction. It involves planning, designing, implementing, and modifying interactive computing systems. Human–Computer Interaction facilitates communication across many medical and healthcare sectors. In contemporary ICUs and CCUs, HCI evaluates operating room apparatus. HCI analyses and manages healthcare data using AI, EHRs, dashboards, and patient portals. HCI facilitates diverse online interactions among physicians, patients, authorities, and families [32].

10.4.9 Quantum Computing

Quantum Computing (QC) uses quantum physics to perform Metaverse computations unattainable by traditional computers. Numerous computationally demanding healthcare applications facilitate quality control. Radiotherapy is a prevalent treatment for cancer. It eradicates or suppresses cancer cells using radiation. A radiation plan is necessary to safeguard healthy tissues and organs from radiation exposure. Optimising radiation techniques necessitates numerous simulations. Consequently, quantum computing assesses numerous choices during each simulation. Consequently, healthcare professionals might conduct numerous simulations to ascertain the optimal strategy. QC's pharmaceutical, healthcare data, and genetic contributions improve medical imaging. Quantum imaging can precisely see molecules. Quantum computing and machine learning help doctors analyse data [33].

10.4.10 3D Reconstruction

3DR has emerged as a vital technology in computer vision for the healthcare sector, especially in medicine. The 3DR employs cancer imaging, MRI, CT scans, and surgical photographs. The 3DR enhances imaging precision through medical picture segmentation to facilitate therapy. The preoperative assessment and surgical planning of 3DR software may improve surgical outcomes and reduce risks. Conversely, virtual reality reveals patients' health issues. Virtual reality technology enhances medical education by providing instructional materials, simulating a realistic learning environment, augmenting educators' competencies, and facilitating the communication of lesson plans and material by instructors [34].

10.5 Digital Nutrition and Anti-Ageing Management

10.5.1 The Rise of Digital Healthcare Technologies

Traditional healthcare uses paper records, prescriptions, analogue medical instruments like X-rays, and other technology to diagnose and treat patients. Traditional healthcare systems are more efficient and accessible thanks to digitalisation. Digital technology has revolutionised healthcare delivery and accessibility, facilitating rapid expansion of the sector. Digital technologies utilise little energy and processing time since they employ electrical systems. Digital technologies have improved communication, data collection and analysis, remote monitoring, and tailored interventions in healthcare. These technologies could improve healthcare, particularly anti-ageing medicines [35]. The disparity between analogue and digital healthcare technologies expands as healthcare institutions progressively adopt digital solutions. Digital technologies enhance efficacy, efficiency, accessibility, and data analysis, hence augmenting patient care. Digitalisation began with the adoption of Electronic Health Records (EHRs), which eliminated paper documentation, enabled data sharing, reduced diagnostic inaccuracies through accurate clinical decision support systems, and improved population health management for disease forecasting.

Technology has diminished the necessity for in-patient treatment, enabling patients in remote regions to consult medical specialists through telemedicine, thereby decreasing travel times and expenses while expediting healthcare delivery. Telemedicine is predominantly beneficial and occasionally essential during pandemics such as COVID-19. Telehealth services use the Internet of Things to collect patient data and send it to a server for expert analysis or response. IoT technologies provide patients with sensors to capture clinical data for analysis. A server acquires values over a connection to perform subsequent operations [36]. This data facilitates the monitoring of chronic diseases, offers early alerts, and permits preventive treatment [37]. The use of algorithms and large databases to analyse data, interpret medical images, diagnose diseases, and predict outcomes has altered healthcare with artificial intelligence. Personal health apps and remote monitoring technologies address healthcare facility and service delivery challenges. These advances enable on-demand vital sign monitoring, medication management, and customised health recommendations for self-management. Efficient data sharing, fast and reliable distant data analysis, reduced redundancies, and improved care coordination have been made possible by Health Information Exchange (HIE) technology [38]. However, digital technology has improved healthcare.

10.5.2 Digital Anti-Ageing Dietary Management

Effective anti-ageing healthcare is needed as the population ages. A balanced diet prevents and delays most age-related diseases [5]. Anti-ageing therapy should include nutritional control. Planning, monitoring, nutrient intake measurement, diet adaptation, nutritional targets, and behavioural adjustment are all part of diet management. Because they rely on memory and honesty, self-reported meal diaries and 24-hour recalls are difficult, imprecise, and inefficient [6]. Tracking dietary limitations in an electronic medical system to assess their anti-ageing benefits for the elderly is an issue [7]. The intricacy of assessing nutritional intake and predicting specific, individualised dietary challenges arises from human genetic variability, subjectivity, adherence problems stemming from neglect and forgetfulness, and delays in measuring the effects of the procedure. Digital technology provides unique dietary regulation solutions that enhance anti-ageing wellness. Digital innovations could change healthcare and anti-ageing. Traditional dietary management difficulties can be addressed by digital technologies [9]. Nutritional assessment data precision, procedure optimisation, and participant burden are improved by digital technology. This may improve public health, clinical research, and personalised nutrition. Mobile apps for food and diet tracking dominate digital dietary management [8]. These applications track user data and generate recommendations through sophisticated analytics to assist healthcare providers in evaluating patients [1]. Remote patient monitoring utilising sensor-based devices and IoT technologies evaluates hydration, stress, and lifestyle to provide dietary and nutritional recommendations [2]. Artificial intelligence, Blockchain, cloud computing, edge computing, 5G connection, nanotechnology, point-of-care technologies, and others improve efficiency in the backend or with these applications. Wearable gadgets can send data to servers over 5G [3]. Advanced nutritional systems use Blockchains for food safety [4]. Digital technologies impact anti-ageing endeavours such as optimal nutrition, BMI regulation, weight reduction, wellness, and healthy living [5].

10.5.2.1 Mobile Applications for Nutritional Tracking

Digital technology for dietary management mostly includes diet and food tracking applications. These programs aim to assist users in monitoring their food consumption, nutrient, and calorie intake to provide tailored suggestions for healthy ageing. Consequently, IT developers and stakeholders create diet-management mobile applications. A multitude of individuals utilise MyFitnessPal to monitor their dietary intake and caloric consumption. The database contains more than 11 million food components. MyFitnessPal enables users to establish weight reduction or muscle gain objectives and offers tailored nutritional guidance. This program reads barcodes to efficiently include food products into the database. The previously mentioned examples show that the United States has led diet control app development for decades. The United States leads this business due to its technologically advanced population, health consciousness, entrepreneurial energy, healthcare expenditure, prevention focus, market demand, and environmental limits. Free apps with limited features are available, but premium services demand a monthly charge. Many nations have health and wellness programs. Asian media reported that Malaysia, South Korea, Thailand, Indonesia, and Japan used health and wellness apps, including dietary control apps, during the COVID-19 pandemic in 2021. These Asian countries use healthcare professionals, stakeholders, and engineers to meet population needs. Japan, South Korea, India, and China will drive the Asia-Pacific diet and nutrition application market to $4,245.82 million by 2028.

In addition to the commercially accessible programs, university researchers are developing innovative mobile applications for anti-ageing healthcare. Technical advancements in nutritional monitoring and precision nutrition were discussed in [29]. The authors initially concentrated on food photography and the use of AI in dietary monitoring, then investigating physical and chemical sensors for detecting dietary intake and meal composition through wearable and mobile devices capable of automating diet reporting. This study also assessed AI-driven nutrition advisory systems based on gut microbiota. The examination of AI-driven diet tracking and health assessment was also conducted [38]. The authors presented a mobile application with a Naive Bayes-classified web chatbot. The proposed application categorises illnesses according to user input and formulates a dietary regimen to enhance health. The chatbots tailor nutrition plans and utilise prior discussions to engage in more profound dialogues with clients. In a healthy lifestyle, article [19] examined how self-monitoring nutrition and physical activity in a technology-assisted behavioural intervention affected weight loss.

Their research investigated the utilisation of mobile applications and wearable technology for weight reduction, emphasising the significance of self-monitoring for optimal weight management outcomes. To comprehend clients' ongoing engagement with mobile applications, paper [9] examined the utilisation of a free diet monitoring application. The study analysed user behaviour and interaction patterns to identify factors influencing the app's sustained acceptance and utilisation for nutritional tracking.

10.5.2.2 Digital Platforms and Remote Coaching

These mobile apps often have a browser-based interface for querying and receiving server responses. They run on desktops without installation. Digital platforms and virtual coaching dominate nutritional management. MyFitnessPal and Noom offer web-based and mobile apps for nutrition tracking and customised advice from healthcare professionals and AI-powered chatbots. Online forums and communities boost healthy eating motivation and accountability. Another example is the Korean web-based nutritional assessment and meal planning tool CAN-Pro [2]. The CAN-Pro database provides Korean food nutrition for menu planning, dietary assessment, education, and research. Digital platforms offer personalised guidance from experts who provide daily exercises and challenges to meet nutritional goals. Zoom, Skype, and Google Meet make virtual dietary management coaching more engaging. Effective virtual coaching improves mental health and ageing.

10.5.2.3 Internet of Things, Sensors, and Wearable Technology

Wearable devices with sensors have enhanced physiological monitoring and the documentation of eating behaviours [3]. Wearable devices assist physicians and patients in monitoring dietary consumption in real time. These gadgets encompass ECG monitors, smartwatches, and fitness trackers that monitor activity, sleep, and caloric consumption. Advanced technology can automatically monitor chewing, swallowing, and food consumption [4]. Wearable sensors, such as accelerometers, gyroscopes, and optical sensors, track physical activity and energy expenditure in real time, enhancing dietary choices and facilitating customised meals [5]. Wearable devices can monitor dietary habits over time, facilitating the identification of areas for enhancement. The dependable data provided by wearables on food consumption, portion sizes, and meal structure facilitates personalised diets [4]. Reference [6] described on-body sensing for automatic dietary monitoring. The researchers automated nutritional monitoring with EMG, IMUs, and food intake sensors. The initiative developed simple and unobtrusive diet tracking technology to help people maintain healthy eating habits and meet nutritional goals.

The study's potential implications highlighted that the suggested technology will encourage healthier lives and enable consumers to make sensor-informed food selections. Additionally, article [7] assessed the efficacy of wearable sensor technology and computer vision for automated nutritional surveillance. Computer vision examines photos and videos to detect and monitor food intake. Moreover, systems utilising wearable sensors collect data on eating behaviours and patterns. This study analysed the advantages, disadvantages, and prospective applications of diverse technologies for automated dietary monitoring. The IoT interlinks devices and the cloud, enabling sensors to transmit data to servers for processing. Dietary tracking applications utilise the IoT to integrate real-time food consumption data with comprehensive user information to evaluate eating patterns and guide decision-making. Kitchen-Mate, a widely used IoT-enabled diet-tracking application, connects intelligent kitchen appliances to monitor users' intake and provide tailored recommendations depending on their objectives. The IoT employs wearable devices to deliver a comprehensive health overview. Customised diets utilising wearable gadgets and mobile sensors. To effectively analyse dietary habits and health trends, they employed IoT and cloud computing technologies. The objective was to deliver personalised nutritional solutions that assist consumers in making healthful dietary selections. An IoT-based nutritional monitoring healthcare solution for women is offered [8]. The system tracks meal frequency and food consumption with an electronic dining table with load sensors and RFID. It tracks portion sizes and consumption with a camera and microphone. The fully automated system evaluates food nutrition using Wi-Fi-enabled sensors and a mobile app. It measures meal weight and sends data to the cloud for analysis. The technology classifies foods by nutrition and diagnoses nutrient deficiencies. It also promotes low-calorie, nutrient-dense meals to fight obesity. Users may make informed nutritional selections and live healthier using the program. Wearable devices, sensors, and the IoT are promising nutritional monitoring tools for anti-ageing treatments that protect older adults' health.

10.5.2.4 Artificial Intelligence

Artificial intelligence seeks to develop systems and robots capable of performing activities analogous to those of humans across various fields. Artificial intelligence automates procedures and generates data-driven forecasts to address intricate issues. AI is being used in disease diagnosis, prognosis, survival analysis, medication discovery, and personalised treatment. Nutritional control is key to customised anti-ageing treatment. AI algorithms can anticipate a diet based on eating patterns, genetic data, personal preferences, health conditions, and goals, improving nutritional interventions [9]. Nutritional monitoring apps, wearable gear, and DRIs are used in many datasets. Dietary Reference Intakes help consumers and healthcare professionals make informed decisions. The DRI comprises scientifically validated nutrient reference values utilised to assess and formulate healthy diets. The DRI is revised every five years to account for demographic shifts, emerging health issues, and advancements in policy and practice. The latest Alexa applications for the United States utilise the 2020–2025 Dietary Reference Intakes (DRIs). Nutrient values like Adequate Intake (AI), Recommended Dietary Allowance (RDA), Estimated Average Requirement (EAR), and Tolerable Upper Intake Level (UL) are important for datasets and training AI models to predict customised diets [10]. The collection includes dietary, clinical, demographic, biochemical, and anthropometric data for customised recommendations. Mobile apps use food image datasets to develop food identification and classification models using computer vision and object detection methods including YOLO, SSD, R-CNN, and HOG. Users take lunch photos with mobile apps. Meal segmentation using computer vision algorithms lets AI systems and nutritional data evaluate food quantities for recommendations or forecasts. Dietary databases provide enough nutritional data for computers to construct user-specific diet plans. AI can analyse dietary patterns, provide recommendations, and change habit using several data sources. AI algorithms can tailor meal plans to dietary preferences, health goals, nutritional needs, age, gender, weight, exercise level, and constraints [12].

Artificial intelligence may utilise image datasets and object detection algorithms to evaluate the nutritional composition of a user's meal, facilitating precise monitoring of calorie consumption, macronutrient distribution, and micronutrient levels [3]. AI algorithms can forecast future eating behaviours based on historical dietary data, which is essential for nutritional assessment and customised nutrition programs. Refrigerators, scales, and culinary tools use artificial intelligence to improve meal preparation, monitor food inventory, and suggest recipes based on components. These methods improve meal planning and diet compliance [4].

Chatbots and voice-activated interfaces offer instant dietary management assistance. Users may request guidance, monitor their progress, and establish reminders to achieve their dietary objectives [5]. The AI algorithms in mobile app backends are imperceptible to users. AI algorithms acquire knowledge from datasets such as Dietary Reference Intakes (DRIs), Food Frequency Questionnaires (FFQs), 24-hour dietary recalls, food diaries, genetic data, wearable technology, and user input to enhance nutritional recommendations tailored to individual requirements. Owing to genetic and medical diversity, artificial intelligence is crucial for sophisticated investigations that can identify markers of ageing and develop robust models incorporating the most pertinent factors [6]. Specific nutritional studies employed AI to meticulously evaluate the dietary content, timing, and long-term behaviours of ageing adults [7]. Reference [8] presented a case study on nutrition monitoring that illustrated an AI-driven reasoning approach. The proposed framework tailors appropriate meals to assist users in recovering from dietary infractions, acknowledging the challenges of sustaining a balanced diet. Conversely, [9] examined AI-driven methodologies for dietary caloric measurement. The scientists employed various algorithms to precisely quantify food caloric content and develop a thorough and uniform nutritional intake plan for individuals. Numerous sophisticated research employed AI computer vision to analyse mobile phone photographs of food items to ascertain their nutritional composition. Computer vision techniques necessitate numerous images and descriptions of various food products to convey textures and lighting conditions from multiple perspectives for model training. The primary problem with computer vision systems is obtaining access to all tagged images. Article [20] developed a smartphone application that scans food items, assesses nutritional value, and provides recommendations aligned with users' objectives to advocate the Ayurvedic diet. Reference [11] describes deep learning-based food segmentation. They sought to recognise food locations and calculate calories in images. Supervised learning algorithms classify food and non-food objects to estimate nutrient intake, improving diet evaluation. A Visually Based Diet Assessment (VBDA) system that uses computer vision algorithms to automatically extract nutritional information from photographs was explored in [2]. Volume and food were investigated. Others used NLP and data mining to help virtual chatbots propose diets and identify eating habits from text and unstructured mobile data [13]. NLP can translate literary descriptions into nutritional information, changing how consumers track food intake. Restaurant menus and descriptions can be analysed by NLP algorithms for items, portions, and cooking methods. This automatic meal logging solution improves dietary data precision for those who struggle with manual meal logging. NLP can analyse text-based nutritional data, opening up new research, healthcare, and nutrition management prospects.

Dietary habits, nutritional intake, and allergenic or intolerant product descriptions can be identified. NLP enhances the usability of food diaries, hence facilitating healthy eating and the management of chronic illnesses. Natural Language Processing can enhance meal journaling by amalgamating textual data with nutritional information, hence refining dietary evaluations for consumers. Effective AI algorithms must work with other technologies. AI reviewed Internet of Things-transmitted wearable sensor data to a cloud server in article [5]. Individuals could enhance their health and age gracefully by making dietary choices informed by real-time data. Nutritional management systems can deliver more accurate and specific anti-ageing dietary recommendations through artificial intelligence [6]. Artificial intelligence also identifies anti-ageing natural extracts and bioactive peptides in meals. These technologies provide nutritional monitoring and customised anti-ageing treatment.

10.5.2.5 Distributed Ledger Technology

Blockchain records transactions securely, openly, and immutably. Blockchain was created by Satoshi Nakamoto in 2008 for Bitcoin and finance. Blockchain is used in many fields and has several benefits. Blockchain improves hospital efficiency, data security, and patient privacy. Blockchain enables anti-ageing healthcare applications like nutritional management. Dietary control using Blockchain technology ensures secure, transparent, and efficient food supply chain data monitoring. Traceability, transparency, food quality, efficacy, and consumer satisfaction are possible. Blockchain allows food safety management and real-time tracing due to its decentralisation and security. Blockchain monitoring food commodities throughout their life cycle reduces risks, improves supply chain efficiency, and improves food safety and quality. Cryptography and decentralisation protect nutritional data in Blockchain technology. Food supply chain systems can improve food safety and quality with Blockchain smart contracts [11]. Blockchain technology can improve nutrition management and health. Blockchain transforms nutritional management by tracking food from manufacturing to consumption [32]. Authentic food with proper nutritional labelling promotes a balanced diet, while fakes can ruin it. Food supply chain transparency with Blockchain technology lets customers verify provenance, nutritional information, and expiration dates. Nutritionists and food specialists use Blockchain smart contracts to create client-specific nutritional recommendations. Blockchain ensures transparency in modification and compliance, while tokens can reward healthy eating and lifestyle advocates. Blockchain technology can monitor food information and reduce the risk of swallowing dangerous ingredients for allergy sufferers. Blockchain facilitates quality assessment, regulatory compliance, and informed consumer choices based on tastes and diets. Blockchain helps numerous companies track and assign supply chain operations from agriculture to consumption. Monitoring food sources improves dietary management by tracing the supply chain and addressing difficulties quickly. Food is also authenticated by Blockchain. The immutability and transparency of Blockchain make it a reliable food tracking system. A Blockchain-based food traceability system allows real-time supply chain monitoring of animal products and tamper-proof data collecting. This reduces the danger of mislabelling and food fraud, which threaten consumer safety and food industry credibility [33]. Blockchain-based dietary management solutions have become popular due to food safety and quality issues that affect consumer health and dietary regulation. These technologies create an immutable distributed ledger allowing food supply chain parties to view transactions in real time. Blockchain frameworks combine many operations, but diet management requires food safety and traceability to protect stakeholders and reduce risk. Popular Blockchain solutions include the following:

- **IBM Food Trust**: A modular Blockchain-based food traceability solution for the food industry's value chain [35]. IBM Food Trust provides rapid quality control, improving supply chain transparency. This technology, used by Walmart, Nestle, and others, may improve food safety.
- **TE-Food**: A permissioned Blockchain for all food businesses, regardless of size. To retain consumer confidence, TE-Food uses Blockchain to monitor food provenance and quality in real time. Swiss supermarket store Migros tracks products with this program.

- **Ambrosus**: Blockchain boosts patients' food safety confidence. Comprehensive traceability ensures food safety and quality at Ambrosus. The Swiss coffee maker Lattesso and Château Latour use it.

Addressing food origin and quality concerns necessitates enhanced transparency, accountability, and traceability. A computerised record of the food supply chain guarantees safety, quality, and regulatory compliance. Robust and efficient data management aids individualised nutrition and dietary planning. The integration of Blockchain with other technologies enhances its functionality. AI-driven technology can be integrated with Blockchain to provide customised nutritional recommendations, enhancing public health by customising nutrition programs to individual need. The decentralisation and security of Blockchain can enhance the transparency, trustworthiness, and personalisation of food intake monitoring, hence assisting individuals in making improved food choices and dietary evaluations.

10.5.2.6 Supplementary Digital Diet Surveillance Technologies

Alternative technology can enhance nutritional strategies in anti-ageing treatments. We have already examined smartphone applications, which are the most used tools for diet tracking. The complete functionalities of these applications necessitate additional technologies contingent upon the objective. Article [8] examines nutrition with Digital Twin (DT) technology. The research examined the potential of nutritional technologies to enhance dietary efficiency and personalisation. The scientists employed a decision tree to model food consumption and nutrient absorption. Data analytics and machine learning enable researchers to replicate and evaluate individual feeding patterns and requirements. Furthermore, research [9] assessed many digital innovations in nutritional monitoring and precision nutrition. Mobile apps, AI, wearable gear, and sensors were tested to create gut microbiota-based nutritional recommendations and continuous glucose monitoring. Three-dimensional printing and AI were used for food printing to customise and fabricate products. Articles present studies. The authors used AI and 3D food printing to find new food protein sources. This study shows that AI can analyse data to improve food protein use. This study studies 3D food printing to create unique, sustainable, and nutritious meals. The main goal was to use AI in 3D food printing to create sustainable and innovative food solutions for future food industry difficulties. Certain mobile application backends can use VR, AR, 5G/6G connection, and edge computing to meet developer and stakeholder goals. 5G/6G connectivity accelerates and consistently transfers digital dietary control data [8]. Point-of-Care (POC) technology can be utilised in anti-ageing healthcare for dietary assessment and clinical decision-making support [14]. Vitamin B and many age-related biomarkers can be continuously assessed using point-of-care equipment. Blood glucose levels, inflammatory indicators, oxidative damage, and hormone dysregulation [12]. These indicators furnish real-time data to assist individuals in comprehending their metabolic wellness and making informed lifestyle choices. Point-of-care devices may utilise biomarker and food consumption data to generate personalised nutritional recommendations aligned with health objectives [13]. Advanced machine learning algorithms and technology can tailor nutritional recommendations to age, gender, metabolic traits, and genetics, improving anti-ageing nutritional therapy. Nanotechnology offers promising treatments, including anti-ageing diet guidance. Nanotechnology's tailored nutrient delivery and precision medicine applications can improve healthy ageing dietary control with wearable sensors, data analytics, and personalised health platforms [15].

Nanosensors for the measurement of hyperglycaemia, oxidative stress, and inflammatory cytokines have progressed significantly. Wearable devices equipped with these sensors can continuously measure metabolic and physiological parameters. Artificial intelligence can examine data to provide dietary and lifestyle suggestions. Nanoparticles and liposomes utilised for nutrient encapsulation and bioavailability have resulted in nanocarriers designed for customised nutrient delivery [14]. Nanocarriers selectively target tissues or cells to facilitate nutrient absorption, hence enhancing precision nutrition and dietary management. This multi-technological integration demonstrates how digital technology enhances dietary management and anti-ageing treatments.

10.6 Obstacles and Developmental Trajectories for Anti-Ageing and Healthcare Metaverse

10.6.1 Metaverse Digital Anti-Ageing Healthcare Challenges

A digital anti-ageing healthcare strategy for the Metaverse must surmount numerous hurdles during its development and implementation. Metaverse healthcare systems can enhance patient outcomes and facilitate healthy ageing, particularly when integrated with supportive technology, although facing hurdles [3]. Figure 10.2 describes various Metaverse digital anti-ageing healthcare challenges.

1. **Apprehensions Regarding Privacy and Security**: There is a significant need for medical data, particularly digital anti-ageing healthcare data inside the Metaverse ecosystem. Cybercriminals persistently attempt to infiltrate unlawful online platforms to expropriate data, notwithstanding the security measures implemented by authorised proprietors. High-quality large datasets are a target for hackers; hence, utilising the Metaverse for healthcare data transmission introduces significant challenges. The huge volume of patient data complicates confidentiality. The encouraging findings in [9] indicate that patients' communication in the Metaverse is contingent upon data confidentiality. Numerous websites jeopardise data security. Metaverse hospitals require enhanced security measures to safeguard patient data and limit access to authorised healthcare staff. HIPAA standards require modification about

Figure 10.2 Metaverse digital anti-ageing healthcare challenges.

the disclosure of information in the Metaverse. Various nations impose distinct data constraints, and physicians are permitted to practise only in specific places, so constraining their capacity to treat patients globally [5]. We contend that the merging of healthcare and the Metaverse may enhance global attractiveness and generate riches innovatively. Figure 10.3 illustrates the methods employed by attackers to infiltrate user devices and the Metaverse platform, emphasising privacy and security issues.

2. **Information Security**: Major healthcare firms may obtain sensitive patient information without consent when delivering healthcare services. The Metaverse has the potential to enhance virtual experiences by enabling physicians to remotely provide care to patients using diverse electronic devices, thereby producing substantial data volumes. Virtual technologies and interpersonal communication facilitate this. The patient's medical status and the physician's replies are transmitted via the same channel. Patient data is safeguarded through the use of robust algorithms and Blockchain technology [6].
3. **Standardisation and Interoperability**: Interoperability, a challenging endeavour in new technologies, is essential to the contemporary healthcare

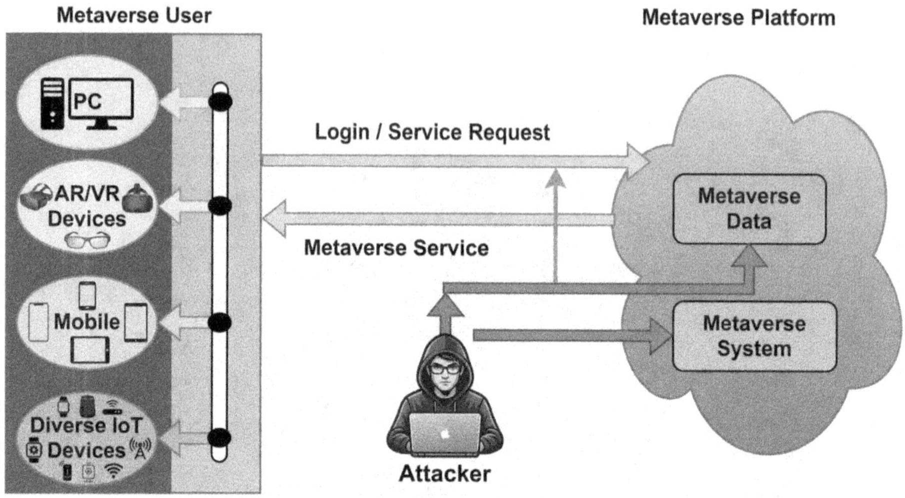

Figure 10.3 Concerns regarding privacy and security in the Metaverse.

framework. The Metaverse may inadvertently influence the interoperability of specific devices across platforms and networks. Data and communication standards must be rapidly established, as the adoption of the Metaverse will be incremental and could yield adverse consequences. Prominent IT businesses could establish the Metaverse by formulating technological standards and protocols. Certain IT companies may modify Metaverse standards to further their corporate objectives. Interoperable technological tools, protocols, and services are crucial for the Metaverse ecosystem's growth, yet developer lock-in, customer choice restrictions, and creative suppression are major difficulties.

4. **Increasing Metaverse User Base**: In what ways may Meta and other IT businesses advance healthcare within the Metaverse? The commercial progress of modern technology is contingent upon its users. The reliability and utilisation of the Metaverse are assessed through several approaches. Can elderly individuals lacking digital proficiency access the Metaverse for treatment? Do Metaverse meetings offer equivalent advantages to in-person meetings? [8].
5. **Inadequate Internet Connectivity in Rural Regions**: Immersive three-dimensional applications necessitate increased bandwidth, potentially limiting rural access to these technologies. Recent integration of AI in ophthalmology has demonstrated that dormancy may lead to anticipatory disruptions in hectic clinical environments, while unreliable internet connectivity remains a significant issue. Recent research is establishing the foundation for a 5G rollout strategy [11]. Numerous small cells must be deployed adjacent to base stations in 5G networks to facilitate signal transmission [12]. The substantial infrastructure requirements in rural regions may complicate the deployment of 5G technology.

6. **Technological Metaverse Sector Misunderstanding**: Insufficient understanding of new technologies impedes the adoption of solutions [14]. A solution may manifest in several forms, complicating the user interface and resulting in device output errors [15]. The commercialisation of behavioural or health data may provoke concerns over privacy and corporate overreach. Qualitative research regarding stakeholders' acceptability of these solutions and their capacity to utilise these technologies can assist in overcoming significant implementation hurdles [16]. Preliminary investigations into immersive technology in ophthalmology revealed that numerous patients expressed a willingness to invest in suitable solutions.
7. **Expensive Equipment**: As Metaverse firms proliferate, innovative AR and VR technologies for enhancing global surgical practices have increased significantly. Wearable sensors, glasses, gloves, and other technologies capable of accurately assessing patients' conditions are required to supplant the Metaverse's healthcare system [17]. The Metaverse's demand for comprehensive connectivity and advanced technology would render healthcare providers' infrastructure costly. The Metaverse in healthcare necessitates the replacement of obsolete wearable devices with adequate software and hardware infrastructure, which is initially costly [18].
8. **Legal and Regulatory Issues**: The Metaverse is revolutionising healthcare by enabling interns to treat patients and training physicians with advanced technologies. Recent advancements in the sector have established the Metaverse as a novel business model. As Metaverse uses proliferate, medical technologies that involve healthcare providers, insurers, and pharmaceutical corporations to treat patients may present legal and regulatory issues. The Metaverse is devoid of standards and conventions, potentially leading to trust concerns and confusion among intellectual property stakeholders. Formulating legislative measures to combat cybercrime is vital.

10.6.2 Prospective Trajectories

A bibliometric analysis of Virtual Reality (VR) and Augmented Reality (AR) indicates that the Metaverse is applicable in the domains of pain management, neurological disorders, stroke, depression, and the diagnosis, treatment, and rehabilitation of cancer. Artificial intelligence can be utilised in cancer prevention, diagnosis, and treatment. Anti-ageing technology in healthcare have augmented life expectancy. A comprehensive DNA study can identify diseases and medical vulnerabilities, facilitating timely prevention. Genetic testing may reveal optimal diets, health conditions, and allergies or drug sensitivities. Immersive virtual and augmented reality technologies may signify the Metaverse 1.0. However, several IT giants use these technologies. Embodied Laboratories provides immersive carer training, XR Health specialises in rehabilitation, and Rend Ever and Silver Adventures develop meaningful geriatric virtual experiences. Also, the Metaverse may enable more authentic ways to communicate remotely.

This is when matters become intriguing. This could be advantageous for elders. Enhanced, more authentic communication will elevate telehealth. A further aspect that requires enhancement is legacy. Establishing a legacy for others to recall you posthumously is challenging. A multitude of individuals is endeavouring to retain their life narratives. The Metaverse will enhance healthcare via telepresence, Digital Twins, and Blockchain, particularly in patient monitoring. Telepresence, often known as telemedicine, delivers medical services remotely. The Metaverse could assist surgeons in executing intricate procedures and enhancing patient care. Surgeons utilise robotics to do surgeries following the collection of vital signs, images, medical records, and additional data. Innovative Metaverse-based solutions can deliver real-time testing data to enhance patient performance. Clinical trials are necessary to validate the surgical efficacy of the Metaverse; hence, its use will occur incrementally.

10.7 Conclusion

Metaverse healthcare has many benefits. This Metaverse study examined digital anti-ageing healthcare approaches. AI, Blockchain, and IoT can improve healthcare, save expenses, and extend patient lives. Further study and development are needed to overcome difficulties and fully utilise Metaverse technology in digital anti-ageing and healthcare. Metaverse technology can improve global health by revolutionising care delivery and reception with proper investment and teamwork. Nutrition-focused digital technologies in anti-ageing healthcare are examined in this study. Digital technologies affect planning, monitoring, tracking, nutrient intake analysis, diet customising, nutritional goal setting, and behavioural modification help. Digital tools help track food intake, identify nutrients, and set dietary goals. This study shows that digitally integrated mobile diet management apps can regulate diets and fight ageing. Despite digital dietary management's drawbacks, affordable and intuitive solutions can improve user experience and adherence. A study reveals digital diet management may extend life.

Chapter 11

Digital Twins in the Metaverse: Unlocking New Realities with Blockchain

11.1 Introduction

The rapid advancement of digital technologies has spurred innovation across numerous sectors, unlocking new potentials and transforming traditional processes [1, 32]. Among these technologies, Digital Twins stand out by enabling real-time monitoring, predictive analytics, and detailed simulation of physical systems. By creating accurate virtual replicas, Digital Twins empower organisations to optimise operational performance, efficiently manage assets, and proactively mitigate risks within increasingly complex environments. Complementing this, Blockchain technology brings essential features such as decentralisation, transparency, and robust security, which significantly enhance the capabilities of Digital Twins. Blockchain provides immutable data records and facilitates trustless data exchanges, ensuring the integrity and security of information shared across interconnected systems [2, 33]. Its ability to govern ownership, automate processes through smart contracts, and maintain tamper-proof transaction histories becomes increasingly critical as systems grow more complex and distributed.

Meanwhile, the Metaverse is rapidly evolving into a fully immersive, shared virtual environment where users can interact, socialise, conduct commerce, and engage with both digital and physical assets in seamless ways [3, 34]. By integrating Digital

DOI: 10.1201/9781003520702-11

Twins and Blockchain technologies within the Metaverse, organisations can construct dynamic, secure, and scalable virtual spaces that closely replicate real-world systems. This integration enhances simulation accuracy, fosters deeper collaboration among stakeholders, and improves asset management through transparent and reliable data flows [4, 35]. This study provides a comprehensive analysis of the benefits and challenges associated with the convergence of Digital Twins, Blockchain, and the Metaverse. Together, these technologies represent the cutting edge of digital innovation, offering improved real-time decision-making, greater automation, and novel economic opportunities enabled by tokenisation and secure data interchange. However, the successful implementation and widespread adoption of this integrated ecosystem hinge on overcoming significant challenges related to technical complexity, scalability constraints, regulatory compliance, and security concerns [5, 36]. Addressing these issues is crucial to unlocking the full transformative potential of this powerful technological synergy.

11.2 Metaverse Digital Twin Technology

11.2.1 Definition of Metaverse Digital Twin Technology

Advanced Metaverse Digital Twin technology uses precise digital replicas to simulate, monitor, and evaluate real-world entities within a virtual environment. These "Digital Twins" continuously update and synchronise the status information of their physical counterparts in real time, accurately reflecting any changes occurring in the physical world. The Metaverse ecosystem currently integrates a range of cutting-edge technologies, including the Internet of Things (IoT), Blockchain, cloud computing, 5G connectivity, Virtual Reality (VR) interactions, Artificial Intelligence (AI), and Digital Twins [6, 37]. Cloud computing and 5G provide the necessary infrastructure, Blockchain technology creates a hybrid economic system, virtual reality technology creates immersive experiences, the Internet of Things provides data, and artificial intelligence acts as the cognitive core of the Metaverse. The development of the Metaverse and the mapping of the real world are made possible by Digital Twin technology. The Metaverse is a synthesis of modern technology. The Digital Twin of the Metaverse is a comprehensive theoretical and technological framework that correlates real and virtual worlds, uses sensors and physical models to gather a variety of real-time data, and uses intelligent optimisation algorithms to simulate the lifecycle of entities. According to the idea of the Metaverse, human technological civilisation has advanced into a new stage of virtualisation, digitisation, and contact with the real environment. Contemporary technology renders the concept feasible. The pandemic has escalated internet engagement to unprecedented heights [7, 38–40]. The majority of activities, such as employment, education, and social interaction, are now conducted online. These phenomena are transient and vital to existence. In 2021, Facebook rebranded as "Meta," unveiling their

Metaverse agenda. This is the firm's rebranding and formal acknowledgement of its leadership in the Metaverse. The result of integrating cutting-edge technology is the Metaverse. The development of the Metaverse is made possible by augmented reality, Blockchain technology, cloud computing, and Digital Twins. This new virtual environment makes it easier to produce, learn, and have fun in the real world [8, 41]. On September 13, 2022, a Metaverse lecture was given by the National Science and Technology Nomenclature Approval Committee. The fundamental elements of the Metaverse were examined by researchers. The definition of "Metaverse," which denotes a major technological advancement, is "a virtual world created by humans via digital technology that either reflects or exceeds the real world and can engage with it." Digital Twin technology accurately models physical objects for the Metaverse, creates virtual worlds that mimic actual campuses, allows for dynamic interactions between the physical and digital worlds, creates virtual avatars, and gives managers, teachers, service providers, and students the ability to oversee, maintain, and teach campuses from a subjective ownership standpoint [9, 42].

11.2.2 Contemporary Research on Metaverse Technology

In the 1992 science fiction book *Avalanche* the words "Avatar" and "Metaverse" are mentioned. Avatars are created by users in the Metaverse, a virtual environment. The book *Real Name and Surname* from 1981 presented a virtual world that could be accessed through a brain-computer connection. Many open multiplayer games appeared between the 1970s and 1990s, and their vast settings laid the groundwork for the Metaverse [10, 43]. In 2021, the Metaverse made its debut. In early 2021, Soul launched a "social Metaverse" for the sector. In March 2021, Roblox, the first Metaverse stock, went public on the New York Stock Exchange. Microsoft CEO Satya Nadella declared in May 2021 that the corporation was creating a "enterprise Metaverse." The Metaverse debuted its first Artificial Intelligence (AI)-generated digital shadow puppets in June 2021. Haier unveiled the first intelligent manufacturing Metaverse platform in August 2021, which combines virtual and physical intelligent manufacturing into a cross-scenario experience that includes "factory, store, and home." In a similar vein, Nvidia revealed the Metaverse-supporting simulation and collaboration platform [12, 44]. Baidu's inaugural domestic Metaverse product, "Xirang," commenced focused internal testing on December 21, 2021. Users can augment their Xirang experience using an invitation code. Gather.town is an educational Metaverse platform that enables students to create virtual avatars for the purpose of learning [11, 45]. Customisable virtual learning settings are available; the platform for extracurricular activities allows for a variety of virtual interactive interactions, and the leisure area allows students to socialise and share ideas with peers and coworkers. The platform can be used for a wide range of offline activities. The virtual STEM course offered by Nagaoka University of Technology and Science in Japan uses VR, AR, and XR technology to create an online learning environment. Educators and learners utilise their terminals for instruction and study, while the platform concurrently records and transmits resources, data, and outputs in real time to the educator's computer for oversight. The University of Cincinnati's Simulation and Virtual Environment Research Centre provides immersive education via a Metaverse learning platform and interdisciplinary courses [13, 46]. Its healthcare and biotechnology research is exceptional. Metaverse technology emulates campus data to virtualise the environment. The subjective and immersive campus administration from an experiential standpoint hinders decision support, complicating the appropriate management and monitoring of global trends across various business environments. Virtualisation enhances campus data management and facilitates the rapid identification of security risks and anomalies. Data visualisation enhances campus administration, decision-making, and information management [14, 47, 48].

11.2.3 Contemporary Research on Digital Twins

Digital Twins were created in 2002 and are credited to Michael Grieves, a professor at the University of Michigan. Originally called the "Information Mirroring Model" in the introductory "Product Lifecycle Management" course, the term was later changed to the "Digital Twin." It was first used to refer to the digital depiction of products in simulation software, but it has now expanded to include the virtual representation of real products as well as the direct link between each product and its virtual equivalent [15]. By 2015, Digital Twin research has accelerated due to developments in cloud computing, wireless networking, and machine learning. According to [3], Digital Twins assist manufacturers in enhancing predictions, judgements, and strategies. They assert that Digital Twins have the potential to enhance simulation technologies. Various experts subsequently deliberated on methodologies for studying Digital Twin technologies. Article [4] advocates for interdisciplinary collaborative simulation in Digital Twin research, whereas article [5] asserts that big data and Digital Twins can enhance intelligent manufacturing. Certain scientists assert that Digital Twins integrate physical and virtual realms. In order to improve the security of industrial control systems, the author of [6] looked at a framework that used Digital Twin technology. They also presented a new attack model, defined security requirements for the state replication model, and suggested a creative security architecture. A thorough analysis of Digital Twin technologies and access control in the context of industrial control network security was carried out by the author of [7, 49, 50]. To test a simplified access control framework for Digital Twins of industrial control systems, they used OpenStack. According to their research, the strategic language can be used to construct access control regulations by articulating the components and relationships found in the Digital Twin of industrial control systems. The author of [8] developed a two-phase deep transfer learning method that uses Digital Twin technology to improve the efficacy, transparency, and adaptability of fault diagnostics. The Internet of Things' Digital Twin creates a digital simulation on an information platform by utilising software analysis, artificial intelligence, machine learning, and physical feedback data. Based on feedback, this simulation responds quickly to changes in physical elements. Digital Twins must effectively assimilate feedback from several sources and accurately represent physical entities in real time. Digital Twin feedback depends on sensors for pressure, tilt, and speed, among others. Machine learning for Digital Twins can utilise sensor feedback, historical data, and integrated network data. The latter typically denotes many analogous physical components performing distinct activities and transmitting data to a common platform. Digital Twins require substantial input for deep learning and precise simulations. The Digital Twin aims to identify and rectify design flaws while enhancing diagnostic models during the development process. Simulation outcomes can be utilised in the physical realm without necessitating model retraining during operation and maintenance. Dual fault detection in both virtual and physical environments mitigates unforeseen failures, enhancing the sustainability, reliability, and efficiency of intelligent manufacturing. According to article [11, 51, 52], Digital Twins enable the monitoring, modelling, optimisation, and forecasting of Cyber-Physical Systems (CPSs), with their fully operational virtual counterparts being crucial for system security. In order to enable unfettered exploration and testing of similar settings without interfering with real-time systems, they created a framework for building and managing Digital Twins that faithfully imitate industrial control devices. The security area at the top enables analysts to oversee CPS status or do security analysis. The security module formulates security protocols based on implicit or explicit user configurations and examines anomalies within the virtual environment during operation. This module detects problematic process states during operation and facilitates virtual simulations to evaluate compliance with established criteria.

11.3 Conceptual Framework of the Metaverse

The Metaverse, as an innovative service, has the potential to transform global technology and enhance urban development, industries, and services. In order to provide a more tactile, visible, and interactive experience, the Metaverse uses XR technologies like AR, VR, and MR to provide user and object data that has been aggregated from many locations and devices (such as homes, workplaces, and Internet of Things devices) in an immersive format. It is novel to interact with processed and aggregated data in the Metaverse. Metaverse services can gain advantages from digital transformation [16, 53]. Digital Twins for Metaverse services would facilitate end-user demand monitoring and furnish the resources necessary to enhance services and attain Quality of Experience (QoE). These services would cater to the various devices, concepts, and processes involved, particularly network resources. Conversely, Digital Twins of tangible objects can establish an authentic Metaverse for an immersive experience [17, 54].

11.3.1 Digital Transformation of Metaverse Services

The Metaverse requires data collection, transmission, manipulation, and production to provide immersive services. The devices of Metaverse participants, including phones, cameras, headsets, and edge nodes, are indispensable. Establishing a tangible Metaverse necessitates advanced networking, communication technologies, machine learning, artificial intelligence, and Digital Twins. Digital Transformation (DT) offers numerous advantages for the management of intricate ecosystems [18, 55]. To supervise and offer a thorough and precise study of the Metaverse service in order to create its Digital Twin, all Digital Twins of relevant procedures, ideas, and things must work together. Because network performance impacts service quality, the Digital Twin (DT) of the Metaverse service needs to communicate with the wireless network DT, which includes the DT for network operations and infrastructure. DT seeks assistance in optimising network resource allocation to enhance Quality of Service and autonomy [19, 56, 57].

11.3.2 Digital Twin for Metaverse Applications

The Metaverse introduces an additional dimension to the digitisation of smart cities. It can improve services and broaden applications. The real-world Metaverse enhances services, businesses, towns, and nations by merging utility, context, and relevance between real and virtual environments. In addition to providing enjoyment, a Metaverse experience that mimics the real world may be used to analyse various real-life situations and understand system dynamics, which will help people make more informed decisions in their daily lives. In the Metaverse, Digital Twins are used to create and depict the physical characteristics of virtual world items [20, 58]. Through real-time data and information obtained from the Digital Twin (DT), the Metaverse makes it possible to create a digital replica of the actual world that accurately reflects physical qualities and offers realistic answers depending on the analysis of the DT [21, 59, 60].

Consequently, DT product visualisation is more comprehensive in this context. Establishing a tangible Metaverse enhances information visualisation and interaction, facilitating system monitoring in healthcare, construction, retail, and tourism. Digital Twins within the Metaverse can enhance forensic investigations and safety in smart cities [22, 61].

11.3.3 Prerequisites for the Metaverse

The 3D environment must encompass the digital counterpart of every entity, thought, or process to construct the real-world Metaverse. Such a system requires a substantial amount of diverse data, including IoT data and high-resolution images (8k film). A substantial volume of terabytes of data is required to construct a real-world Metaverse [23]. The data must be analysed with AI and ML to generate the Digital Twin and exhibit its three-dimensional depiction. The Metaverse facilitates interaction with manufactured objects by enabling users to grasp, manipulate, and magnify them. Using certain technologies and techniques to track user movements will make it easier to gather information that can be evaluated and converted into requests and comments. This improves participation in the Metaverse. Data must be gathered, sent, analysed, processed, and distributed to Metaverse users in a sequential manner. All actions must be performed accurately and with the least amount of latency in order to achieve full participant synchronisation and instantaneous 3D object reactions [24, 63]. Each 3D object's Digital Twin interacts and engages with the real-world Metaverse. There are many accessibility, availability, and integrity concerns with the access and transfer of this data. Moreover, data can substantially influence system latency, responsiveness, and accuracy. Various parties must collaborate to achieve the necessary level of service. Methodological complexity, algorithm standardisation, transparency, and trust are significant hurdles in this collaboration [25, 62].

11.4 System Model: Blockchain-enabled Metaverse Digital Twin

This framework employs Digital Twins to delineate the Blockchain underpinnings of the Metaverse. This framework comprises four tiers: physical, Digital Twin, Metaverse, and Blockchain. Concise descriptions of each tier are provided in Figure 11.1.

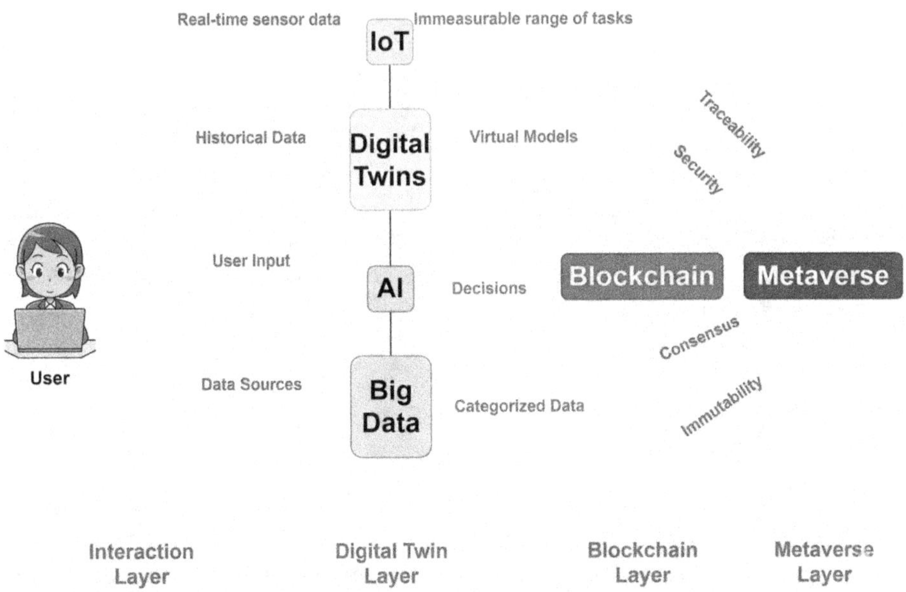

Figure 11.1 Blockchain-enabled Metaverse Digital Twin.

1. **Interaction Layer**: The physical layer encompasses all entities within the system, including human and non-human. Individuals provide operational data such as medical records, proprietary corporate information, governmental data, and additional types. Monitoring devices, sensors, robotics, and smart devices constitute non-human entities. The Digital Twin layer receives input from diverse nodes to create a virtual version of the actual system [26, 64].
2. **Digital Twin Layer**: Information technology converts physical entities into virtual and digital representations within the Digital Twin Layer. Digitising the qualities, functions, features, and parameters of physical entities into the Metaverse generates approximate counterparts in the real world [15, 65]. This layer integrates simulators, historical data analytics, and streaming data models to execute accurate operations. The learning process depends on the continuous updating of the Digital Twin to produce timely, accurate forecasts for informed decision-making [16, 66].
3. **Metaverse Layer**: The Metaverse employs Digital Twins within a shared online virtual reality environment to engage with the physical world [17, 67]. MSPs deliver services and facilitate relationships with Metaverse Users (MUs) at this level. Each system node—MSPs and MUs—maintains tokens, assets, and money for transactions among themselves and with the MSPs. Members can utilise currencies or assets to access MSP services. The Blockchain, as the subsequent layer of the system paradigm, oversees and documents the interactions inside this layer. Simulation and high-definition rendering technologies sustain and enhance the Metaverse's virtual representation. These technologies offer longevity, scalability, quality, interoperability, and an immersive node experience [18, 68].
4. **Blockchain Layer**: The Blockchain Layer addresses significant security and privacy issues, reflecting real-world challenges. Blockchain technology facilitates the interaction between Managed Service Providers (MSPs) and Metaverse Users (MUs) at the Metaverse layer. The transactions of these businesses are securely documented on the Blockchain, guaranteeing privacy and anonymity while automating the procedure. Blockchain ensures secure and seamless asset transactions between MSPs and MUs. All network nodes gain advantages from the transparency and immutability of the Blockchain-based system concept [20, 69].

11.5 Dependable Metaverse DTs

Blockchain and Digital Twin technology make it easier to create a safe, unchangeable virtual version of a genuine product or industrial system for information security, data traceability, and real-time data monitoring and analysis. Blockchain-based smart contracts for Digital Twin data governance improve information management and guarantee the safety and openness of automated transactions. This section analyses the integration of Digital Twins with Blockchain. We study the Ethereum Blockchain as our design and implementation reference, which has developed from the Bitcoin network and incorporated functionality to function as a complete platform for decentralised application development [70].

11.5.1 Core Structure and Status of the Digital Twin

Recent scientific research [14] has delineated Digital Twins (DTs) via a unique spectrum of abstract roles and capabilities, enabling the identification of a common set of characteristics and the provision of a cohesive conceptual framework applicable across several domains. They have been conceptualised and analysed from an ecosystem viewpoint, wherein each Digital Twin (DT) functions as an autonomous software component that digitises its physical counterpart and interacts with digital applications and other twins to fulfil application objectives. This study employs these principles to align with the current state of the art while characterising the relationships and applications of Blockchain technology to enhance Digital Twins. Each Digital Twin (DT) must function independently to accurately model and represent its physical equivalent within its operational context, as per Representativeness and Contextualisation capabilities [14, 71]. It is essential to document pertinent attributes (such a robot's joint positions, picker setup, or responsibilities), behaviours (such as target industrial robot activities), and relationships. The Digital Twin Model governs the transmission of inputs and actions from the twin to the physical entity, as well as the mapping of discrepancies from the real world into the digital replica. The Digital Twin State organises, preserves, and conveys all computed properties and relationships, including temporal variations, to other components. Physical Adapters ensure accurate, reciprocal communication with the physical counterpart over time and define the twin's Physical Interface. During the process, the robot's picker configuration, joint orientation, and rotation can be changed to match the modelled state (e.g., signal resampling or representation adaptation) or directly obtained from the actual environment [27, 72].

This procedure can get or autonomously ascertain physical relationships between the target Digital Twin and other external entities or Digital Twins. The Augmentation capacity enables the Digital Twin to utilise its digitalisation capabilities to modify, update, and enhance its representation throughout time, as physical entities possess static characteristics and services. Augmentation and the Digital Twin A physical asset's functions can expand its capabilities and provide new attributes or connections, such coordinating a robot's tasks with client demands and production goals [28, 73]. By establishing a Digital Interface with one or more Digital Adapters, the Digital Twin (DT) bridges the gap between the physical and virtual worlds. This enables each DT to show its present state and accept commands to do tasks or change its behaviour on the go. Developed according to these principles, structured and interoperable Digital Twins create a digital overlay that allows Metaverse applications to engage with reality without incurring the direct costs of its complexity and fragmentation, while providing access to augmented and integrated data and functionalities. In addition to highlighting the critical role of Digital Twins, this scenario raises a number of new and little-studied issues about the responsibility, integrity, and dependability of virtual applications in connection to the effectiveness of application logic [29, 74].

Consequently, a Digital Twin must be reliable in its cyber-digital linkage to reality and its temporal progression regarding state fluctuations and their origins. These difficulties require analysis and can be addressed through the use of Digital Twins, Blockchain, and Ethereum technology, as detailed in the subsequent sections [30, 75].

11.5.2 Smart Contract for Digital Twin

Digital applications, like Metaverse services that provide a virtualised representation of reality or other Digital Twins that are in charge of creating and aggregating numerous sub-twins, need to have access to a certified layer that can confirm their structure, relationships with physical counterparts, and other characteristics in order to build trust and dependability in distributed cyber-physical systems [31]. The correct operation of DT-dependent apps and services will be ensured by this trustworthy, transparent, and unchangeable data. To establish a robust, cohesive, and dependable digital overlay, the subsequent components of Digital Transformation (DT) must be assessed and sanctioned:

- **Cyber-Physical Association**: verifying the linkage between a Digital Twin and its physical counterpart(s) guarantees that the Digital Twin faithfully represents reality and assists applications in recognising cyber-physical relationships, thereby identifying the optimal digital representation.
- **DT Structure**: it assesses the Digital Twin's architecture concerning its attributes, occurrences, behaviours, and interrelations, ensuring it remains unchanged, coherent, and only governed by the Digital Twin, in alignment with modifications to the physical counterpart.
- **Ownership Verification**: this validates the proprietor of the Digital Twin (DT) and other critical characteristics, including the software version and deployment environment (e.g., Cloud or Edge), to ascertain the twin's legitimacy and enable apps to select between various DT implementations [1].
- **State Management**: this assesses the Digital Twin's attributes about traits, events, behaviours, and relationships. It guarantees that the Digital Twin's condition is consistently checked throughout its life cycle, remains stable amid variances, ensures reliability for exposed data, and is governed by the Digital Twin itself.
- **History Visibility**: this enables users to examine a Digital Twin's historical context and the events that influenced its development. It guarantees the

transparency and accessibility of the DT's history by securely documenting every operation about its state attributes prior to and following alteration [2].

- **Communication Channels**: real-time communication and observation without Blockchain transit are made possible by authenticating DT's communication channels and access points, which let programs to identify reliable endpoints for direct interaction with the twin. Because DT endpoints are authorised, there is less chance that users may communicate with unprotected, fraudulent, or untrusted twin instances.

The development of a structured and flexible smart contract technology for the suggested integrated and reliable cyber-physical flow requires a Blockchain network. We claim that Ethereum is the best Blockchain option for each of the specified uses. The creation of decentralised apps and smart contracts is made easier by this open-source platform. It was designed to allow developers to create other apps on its network, unlike Bitcoin, which was initially developed as a decentralised digital money. It is a permissionless Blockchain, in contrast to Hyperledger Fabric [16], allowing universal participation. Ethereum transactions encompass cryptocurrency transfers and the execution of smart contracts, which are implemented as executable code. A dedicated transaction block documents all network modifications from the past to the present. Ethereum smart contracts autonomously enforce contractual commitments in the absence of intermediaries upon the fulfilment of specified criteria, guaranteeing transparency, security, and resilience to tampering. Publicly verifiable computer code encapsulates the contract's provisions and functionalities, obviating the necessity for third-party trust and guaranteeing timely and agreed-upon implementation. Ethereum contracts describe the condition of a Digital Twin (DT) on the Blockchain network and the basic ways to access or modify the contract and track its changes over time. Every smart contract has a Blockchain address that serves as its public identification when it is deployed [3]. Ethereum accounts, data, and assets including smart contracts are stored, managed, and interacted with via the wallet. To effectively participate in the Ethereum network, the proposed approach calls for each Digital Twin (DT) to use a Blockchain adapter to handle its contracts and wallet.

A setValue function is used to assign a value to the corresponding attribute, a getValue procedure is used to retrieve a single attribute value, a getAll method is used to obtain all available attributes and their associated values, and an add method (such as addProperty) is used to register a new field in the DT structure description. Every process produces. The data of the smart contract, which is based on the basic state characteristics of the Digital Twin, including attributes, events, behaviours, and relationships, is shown graphically in Figure 11.2. This information encompasses details about the target Digital Twin's software, including its version and dependencies, deployment parameters such as resource requirements and architectural preferences (e.g., edge or cloud computing), ownership, and its cyber-physical linkage to

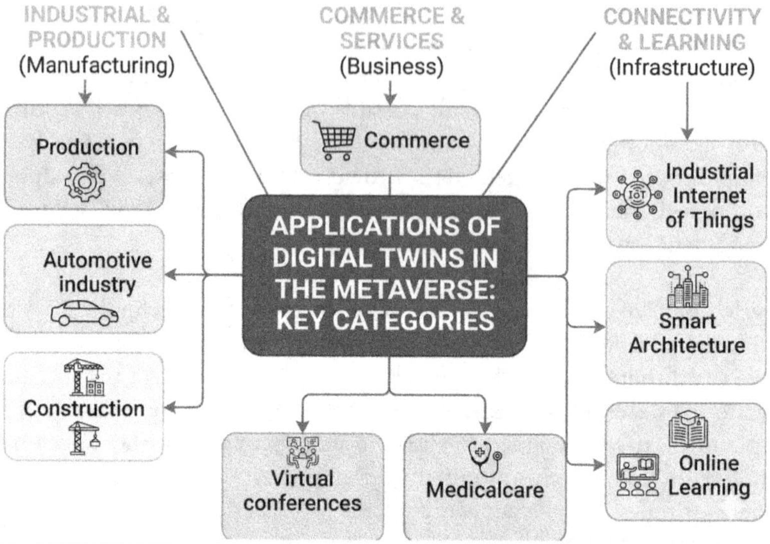

Figure 11.2 Applications of Digital Twin technology in the Metaverse.

the corresponding physical entity [4]. The smart contract architecture leverages dictionary-based data structures, allowing it to flexibly incorporate attributes relevant to each category according to the specific application design and context. For this architecture to function effectively, decentralised technologies and applications must support processes that can both write data to and retrieve data from the Blockchain, thereby creating a secure and trustworthy environment [5].

11.6 Principal Advantages of Metaverse–Digital Twin Integration

Blockchain, Digital Twin, and the Metaverse create a potent combination that offers numerous advantages in security, transparency, and interactivity. The primary advantages are as follows:

- **Data Integrity**: Blockchain ensures tamper-proof, transparent records for Digital Twin data, crucial for sensitive sectors.
- **Ownership and Identity**: Blockchain verifies digital asset ownership and authenticates user identities, reducing fraud.
- **Asset Monitoring**: Real-time tracking and auditable histories improve management and supply chain transparency.
- **Automation**: Smart contracts enable efficient, automated, trustless interactions within the Metaverse.

- **Governance and Interoperability**: Decentralised control and cross-platform compatibility enhance collaboration.
- **Monetisation**: Tokenisation and secure data exchange open new revenue streams and marketplaces.
- **Resilience**: Distributed backups and secure logs support disaster recovery and risk management.
- **Collaboration**: Secure data sharing fosters new ecosystems across industries.
- **Data Privacy**: Users control data access, ensuring confidential and authorised sharing.
- **Scalability**: Supports large-scale, dynamic virtual environments with real-time updates and adaptability.

11.7 Applications of Digital Twin Technology in the Metaverse

Investigating the diverse applications of Digital Twin technology reveals its transformative influence across various industries, bolstered by tangible success narratives. This research will examine many domains where Digital Twins have demonstrated remarkable success, as well as those with significant potential for synergy with the Metaverse [13]. Figure 11.2 explains various applications of Digital Twins in the Metaverse environment.

11.7.1 Production

The industrial Metaverse introduces a new dimension to the Metaverse narrative, asserting its potential to impact society and the economy beyond advanced entertainment and retail contexts. The Metaverse's incorporation of Industry 4.0 principles, which indicate the merging of advanced technology implementation and the indistinction between physical, digital, and biological realms, is significant. Digital Twins have traditionally been utilised in manufacturing; however, their incorporation into the Metaverse establishes the "meta factory," a virtual ecosystem characterised by perpetual operation and remote accessibility, facilitating collaboration among experts from diverse fields and significantly diminishing project timelines. Despite the utilisation of Digital Twins, professionals were required to travel to designated sites for repairs, resulting in extended equipment downtime and the recognition of issues only upon arrival. The Metaverse enables experts to evaluate and initiate maintenance remotely, transforming this process [14]. The immersive characteristics of the Metaverse enable teams to swiftly identify production difficulties and enhance processes. This mitigates process disruptions and equipment inactivity. Creators of the Metaverse construct immersive environments for Digital Twins, integrating the virtual and the real. The integration of Digital Twins with the Metaverse allows professionals to interact with and modify real-time digital replicas of physical assets, significantly boosting industrial efficiency, productivity, and connectivity [15]. This collaboration aligns with the principles of the Fourth Industrial Revolution by seamlessly merging digital innovation with industrial operations. As a result, the synergy between Digital Twins and the Metaverse has become a cornerstone of modern industrial strategy, driving businesses towards a future where virtual and physical worlds converge to improve problem-solving, operational effectiveness, and overall efficiency [16].

11.7.2 Automotive Industry

Digital Twins within the Metaverse are revolutionising the automotive sector. Companies now develop digital prototypes of upcoming vehicle models, moving away from traditional physical prototypes, scale models, and testing methods to embrace advanced virtual technologies. Design teams can create and analyse vehicle Digital Twins using cloud platforms, while the Metaverse provides a virtual space to explore and experiment with these models like never before [17]. This virtual testing environment simulates real-world conditions, offering benefits such as improved efficiency, cost reduction, and increased safety by reducing the need for physical test drives. The Metaverse allows experts to assess and optimise vehicle aspects such as aerodynamics and safety features. Thanks to the rapid adaptability of Digital Twins, teams worldwide can collaborate within the Metaverse on iterative design and development, enhancing automotive innovation and functionality [18]. Creating detailed and realistic vehicle simulations in the Metaverse demands extensive technological and automotive expertise, heralding a new era of innovative, safe, and sustainable automobile manufacturing [19].

11.7.3 Commerce

The retail sector stands to be transformed by Digital Twins and the Metaverse, especially through immersive virtual shopping experiences. Virtual stores enable consumers to explore products and brands from anywhere, giving retailers unprecedented access to new customers and markets. Retailers can build intricate Digital Twin replicas of physical stores, offering shoppers an engaging experience that blends online browsing with the feel of in-store shopping. Beyond customer interaction, Metaverse Digital Twins also optimise supply chain and inventory management. By simulating these processes virtually, retailers can better forecast demand, speed up restocking, and improve logistics, which reduces costs and increases efficiency [20]. Digital Twins provide a dynamic view of supply chains, helping predict shortages and optimise inventory levels. Additionally, Digital Twins enable personalised retail experiences by aggregating and analysing customer data—ranging from buying habits to preferences—creating detailed consumer profiles. This enables retailers to tailor product offerings and marketing strategies with high precision. The integration of Digital Twins and the Metaverse is poised to revolutionise retail by enhancing customer experience, streamlining operations, and increasing satisfaction [21].

11.7.4 Medical Care

The Metaverse is transforming healthcare through collaborative medicine, predictive analytics for treatment outcomes, immersive virtual training, and augmented reality-enhanced operations. This transformation depends on Digital Twin and Metaverse technologies to assist physicians in diagnosing and treating patients through virtual organs or anatomies. Digital Twins are transforming healthcare treatment and surgical procedures. Generating accurate digital replicas of patient-specific organs or physiological systems enables physicians to simulate and evaluate treatment protocols in a secure setting. Comparable skills enhance the precision and efficacy of medical interventions, facilitating patient-specific treatment options. Medical augmented reality and Digital Twins enhance surgical procedures. Augmented reality glasses or screens enable surgeons to superimpose Digital Twins onto the surgical field, providing unparalleled clarity and precision. This technology presents real-time placement and trajectory of surgical instruments [22]. Cloud-based Digital Twins facilitate remote collaboration among global professionals during surgical procedures. The Metaverse is transforming medical education and training. Digital Twins in Metaverse settings enable medical students and trainees to rehearse surgical, diagnostic, and therapeutic techniques on virtual patients. This training method addresses the ethical and practical limitations of conventional training on patients or cadavers, establishing a scalable and efficient learning platform capable of simulating many clinical environments and disorders. Digital Twin and Metaverse technologies enhance clinical procedures, surgical accuracy, and medical education, facilitating more accessibility to advanced training. The integration facilitates superior healthcare providers, more personalised and effective medicines, and broader dissemination and accessibility of medical knowledge within the immersive and interactive Metaverse [23].

11.7.5 Construction

Advancements in the Metaverse are revolutionising construction and real estate. Construction enterprises are utilising Digital Twins to create virtual representations of buildings. Digital Twins provide ongoing surveillance and adjustments across a building's lifecycle, enhancing maintenance and durability. The Metaverse is concurrently generating Digital Twins for entire cities, transforming urban administration. An exemplary instance of this creative approach is South Korea's Digital Twin initiative for Incheon. This ambitious effort employs Digital Twin technologies to transform Incheon into a fully integrated smart city. Providing virtual tours of international cities such as Paris via meticulously crafted Metaverse digital replicas has the potential to transform tourism. Digital Twin and Metaverse technologies are revolutionising urban planning, development strategies, and the construction of buildings and entire cities. Urban planners and developers can leverage Metaverse-based Digital Twins to simulate various scenarios, evaluate the effects of policies, and make informed, data-driven decisions that improve city operations and services. Beyond structural and planning aspects, Digital Twins play a crucial role in promoting sustainability. By analysing Digital Twin data, cities can optimise energy use, waste management, and resource allocation, thereby advancing environmental conservation efforts [24]. The integration of Digital Twins within Metaverse environments highlights their transformative potential in building smarter, more efficient, and sustainable urban spaces. The city of Incheon serves as a leading example of how these technologies can drive urban innovation and inspire similar advancements worldwide [25].

11.7.6 Smart Architecture

Intelligent architecture employs Digital Twins to develop sustainable, occupant-centric designs. Architects committed to sustainability, such as Foster + Partners, are investigating Digital Twins for design optimisation. Siemens, a worldwide leader in intelligent buildings and infrastructure, additionally employs Digital Twins [18]. The implementation of innovative Digital Twins transcends conventional design practices. Digital Twins assist architects in assessing energy efficiency and occupant comfort. This dynamic and iterative design methodology enables architects to adjust their ideas to meet the highest standards of sustainability, aesthetics, and functionality [26]. The Shard in London and several architectural endeavours have employed Digital Twins for pragmatic purposes. A Digital Twin monitored and optimised energy consumption, rendering the Shard one of the globe's most energy-efficient towers. This tangible achievement demonstrates how Digital Twins may assist architects in achieving sustainability and efficiency [27].

11.7.7 Industrial Internet of Things

Digital Twins revolutionise predictive maintenance within Industrial IoT by forecasting equipment failures in real time, hence facilitating preventive maintenance. This minimises downtime and enhances manufacturing operations across industries. Digital Twins can replicate and enhance pharmaceutical production line configurations, increasing efficiency and reducing expenses. The integration of Digital Twins in Industrial IoT transforms industrial productivity and reduces costs.

11.7.8 Engage in Online Learning

Digital Twin technology can replicate classrooms and educational settings for online learning. Students can engage with digital replicas of tangible objects and sites for a more individualised and immersive educational experience. Institutions may create Digital Twins of laboratories for science students to conduct virtual experiments. This technology facilitates real-time monitoring of student progress and behaviour for precise feedback and assistance. Digital Twins enable educators to evaluate innovative teaching methodologies and concepts, hence enhancing online instruction [28].

11.7.9 Virtual Conferences

Digital Twin technology enables virtual meeting participants to engage with digital representations of physical items and environments. Despite the emergence of real-world instances, the potential remains substantial. A firm may employ Digital Twins to replicate a conference room, enabling meeting participants to engage with virtual objects. Immersive experiences enhance the quality of interaction and productivity. It aids in time management by tracking and enhancing meeting efficiency in real time. Digital Twins can imitate meeting environments to evaluate alternative formats and methodologies, enhancing the efficiency and engagement of virtual meetings.

11.8 Obstacles and Factors for the Adoption and Integration of These Technologies

Some major challenges must be addressed to implement Digital Twin, Blockchain, and the Metaverse:

1. **Integrating with Complexity**
   a. *Interoperability*: Data must transfer effortlessly between platforms to synchronise Digital Twins, Blockchain technology, and the Metaverse. Standardisation and interoperability among suppliers are challenging.
   b. *The technologies are at different levels of maturity*. Blockchain scalability, Digital Twin models, and Metaverse platforms may provide conflicts, complicating integration.
2. **Data Privacy and Security**
   a. *Transparency versus Privacy*: The transparency of Blockchain may conflict with the need for data privacy, particularly when handling sensitive Digital Twin information such as healthcare data.
   b. *Cybersecurity*: Various technologies expand the attack surface. Compromised Blockchain nodes, flaws in smart contracts, or data breaches within the Metaverse might jeopardise the ecosystem [29].
3. **Issues of Scalability**
   a. *Blockchain Scalability*: Public Blockchains face challenges regarding transaction velocity and scalability. The storing and verification of extensive real-time data for Digital Twins via Blockchain can overwhelm existing infrastructure.

   b. *Data Overload*: The management of extensive datasets from Digital Twins in real time within Blockchain and immersive Metaverse systems may lead to performance challenges.
4. **Regulatory and Legal Ambiguity**
   a. *Lack of Legal Frameworks*: Regulatory frameworks governing Digital Twins, Blockchain, and the Metaverse are limited. The concepts of intellectual property, digital asset ownership, and cross-border transactions lack clarity.
   b. *Jurisdiction*: The decentralisation of Blockchain and the global scope of the Metaverse complicate legal compliance and data governance [30].
5. **Expensive and Resource-Demanding**
   a. *Infrastructure and Maintenance Expenditures*: The development and upkeep of an integrated system necessitate substantial investment in cloud infrastructure, Blockchain networks, data storage, and skilled personnel.
   b. *Equipment and Bandwidth*: Immersive Metaverse experiences, Blockchain operations, and real-time Digital Twin simulations necessitate robust computing power and substantial bandwidth.
6. **Utilisation of Energy**
   a. *Excessive Energy Consumption*: Blockchain, particularly proof-of-work consensus mechanisms, Digital Twins, and Metaverse platforms, raise environmental issues.
   b. *Environmental Impact*: Without the adoption of more sustainable technologies such as proof-of-stake, the energy requirements of integrated systems may significantly elevate their carbon footprint.
7. **Competency Deficiency and User Acceptance**
   a. *Significant Learning Curve*: The integration of Digital Twins, Blockchain, and the Metaverse necessitates specialist expertise and training, impeding both business and consumer adoption.
   b. *Resistance to Change*: Established industries and users may resist the adoption of new technology due to substantial costs and perceived risks, hence constraining adoption [1].
8. **Deficiencies in Smart Contracts**
   a. *Coding Vulnerabilities*: Smart contracts, which facilitate transactions in Digital Twin-Metaverse environments, may be susceptible. Defects or poorly constructed code can lead to vulnerabilities, monetary losses, or system malfunctions.
   b. *Immutability Issues*: Smart contracts are immutable once executed. In decentralised ecosystems, errors or unforeseen consequences may be irreversible, complicating risk management.
9. **Societal and Ethical Considerations**
   a. *Digital Divide*: The digital divide may be exacerbated by unequal access to the Metaverse and Blockchain technologies, so restricting inclusivity.
   b. *Moral Concerns*: The Digital Twins within the Metaverse can replicate real-world environments, presenting challenges related to surveillance, identity alteration, and control over virtual representation.

10. **Intellectual Property and Proprietorship**
    a. *Ownership Disputes*: Analysing Metaverse digital assets and data produced by Digital Twins presents challenges. Blockchain monitors ownership; yet intellectual property concerns may persist.
    b. *Data Governance*: Regulating the management and access to the extensive data of Digital Twins in decentralised systems poses challenges, particularly with several stakeholders engaged [31].

11.9 Conclusion

Digital Twin technology, Blockchain, and the Metaverse have the potential to transform manufacturing, healthcare, urban planning, and entertainment. By integrating these technologies, businesses can enhance real-time simulation, secure data management, decentralised collaboration, and monetisation. The integration facilitates more immersive, safe, and dynamic virtual environments with direct physical connections. Nevertheless, the integration of these advanced technologies is hindered by platform complexity, data protection difficulties, scalability challenges, and regulatory ambiguities. Significant resource requirements, energy consumption, and advanced technical proficiency may impede adoption and implementation. Industries, governments, and technology developers must cooperate to implement and optimise these technologies. Interoperability, sustainability, security, and explicit restrictions are essential. Should these obstacles be surmounted, Digital Twins, Blockchain, and the Metaverse will revolutionise our engagement with both physical and virtual realms, unlocking new possibilities for innovation, efficiency, and connectivity.

References

1. Panda, S.K., Satapathy, S.C. (2021). An Investigation into Smart Contract Deployment on Ethereum Platform Using Web3.js and Solidity Using Blockchain. In: Bhateja V., Satapathy S.C., Travieso-González C.M., Aradhya V.N.M. (eds.), *Data Engineering and Intelligent Computing*. Advances in Intelligent Systems and Computing, vol. 1. Springer, Singapore. https://doi.org/10.1007/978-981-16-0171-2_52
2. Panda, S.K., Rao, D.C., Satapathy, S.C. (2021). An Investigation into the Usability of Blockchain Technology in Internet of Things. In: Bhateja V., Satapathy S.C., Travieso-González C.M., Aradhya V.N.M. (eds.), *Data Engineering and Intelligent Computing*. Advances in Intelligent Systems and Computing, vol. 1. Springer, Singapore. https://doi.org/10.1007/978-981-16-0171-2_53
3. Panda, S.K., Dash, S.P., Jena, A.K. (2021). Optimization of Block Query Response Using Evolutionary Algorithm. In: Bhateja V., Satapathy S.C., Travieso-González C.M., Aradhya V.N.M. (eds.), *Data Engineering and Intelligent Computing*. Advances in Intelligent Systems and Computing, vol. 1. Springer, Singapore. https://doi.org/10.1007/978-981-16-0171-2_54
4. Nanda, S.K., Panda, S.K., Das, M., Satapathy, S.C. (2022). Automating Vehicle Insurance Process Using Smart Contract and Ethereum. In: Chakravarthy, V.V.S.S.S., Flores-Fuentes, W., Bhateja, V., Biswal, B. (eds.), *Advances in Micro-Electronics, Embedded Systems and IoT*. Lecture Notes in Electrical Engineering, vol. 838. Springer, Singapore. https://doi.org/10.1007/978-981-16-8550-7_23
5. Varaprasada Rao, K., Panda, S.K. (2023). Secure Electronic Voting (E-Voting) System Based on Blockchain on Various Platforms. In: Satapathy, S.C., Lin, J.C.W., Wee, L.K., Bhateja, V., Rajesh, T.M. (eds.), *Computer Communication, Networking and IoT*. Lecture Notes in Networks and Systems, vol. 459. Springer, Singapore. https://doi.org/10.1007/978-981-19-1976-3_18
6. Varaprasada Rao, K., Panda, S.K. (2023). A Design Model of Copyright Protection System Based on Distributed Ledger Technology. In: Satapathy, S.C., Lin, J.C.W., Wee, L.K., Bhateja, V., Rajesh, T.M. (eds.), *Computer Communication, Networking and IoT*. Lecture Notes in Networks and Systems, vol. 459. Springer, Singapore. https://doi.org/10.1007/978-981-19-1976-3_17
7. Panda, S.K., Elngar, A.A., Balas, V.E., & Kayed, M. (Eds.). (2020). *Bitcoin and Blockchain: History and Current Applications* (1st ed.). CRC Press. https://doi.org/10.1201/9781003032588
8. Panda, S.K., Jena, A.K., Swain, S.K., Satapathy, S.C. (Eds.). (2021). *Blockchain Technology: Applications and Challenges*. Intelligent Systems Reference Library. Springer, Cham. https://doi.org/10.1007/978-3-030-69395-4.

9. Sathya, A.R., Panda, S.K., Hanumanthakari, S. (2021). Enabling Smart Education System Using Blockchain Technology. In: Panda, S.K., Jena, A.K., Swain, S.K., Satapathy, S.C. (eds.), *Blockchain Technology: Applications and Challenges*. Intelligent Systems Reference Library, vol. 203. Springer, Cham. https://doi.org/10.1007/978-3-030-69395-4_10
10. Lokre, S.S., Naman, V., Priya, S., Panda, S.K. (2021). Gun Tracking System Using Blockchain Technology. In: Panda, S.K., Jena, A.K., Swain, S.K., Satapathy, S.C. (eds.), *Blockchain Technology: Applications and Challenges*. Intelligent Systems Reference Library, vol. 203. Springer, Cham. https://doi.org/10.1007/978-3-030-69395-4_16
11. Panda, S.K., Daliyet, S.P., Lokre, S.S., Naman, V. (2022). Distributed Ledger Technology in the Construction Industry Using Corda. In: Panda, S.K., Mohapatra, R.K., Panda, S., Balamurugan, S. (eds.), *The New Advanced Society: Artificial Intelligence and Industrial Internet of Things Paradigm*, pp. 15–41. Wiley. https://doi.org/10.1002/9781119884392.ch2
12. Panda, S.K., Mohammad, G.B., Nandan Mohanty, S., Sahoo, S. (2021). Smart Contract-Based Land Registry System to Reduce Frauds and Time Delay. *Security and Privacy*, e172. https://doi.org/10.1002/spy2.172
13. Panda, S.K., Satapathy, S.C. (2024). Drug Traceability and Transparency in Medical Supply Chain Using Blockchain for Easing the Process and Creating Trust Between Stakeholders and Consumers. *Personal and Ubiquitous Computing* 28, 75–91. https://doi.org/10.1007/s00779-021-01588-3
14. Niveditha, V.R., Sekaran, K., Singh, K.A., Panda, S.K. (2021). Effective Prediction of Bitcoin Price Using Wolf Search Algorithm and Bidirectional LSTM on Internet of Things Data. *International Journal of System of Systems Engineering* 11(3–4), 224–236.
15. Arza, M.A., Panda, S.K. (2022). An Integration of Blockchain and Machine Learning into the Health Care System. In: Jena, O.P., Pramanik, S., Elngar, A.A. (eds.), *Machine Learning Adoption in Blockchain-Based Intelligent Manufacturing*, vol. 1, pp. 33–58. CRC Press. https://doi.org/10.1201/9781003252009-3
16. Murala, D.K., Panda, S.K., Swain, S.K. (2019). A Survey on Cloud Computing Security and Privacy Issues and Challenges. *Journal of Advanced Research in Dynamical and Control Systems* 11, 1276–1290.
17. Murala, D.K., Panda, S.K. (2019). Secure Dynamic Groups Data Sharing with Modified Revocable Attribute-Based Encryption in Cloud. *International Journal of Recent Technology and Engineering* 8(4), 9508–9512.
18. Murala, D.K., Panda, S.K., Swain, S.K. (2019). A Novel Hybrid Approach for Providing Data Security and Privacy from Malicious Attacks in the Cloud Environment. *Journal of Advanced Research in Dynamical and Control Systems* 11, 1291–1300.
19. Panda, S.K., Swain, S.K., & Mall, R. (2015). An Investigation into Usability Aspects of E-Commerce Websites Using Users' Preferences. *Advances in Computer Science: An International Journal* 4(1), 65–73.
20. Panda, S.K., Swain, S.K., Mall, R. (2015). Measuring Web Site Usability Quality Complexity Metrics for Navigability. In: Jain, L., Patnaik, S., Ichalkaranje, N. (eds.), *Intelligent Computing, Communication and Devices*. Advances in Intelligent Systems and Computing, vol. 308. Springer, New Delhi. https://doi.org/10.1007/978-81-322-2012-1_41
21. Panda, S.K. (2014). A Usability Evaluation Framework for B2C E-Commerce Websites. *Computer Engineering and Intelligent Systems* 5(3), 66–85.

22. Bhalerao, V., Panda, S.K., Jena, A.K. (2021). Optimization of Loss Function on Human Faces Using Generative Adversarial Networks. In: Bandyopadhyay, M., Rout, M., Chandra Satapathy, S. (eds.), *Machine Learning Approaches for Urban Computing*. Studies in Computational Intelligence, vol. 968. Springer, Singapore. https://doi.org/10.1007/978-981-16-0935-0_9
23. Panda, S.K., Dwivedi, M. (2020). Minimizing Food Wastage Using Machine Learning: A Novel Approach. In: Satapathy, S., Bhateja, V., Mohanty, J., Udgata, S. (eds.), *Smart Intelligent Computing and Applications*. Smart Innovation, Systems and Technologies, vol. 159. Springer, Singapore. https://doi.org/10.1007/978-981-13-9282-5_44
24. Panda, S.K., Sathya, A.R., Mishra, M., Satpathy, S. (2019). A Supervised Learning Algorithm to Forecast Weather Conditions for Playing Cricket. *International Journal of Innovative Technology and Exploring Engineering* 9(1), 1560–1565.
25. Panda, S.K. (2020). Fraud-Resistant Crowdfunding System Using Ethereum Blockchain. In: Panda, S.K., Elngar, A.A., Balas, V.E., Kayed, M. (eds.), *Bitcoin and Blockchain*, pp. 237–276. CRC Press.
26. Panda, S.K., Mishra, V. Balamurali, R., Elngar, A.A. (2021). *Artificial Intelligence and Machine Learning in Business Management Concepts, Challenges, and Case Studies*, pp. 1–278. CRC Press. https://doi.org/10.1201/9781003125129.
27. Joshi, S., Panda, S.K., Sathya, A.R. (2020). Optimal Deep Learning Model to Identify the Development of Pomegranate Fruit in Farms. *International Journal of Innovative Technology and Exploring Engineering* 9(3), 2352–2356.
28. Puranam, K.S.R., Gaddam, M.C.T., Panda, S.K., Reddy, G. (February 18, 2019). Anatomy and Lifecycle of a Bitcoin Transaction. In: *Proceedings of International Conference on Sustainable Computing in Science, Technology and Management (SUSCOM)*. Amity University Rajasthan, Jaipur, India, Available at SSRN: https://ssrn.com/abstract=3355106 or http://dx.doi.org/10.2139/ssrn.3355106
29. Panda, S.K., Swain, S.K. (2016). *Quality Assurance Aspects of Web Design, Design Solutions for Improving Website Quality and Effectiveness*, pp. 87–129. IGI Global.
30. Panda, S.K., Bhalerao, V., Sathya, A.R. (2020), A Machine Learning Model to Identify Duplicate Questions in Social Media Forums. *International Journal of Innovative Technology and Exploring Engineering* 9(4), 370–373.
31. Ahmareen, S., Raj, A., Potluri, S., Panda, S.K. (2020). Book Shala: An Android-Based Application Design and Implementation of Sharing Books. In: Satapathy, S., Bhateja, V., Mohanty, J., Udgata, S. (eds.), *Smart Intelligent Computing and Applications*. Smart Innovation, Systems and Technologies, vol. 159. Springer, Singapore. https://doi.org/10.1007/978-981-13-9282-5_28
32. Panda, S.K., Das, S.S., Swain, S.K. (2013). S-Model for Service-Oriented Applications in Web Engineering. *Regional College of Management* 10(3), 38–46.
33. Panda, S.K. An Investigation into Usability and Productivity of ECommerce Websites. *Introduction to Hyper-Intelligent Networks* 27, 28.
34. Panda, S.K., Chandrasekhar, A., Gantayat, P.K., Panda, M.R. (2022). Detecting Brain Tumor Using Image Segmentation: A Novel Approach. In: Bhateja, V., Khin Wee, L., Lin, J.C.W., Satapathy, S.C., Rajesh, T.M. (eds.), *Data Engineering and Intelligent Computing*. Lecture Notes in Networks and Systems, vol. 446. Springer, Singapore. https://doi.org/10.1007/978-981-19-1559-8_35
35. Sanghi, P., Panda, S.K., Pati, C., Gantayat, P.K. (2022). Learning Deep Features and Classification for Fresh or Off Vegetables to Prevent Food Wastage Using Machine Learning Algorithms. In: Satapathy, S.C., Peer, P., Tang, J., Bhateja, V., Ghosh, A. (eds.), *Intelligent Data Engineering andAnalytics*. Smart Innovation, Systems and Technologies, vol. 266. Springer, Singapore. https://doi.org/10.1007/978-981-16-6624-7_44

36. Gantayat, P.K., Mohapatra, S., Panda, S.K. (2022). Secure Trust Level Routing in Delay-Tolerant Network with Node Categorization Technique. In: Satapathy, S.C., Peer, P., Tang, J., Bhateja, V., Ghosh, A. (eds.), *Intelligent Data Engineering and Analytics*. Smart Innovation, Systems and Technologies, vol. 266. Springer, Singapore. https://doi.org/10.1007/978-981-16-6624-7_45
37. Panda, S.K., Urkude, S.V., Urkude, V.R., Vairachilai, S. (2022). An Investigation into COVID 19 Pandemic in India. In: Panda, S.K., Mohapatra, R.K., Panda, S., Balamurugan, S. (eds.), *The New Advanced Society: Artificial Intelligence and Industrial Internet of Things Paradigm*, vol. 1, pp. 289–305. Wiley.
38. Panda, S.K., Das, S., Swain, S.K. (October 12, 2015). Web Site Productivity Measurement Using Single Task Size Measure. *Journal of Information Sciences and Computing Technologies (JISCT)* 4(3).
39. Hanumanthakari, S., Panda, S.K. (2022). Detecting Face Mask for Prevent COVID-19 Using Deep Learning: A Novel Approach. In: Satapathy, S.C., Bhateja, V., Favorskaya, M.N., Adilakshmi, T. (eds.), *Smart Intelligent Computing and Applications, Volume 2*. Smart Innovation, Systems and Technologies, vol. 283. Springer, Singapore. https://doi.org/10.1007/978-981-16-9705-0_45
40. Panda, S.K., Sathya, A.R., Das, S. (2023). Bitcoin: Beginning of the Cryptocurrency Era. In: Panda, S.K., Mishra, V., Dash, S.P., Pani, A.K. (eds.), *Recent Advances in Blockchain Technology*. Intelligent Systems Reference Library, vol. 237. Springer, Cham. https://doi.org/10.1007/978-3-031-22835-3_2
41. Murala, D.K., Panda, S.K., Sahoo, S.K. (2023). Securing Electronic Health Record System in Cloud Environment Using Blockchain Technology. In: Panda, S.K., Mishra, V., Dash, S.P., Pani, A.K. (eds.), *Recent Advances in Blockchain Technology*. Intelligent Systems Reference Library, vol. 237. Springer, Cham. https://doi.org/10.1007/978-3-031-22835-3_4
42. Rao, K.V., Murala, D.K., Panda, S.K. (2023). Blockchain: A Study of New Business Model. In: Panda, S.K., Mishra, V., Dash, S.P., Pani, A.K. (eds.), *Recent Advances in Blockchain Technology*. Intelligent Systems Reference Library, vol. 237. Springer, Cham. https://doi.org/10.1007/978-3-031-22835-3_9
43. Panda, S.K., Mishra, V., Dash, S.P., Pani, A.K. (2023). *Recent Advances in Blockchain Technology Real-World Applications, Vol. 1*. Intelligent Systems Reference Library (ISRL), vol. 237, pp. 1–317. Springer.
44. Panda, S.K., Mohapatra, R.K., Panda, S., Balamurugan, S. (2022). *The New Advanced Society: Artificial Intelligence and Industrial Internet of Things Paradigm*, vol. 1, pp. 1–512. Wiley. https://doi.org/10.1002/9781119884392
45. Nanda, S.K., Panda, S.K., Das, M., Satapathy, S.C. (2023). Decentralization of Car Insurance System Using Machine Learning and Distributed Ledger Technology. In: Bhateja, V., Yang, X.S., Chun-Wei Lin, J., Das, R. (eds.), *Intelligent Data Engineering and Analytics (FICTA 2022)*. Smart Innovation, Systems and Technologies, vol. 327. Springer, Singapore. https://doi.org/10.1007/978-981-19-7524-0_52
46. Nanda, S.K., Panda, S.K. & Dash, M. (2023). Medical Supply Chain Integrated with Blockchain and IoT to Track the Logistics of Medical Products. *Multimedia Tools and Applications* 82, 32917–32939. https://doi.org/10.1007/s11042-023-14846-8
47. Panda, S.K., Jena, A.K., Panda, M.R., Panda, S. (2023). Speech Emotion Recognition Using Multimodal Feature Fusion with Machine Learning Approach. *Multimedia Tools and Applications* 82, 42763–42781. https://doi.org/10.1007/s11042-023-15275-3
48. Panda, S.K., Mohanty, S.N. (2023). Time Series Forecasting and Modeling of Food Demand Supply Chain Based on Regressors Analysis. *IEEE Access* 11, 42679–42700. https://doi.org/10.1109/ACCESS.2023.3266275.

49. Desai, D.D., Dey, J., Satapathy, S.K., Mishra, S., Mohanty, S.N., Mishra, P., Panda, S.K. (2023). Optimal Ambulance Positioning for Road Accidents with Deep Embedded Clustering. *IEEE Access* 11, 59917–59934. https://doi.org/10.1109/ACCESS.2023.3284993.
50. Lakshmi, L., Devi, K.D.S., Gupta, S., Reddy, K.A.N., Grandhi, S.K., Panda, S.K. (2023). WOMT: Wasserstein Distribution Based Minimization of False Positives in Breast Tumor Classification Using Deep Learning. *IEEE Access* 11, 57831–57842. https://doi.org/10.1109/ACCESS.2023.3279496.
51. Mishra, P., Panda, S.K. (2023). Dependency Structure-Based Rules Using Root Node Technique for Explicit Aspect Extraction from Online Reviews. *IEEE Access* 11, 65117–65137. https://doi.org/10.1109/ACCESS.2023.3287830.
52. Routray, N., Rout, S.K., Sahu, B., Panda, S.K., Godavarthi, D. (2023). Ensemble Learning with Symbiotic Organism Search Optimization Algorithm for Breast Cancer Classification and Risk Identification of Other Organs on Histopathological Images. *IEEE Access* 11, 110544–110557. https://doi.org/10.1109/ACCESS.2023.3322222.
53. Agarwal, R., Pande, S.D., Mohanty, S.N., Panda, S.K. (2023). A Novel Hybrid System of Detecting Brain Tumors in MRI. *IEEE Access* 11, 118372–118385. https://doi.org/10.1109/ACCESS.2023.3326447
54. Nayak, S.K., Garanayak, M., Swain, S.K., Panda, S.K., Godavarthi, D. (2023). An Intelligent Disease Prediction and Drug Recommendation Prototype by Using Multiple Approaches of Machine Learning Algorithms. *IEEE Access* 11, 99304–99318. https://doi.org/10.1109/ACCESS.2023.3314332
55. Gupta, A., Gandhi, R., Jatana, N., Jatain, D., Panda, S.K., Ramesh, J.V.N. (2023). A Severity Assessment of Python Code Smells. *IEEE Access* 11, 119146–119160. https://doi.org/10.1109/ACCESS.2023.3327553
56. Murala, D.K., Panda, S.K., Dash, S.P. (2023). MedMetaverse: Medical Care of Chronic Disease Patients and Managing Data Using Artificial Intelligence, Blockchain, and Wearable Devices State-of-the-Art Methodology. *IEEE Access* 11, 138985. https://doi.org/10.1109/ACCESS.2023.3340791.
57. Sethi, B.K., Singh, D., Rout, S.K., Panda, S.K. (2024). Long Short-Term Memory-Deep Belief Network-Based Gene Expression Data Analysis for Prostate Cancer Detection and Classification. *IEEE Access* 12, 1508–1524. https://doi.org/10.1109/ACCESS.2023.3346925.
58. Mahapatra, A., Majhi, S.K., Mishra, K., Pradhan, R., Rao, D.C., Panda, S.K. (2024). An Energy-Aware Task Offloading and Load Balancing for Latency-Sensitive IoT Applications in the Fog-Cloud Continuum. *IEEE Access* 12, 14334–14349. https://doi.org/10.1109/ACCESS.2024.3357122.
59. Mishra, P., Sharma, O., Panda, S.K. (2023). ADN-BERT: Attention-Based Deep Network Model Using BERT for Sarcasm Classification. In: Bhateja, V., Yang, X.S., Ferreira, M.C., Sengar, S.S., Travieso-Gonzalez, C.M. (eds.), *Evolution in Computational Intelligence (FICTA 2023)*. Smart Innovation, Systems and Technologies, vol. 370. Springer, Singapore. https://doi.org/10.1007/978-981-99-6702-5_51
60. Varaprasada Rao, K., Panda, S.K. (2024). Initiation, Innovation, Implementation and Integration of CBDC in Digital Virtual Payment Systems. In: Chakravarthy, V.V.S.S.S., Bhateja, V., Anguera, J., Urooj, S., Ghosh, A. (eds.), *Advances in Microelectronics, Embedded Systems and IoT (ICMEET 2023)*. Lecture Notes in Electrical Engineering, vol. 1156. Springer, Singapore. https://doi.org/10.1007/978-981-97-0767-6_20
61. Murala, D.K., Panda, S.K. (2023). Artificial Intelligence in the Development of Metaverse. In: Chandrashekhar, A., Saheb, S.H., Panda, S.K., Balamurugan, S., Peng, S.-L. (eds.), *Metaverse and Immersive Technologies: An Introduction to Industrial Business and Social Applications*, pp. 407–436. Wiley, Hoboken, NJ.

62. Murala, D.K., Panda, S.K. (2023). Metaverse: A Study on Immersive Technologies. In: Chandrashekhar, A., Saheb, S.H., Panda, S.K., Balamurugan, S., Peng, S.-L. (eds.), *Metaverse and Immersive Technologies: An Introduction to Industrial Business and Social Applications*. Wiley, Hoboken, NJ.
63. Murala, D.K., Panda, S.K. (2023). The Internet of Things in Developing Metaverse. In: Chandrashekhar, A., Saheb, S.H., Panda, S.K., Balamurugan, S., Peng, S.-L. (eds.), *Metaverse and Immersive Technologies: An Introduction to Industrial Business and Social Applications*. Wiley, Hoboken, NJ.
64. Murala, D.K., Panda, S.K. (2023). Blockchain in the Development of Metaverse. In: Chandrashekhar, A., Saheb, S.H., Panda, S.K., Balamurugan, S., Peng, S.-L. (eds.), *Metaverse and Immersive Technologies: An Introduction to Industrial Business and Social Applications*. Wiley, Hoboken, NJ.
65. Murala, D.K., Panda, S.K. (2023). The Role of Immersive Reality (AR/VR/MR/XR) in Metaverse. In: Chandrashekhar, A., Saheb, S.H., Panda, S.K., Balamurugan, S., Peng, S.-L. (eds.), *Metaverse and Immersive Technologies: An Introduction to Industrial Business and Social Applications*, pp. 159–189. Wiley, Hoboken, NJ.
66. Panda, S.K. (2023). Revolution of the Metaverse and Blockchain Technology. In: Chandrashekhar, A., Saheb, S.H., Panda, S.K., Balamurugan, S., Peng, S.-L. (eds.), *Metaverse and Immersive Technologies: An Introduction to Industrial Business and Social Applications*. Wiley, Hoboken, NJ.
67. Sahoo, S.K., Das, S., Panda, S.K. (2024). Alzheimer's Disease Classification Using Brain MRI Based on 2D CNN and Transfer Learning. In: Kumar, A., Mozar, S. (eds.), *Proceedings of the 6th International Conference on Communications and Cyber Physical Engineering (ICCCE 2024)*. Lecture Notes in Electrical Engineering, vol. 1096. Springer, Singapore. https://doi.org/10.1007/978-981-99-7137-4_1
68. Panda, S.K., Ramesh, J.V.N., Ghosh, H., Rahat, I.S., Sobur, A., Bijoy, M.H., Yesubabu, M. (2024). Deep Learning in Medical Imaging: A Case Study on Lung Tissue Classification. *EAI Endorsed Transactions on Pervasive Health and Technology*, 10.
69. Paruchuri, V.N.L.L., Shaik, A.H., Murala, D.K., Panda, S.K. (2024). IoT-Enabled Neural Network Analysis for Early Detection and Prediction of Mental Depression. In: Bhateja, V., Tang, J., Sharma, D.K., Polkowski, Z., Ahmad, A. (eds.), *Information System Design: Communication Networks and IoT (ISDIA 2024)*. Lecture Notes in Networks and Systems, vol. 1057, pp. 257–268. Springer, Singapore. https://doi.org/10.1007/978-981-97-4895-2_21
70. Paruchuri, V.N.L.L., Malaviya, M.P., Murala, D.K., Panda, S.K. (2024). Connecting IoT Sensors for Enhanced Dementia Disease Monitoring and Intervention. In: Bhateja, V., Tang, J., Sharma, D.K., Polkowski, Z., Ahmad, A. (eds.), *Information System Design: Communication Networks and IoT (ISDIA 2024)*. Lecture Notes in Networks and Systems, vol. 1057, pp. 269–281. Springer, Singapore. https://doi.org/10.1007/978-981-97-4895-2_22
71. Panda, S.K., Das, S., Sahoo, S.K. (2025). Predominant Music Genre Classification Using Machine Learning Approach. In: Bhateja, V., Chakravarthy, V.V.S.S.S., Anguera, J., Ghosh, A., Flores Fuentes, W. (eds.), *Signal Processing, Telecommunication and Embedded Systems with AI and ML Applications (ICMEET 2023)*. Lecture Notes in Electrical Engineering, vol. 1281. Springer, Singapore. https://doi.org/10.1007/978-981-97-8422-6_17
72. Panda, S.K., Das, S., Sahoo, S.K. (2025). Vehicle Detection and Classification Using Intelligent Systems. In: Bhateja, V., Chakravarthy, V.V.S.S.S., Anguera, J., Ghosh, A., Flores Fuentes, W. (eds.), *Signal Processing, Telecommunication and Embedded Systems with AI and ML Applications (ICMEET 2023)*. Lecture Notes in Electrical Engineering, vol. 1281. Springer, Singapore. https://doi.org/10.1007/978-981-97-8422-6_18

73. Chandrasekhar, A., Dodhiawala, Z., Panda, S.K. (2025). An Investigation into Chronic Kidney Disease Based-on Classification Model. In: Bhateja, V., Chakravarthy, V.V.S.S.S., Anguera, J., Ghosh, A., Flores Fuentes, W. (eds.), *Signal Processing, Telecommunication and Embedded Systems with AI and ML Applications (ICMEET 2023)*. Lecture Notes in Electrical Engineering, vol. 1281. Springer, Singapore. https://doi.org/10.1007/978-981-97-8422-6_19
74. Chandrashekhar, A., Saheb, S.H., Panda, S.K., Balamurugan, S., Peng, S.-L. (2023). *Metaverse and Immersive Technologies: An Introduction to Industrial, Business and Social Applications*. Wiley.
75. Rao, K.V., Murala, D.K., Panda, S.K. (2025). Design and Develop the Business Process Model for Open Access Copyright Management System Using Permission Less Blockchain. *International Journal of Safety and Security Engineering* 15(2), 369–382. https://doi.org/10.18280/ijsse.150218
76. Murala, D.K. (2024). METAEDUCATION: State-of-the-Art Methodology for Empowering Feature Education. *IEEE Access* 12, 57992–58020.
77. Murala, D.K. (2013). Divide and Conquer Method for Clustering Mixed Numerical and Categorical Data. *International Journal of Computer Science and Information Technologies* 4(1), 103–106.
78. Balintfy, J.L. (1964). On a Basic Class of Multi-Item Inventory Problems. *Management Science* 10(2), 287–297. https://doi.org/10.1287/mnsc.10.2.287

Index

O

P

Q

R

S

T

U

V

W

Z

For Product Safety Concerns and Information please contact our EU representative GPSR@taylorandfrancis.com
Taylor & Francis Verlag GmbH, Kaufingerstraße 24, 80331 München, Germany

www.ingramcontent.com/pod-product-compliance
Lightning Source LLC
Chambersburg PA
CBHW070249230726
48635CB00030B/363
* 9 7 8 1 0 3 2 8 5 9 6 9 9 *